Staging Technology

RELATED TITLES

Theatre in the Dark: Shadow, Gloom and Blackout in Contemporary Theatre
Edited by Adam Alston and Martin Welton
ISBN 978-1-3500-9940-1

Brecht in Practice: Theatre, Theory and Performance
David Barnett
ISBN 978-1-4081-8503-2

Postdramatic Theatre and Form
Edited by Michael Shane Boyle, Matt Cornish and Brandon Woolf
ISBN 978-1-3500-4316-9

Rethinking the Theatre of the Absurd: Ecology, the Environment and the Greening of the Modern Stage
Edited by Carl Lavery and Clare Finburgh
ISBN 978-1-4725-0667-2

Digital Scenography: 30 Years of Experimentation and Innovation in Performance and Interactive Media
Neill O'Dwyer
ISBN 978-1-3501-0731-1

Contemporary Scenography: Practices and Aesthetics in German Theatre, Arts and Design
Edited by Birgit E. Wiens
ISBN 978-1-3501-9486-1

Staging Technology

Medium, Machinery, and Modern Drama

Craig N. Owens

methuen | drama

LONDON • NEW YORK • OXFORD • NEW DELHI • SYDNEY

METHUEN DRAMA
Bloomsbury Publishing Plc
50 Bedford Square, London, WC1B 3DP, UK
1385 Broadway, New York, NY 10018, USA
29 Earlsfort Terrace, Dublin 2, Ireland

BLOOMSBURY, METHUEN DRAMA and the Methuen Drama logo are trademarks of Bloomsbury Publishing Plc

First published in Great Britain 2021
Paperback edition published 2022

Copyright © Craig N. Owens, 2021, 2022

Craig N. Owens has asserted his right under the Copyright, Designs and Patents Act, 1988, to be identified as the Author of this work.

For legal purposes the Acknowledgments on pp. ix–x constitute an extension of this copyright page.

Cover design by Charlotte Daniels
Cover image: Melody Moore as Marguerite and Toby Spence as Faust in the English National Opera's production of Charles Gounod's *Faust* directed by Des McAnuff, conducted by Edward Gardner at the London Coliseum. (© Robbie Jack / Corbis / Getty Images)

All rights reserved. No part of this publication may be reproduced or transmitted in any form or by any means, electronic or mechanical, including photocopying, recording, or any information storage or retrieval system, without prior permission in writing from the publishers.

Bloomsbury Publishing Plc does not have any control over, or responsibility for, any third-party websites referred to or in this book. All internet addresses given in this book were correct at the time of going to press. The author and publisher regret any inconvenience caused if addresses have changed or sites have ceased to exist, but can accept no responsibility for any such changes.

A catalogue record for this book is available from the British Library.

A catalog record for this book is available from the Library of Congress.

ISBN: HB: 978-1-3501-6857-2
PB: 978-1-3501-9670-4
ePDF: 978-1-3501-6859-6
eBook: 978-1-3501-6858-9

Typeset by Newgen KnowledgeWorks Pvt. Ltd., Chennai, India

To find out more about our authors and books visit www.bloomsbury.com and sign up for our newsletters.

*For Graham,
ever game*

Contents

Acknowledgments	ix
Introduction: Staging Technology	1
1 Avant-Garde Assemblages: Tristan Tzara, Jean Cocteau, and Eugène Ionesco	35
2 Machineries of Nostalgia and American Modernity: Sophie Treadwell, Elmer Rice, Arthur Miller, and Isaac Gomez	69
3 Alienating Devices: Bertolt Brecht & Kurt Weill, John Adams & Alice Goodman, Don DeLillo, and Athol Fugard	101
4 Machineries of Constraint: Samuel Beckett, Harold Pinter, and Badal Sircar	149
5 Post-Human Recursivity: Heiner Müller, Julie Taymor, and Tod Machover & Robert Pinsky	185
Coda: Medium, Machinery, and the Present Moment	223
Notes	229
Bibliography	257
Index	269

Acknowledgments

I am grateful for the support of numerous people and organizations during the many years of research and writing that have led to this book. Drake University's English Department, Center for the Humanities, College of Arts and Sciences, and Office of the Provost provided essential research, sabbatical, and travel funding. Students in my course "Staging the Machine" in fall 2017 engaged thoughtfully with the theory, works, and methods that would come to guide this book in ways that profoundly shaped its development.

SteinSemble Performance Group, dedicated to the interpretation and production of modernist avant-garde works, The Harold Pinter Society, and Detour Productions have given me the opportunity to design, direct, or perform in productions of many of the pieces discussed here.

Fellow scholars, including Judith Roof of Rice University, Stephen M. Watt of Indiana University, Ann C. Hall of the University of Louisville, Lance Norman of Lansing Community College, and Terence Hartnett of Rose-Hulman Institute of Technology have provided valuable insights in response to the conference papers and essays from which this project has evolved. Daniel Alexander showed immense generosity and patience in leading me through fractal theory. Amelia Hugill-Fontanel of The Rochester Institute of Technology's Cary Graphic Arts Collection, Ole Lund of the Department of Design of Norwegian University of Science and Technology, David Goodrich of the American Printing History Association offered valuable help in tracking down source material, and Brian Mitchell, archivist for The Houston Grand Opera, provided stage director's notes and other source material pertaining to the 1987 world premiere staging of John Adams and Alice Goodman's *Nixon in China*.

My thanks to the Robert A. Freedman agency for permission to quote from Elmer Rice's *The Adding Machine*; to Éditions Gallimard for permission to quote from Jean Cocteau's *Les Mariés de la Tour Eiffel* from

Theatre complet (Biliothèque de la Pléiade © 1957) and from Eugène Ionesco's *L'Avenir est dans les oeufs* (© 1954); to Calder Publications and Alma Books, Ltd., for permission to quote from Derek Prouse's translation of Ionesco's *The Future is in Eggs* (1960); to Nick Hern Books for permission to quote from Sophie Treadwell's *Machinal*; to New York Review of Books, publisher of Alice Goodman's libretto *Nixon in China* ((©) 1987); and to Grove Press for permission to quote from Harold Pinter's *Dumb Waiter*. Excerpts from *Death of a Salesman* by Arthur Miller, © 1949, renewed copyright © 1977 by Arthur Miller, are used by permission of The Wylie Agency and of Viking Books, an imprint of Penguin Publishing Group, a division of Penguin Random House LLC—all rights reserved. I am especially grateful to Tucker Smith, of the Wylie Agency, for critical assistance in securing some last-minute permissions without which this project would have been much impoverished. And a huge thank you to Mark Dudgeon and Lara Bateman at Methuen Drama for their patience, wisdom, and guidance throughout the publication process.

And finally, Yasmina Din Madden and Graham Madden Owens: Without your love, encouragement, and patience, this project—and much, much more—could never have been possible.

Introduction: Staging Technology

Hier is der Apparat.
Steig Ein!

—Bertolt Brecht[1]

Imagine the empty stage—void of set and properties, swept clean at the end of the last show's strike, maybe a single safety light and a pair of exit signs casting their meager glow upon the playing space. The curtains are flown, the torms and legs drawn back; the overhead door leading through the cinder-block back wall into the scene shop and loading dock beyond is shut. Cables and rigging coiled, bound, and hung, grid and rails bare of instruments, circuit couplings decoupled, and the catwalk cleared of obstacles, the iron and steel networks overhead are as empty as the stage and auditorium below. There is no sound. And yet, a kind of performance is taking place: the still dance and dumb show of dramatic theatre's millennia-long technological accrual. The space performs a motionless, silent retrospective of its own history, the centuries of innovations and innovators, the mores and aesthetics that have made theatre production possible. In this moment, the theatre reveals itself as an apparatus and, as such, a paean to the conditions of its own possibility—social, economic, technological, and ideological.

For theatre, unlike other modes of artistic and literary representation, stubbornly preserves its most ancient technologies, deploying them along with its most advanced. Digitally synthesized sound effects mingle with the human voice, with the catgut and horsehair of the strings in the pit and with the footfalls of actors strutting boards, both literal and metaphorical. The robot and the puppet interact with the human body and attenuate and extend it. Sunlight, firelight, flashlight, lightbulb, and diode illuminate the scenes, often simultaneously, while painters and carpenters ply their craft alongside electricians, videographers, projectionists, computer programmers, and advanced materials engineers. The light board's analog rheostats and the manually controlled follow spots consort with their programmable, digital progeny. Pulleys, cables, inclines, augers, hinges, levers, revolves, and windlasses, the simple machines of ancient, medieval, and renaissance theatre, articulate to electric motors literally plugged into the power grid and, figuratively, into a webwork of regulation, finance, and global trade. Theatre's machineries, overseen by professionals whose conditions of employment are determined, in part, by the kind of collective action that grew out of industrial labor, often also answer to digital code first developed for applications in aerospace, communications, professional athletics, and warfare. The theatre, in other words, is not simply an architectural artifact; it is also a machine and an archaeology, a cabinet of curiosities collected over thousands of years, always on the verge of reawakening into a radically synchronic choreography. More than any other art form, theatre manifests its entanglement in the flows of capital and power, flows it receives as inputs, transforms in its internal dynamics, and dispenses as outputs.

From the moment the first stage was built, wherever in the world it happened, the theatre has been a technological space, a "machine" that one must continually "step into," to echo the first sung line of Bertolt Brecht and Kurt Weill's *Lindbergh's Flight* (1929), quoted in the epigraph above. But, as in other forms of creative expression and cultural production, the early technological innovations that made theatre possible were, for most of the history of the form, secondary—or tertiary—to other matters. Through the twentieth century, however, painting and dance, and in the early twenty-first century, narrative started to come to terms with the materiality of their media. Clement Greenberg's remarks on the rise of abstraction in European and American painting, dance's reckoning with the surfaces and technologies of the spaces it occupied, and Marshall McLuhan's oft-quoted maxim "the medium is the message" laid the groundwork for a new awareness of materiality in the study of the fine arts and media.[2] N. Katherine Hayles's slim volume *Writing Machines* (2002)—part theory, part criticism, part autobiography, and part manifesto—called for a similar shift in perspective with respect to the reception and interpretation of texts in the age of electronically produced and mediated writing, and fifteen years or so hence, new media studies are mainstays of many rhetoric, English, and writing studies programs. Since the 1980s, some strains of the academic study of avant-garde performance, often situating the performing body within highly technologically mediated environments—and sometimes blurring the lines between the organic and inorganic elements of performance—have also taken note of technology and technologically sustained media as an important element of the performance event.[3] The academic study of narrative drama, by contrast, has yet to attend fully to the materiality, mediation, and the technological conditions of performance production and reception as sites of critical analysis and interpretation.

In some ways, the persistence of text-centered orientations in drama studies in contrast to the practical, application-focused considerations of technical theatre studies would seem surprising, especially given the degree to which theatre and drama are so technologically circumscribed and enmeshed in their own media. We might have expected the emergence of dramatic theatre's media and technologies into stark salience to have preceded that in other arts. For drama would seem especially well positioned to reveal the resonances among representation, the technologies of staging, and the conditions that govern and mediate the everyday lives of its participants and audiences. After all, over the past five hundred years, and especially the last two hundred years, dramatic representation, as a practice, and theatres themselves, as technologically mediated spaces, have seen quite rapid and frequently transformative innovation. The salience of theatre's production technologies not only as enablers but also as bearers of meaning would seem to follow naturally upon highly synthetic nature of dramatic theatre itself as a set of representational practices, which combine elements of sound, embodied performance, lighting, painting, architecture, movement and rhythm, music, and, especially since the final decades of the twentieth century, film, video, and digital programming, so that innovations in any one of these areas have repercussions in theatrical production practices. While technological innovation in musical instruments or architecture may occur relatively slowly, or in bursts of novelty punctuating otherwise long spells of stasis, in bringing these various media together, dramatic theatre finds itself in an almost constant state of technological flux and high innovation density. Because innovation in theatre, and particularly in dramatic theatre, comprises innovation in all other arts, no medium of artistic or creative expression has changed as much as theatre has over the past five hundred years, for theatre always embeds any other individual medium's changes within its expansive repertoire of technologies and techniques. Indeed, in the context of such rapid technological change, we should be surprised in noting that a great deal of formal stability has endured in Western dramatic drama since even before the time of Aristotle's *Poetics*.

It is curious, then, that theatrical production and the study of drama and dramatic theatre so often elide their medium's technological positionality and the multiple materialities of its machineries. With relatively rare exceptions, the technologies of production—the material substrate of the visual and auditory spectacle—seem to fade or disappear entirely into the dramatic effects they produce, including, principally, character, narrative, and scene. The projected images, the cascades of light, the scenic transformations, the sounds of wind, weather, tumult, and triumph often present themselves, as if ex nihilo, as the effects of the staged environment rather than products of a technologically sophisticated, professionally designed, carefully managed techne. Even when we can clearly perceive the mechanisms that produce the effects— the concentric revolves that move actors and properties from place to place, for instance, in Lin-Manuel Miranda's Broadway hit *Hamilton* (2015) or the modest *periaktoi* manually turned between scenes of Jeff Talbot's *The Submission* at the off-Broadway Lucille Lortel Theatre (2010)—conventions of spectation insist that we not acknowledge them or that we bracket them off as something other than representation, the way readers might ignore a book's page numbers, chapter headings, copyright pages, and other paratexts typical of a printed work. *Paratext*, Gerard Genette's term for such seemingly ancillary texts that frame and render legible a central text—a narrative, an account, an argument—offers one way of naming the machineries and systems on the margins of theatrical representation, and thus of making the materialities of dramatic performance available as part of a sign system subject to analysis and interpretation. Genette characterizes a printed text's paratexts as "more than a boundary or a sealed border" marking an "undefined zone" or "vestibule" that both demarcates a central text from the world and connects it to that world: they are "thresholds of interpretation," to quote the subtitle of Genette's book on the subject[4]:

> [A]lthough we do not always know whether these productions are to be regarded as belonging to the text, in any case they surround it and extend it, precisely to *present* it, in the usual sense of this verb but also in the strongest sense: to *make present*, to ensure the text's presence in the world, its reception and consumption in the form (nowadays, at least) of a book.[5]

Much the same can be said for the theatre's apparatus: Like a book's paratexts, they are essential to mounting a dramatic performance, making it present to its audience, enabling "its reception and consumption in the form" of a theatrical production. Like a book's paratexts, in dramatic theatre in particular, production technologies typically do not present themselves as objects of inquiry, scrutiny, or analysis; the spectator must intentionally pay critical attention to them, a task often rendered difficult by the more central spectacle of these technologies' effects. By virtue of their articulation to literal and metaphorical systems of power, they too are "more than a boundary or sealed border": They frame a production without quite enclosing it, suturing it to more or less attenuated, more or less abstract notions of systematicity and technology outside theatre practice.

In order to make these technologies and their function as interpretive "thresholds" visible and available to analysis, *Staging Technology* approaches the intersection of dramatic theatre, production, and technology from a perspective informed in part by the strain of continental and post-structuralist theory, philosophy, and linguistics that focuses its attention on materiality as it emerges at the margins of representation and on recovering, revealing, or making newly visible often overlooked or forgotten, elements of a "text" rendered in any medium. Such a perspective allows us to examine the interconnections among dramatic text, production, and technology and between them and the conditions of their existence and persistence. This way of reading, seeing, and knowing draws partly upon a combination of Foucaultian "archaeology," deconstruction's attention to the margins—the *outwork*, *hors-du-texte*, and *exergues*, to use Jacques Derrida's terminology— and the rhizomic, playful flux central to Gilles Deleuze and Félix Guattari's analysis of culture, power, and signification. As Michel Foucault explains in the introduction to *The Archaeology of Knowledge*, "Beneath the great continuities of thought […] are the *epistemological acts and thresholds* [,] *displacements* and [,] the distinction […] between *microscopic* and *macroscopic scales* [, *r*]*ecurrent redistributions* [, and] *architectonic unities* of systems."[6] While Foucault's remarks pertain to historiography, and to the history of scientific knowledge in particular, these elements complicate the practice of dramatic theatre and lay them open to analyses that re-center the marginal, the technological, and the material elements so frequently elided from these fields.

Likewise, Deleuze and Guattari's notion of the "assemblage," the loosely connected, hybrid, contingent, temporary, and discontinuous systems of knowledge production and dissemination, power consolidation and distribution, and social ordering and reordering, becomes particularly useful to the project of making visible and making sense of the materialities of theatre, drama, and performance.[7] Deleuze and Guattari's analyses disrupt the linear, unified, and hegemonic coherence of the systems they examine by tracing "the minor"—that is, the marginal, deprivileged remainders that persist within dominant or conventional forms.⁸ Thus, a Deleuzo-Guattarian reading of theatre, drama, and performance, following lines of flight, flows of information, and rhizomic vectors as they coalesce into nodes and plateaus of more or less organized sense, reveals systematicities that, if they do not quite undermine conventions of narrative, spectacle, and performed representation, offer possibilities for seeing alternative structures of meaning. In the chapters to follow, such a perspective, while it will often remain implicit, animating my analyses without my continuously invoking its theoretical discourse, will frequently inform my readings.

More generally, useful as post-structuralist perspectives are in bringing to light the elements of performance and production necessary to this project, throughout *Staging Technology* I have as far as possible avoided the dense, often elliptical prose stylings for which deconstructive, rhizomatic, and Foucaultian analyses are so often derided. While I appreciate, and indeed enjoy, the ways such prosody does not just convey but also enacts its own critique of language, meaning, and ideology, I am much more concerned that the theoretical and critical moves *Staging Technology* makes are as clear and readable as I can make them, especially since drama studies so rarely disports with this body of theory in the first place, particularly in contrast to performance studies and analyses of postdramatic or postmodern theatre practices. With apologies to high theorists among my readers, I do not see the value in reproducing the kind of opacity that marks the writing of Derrida, Foucault, and Deleuze and Guattari if my hope is to establish the usefulness of a critical perspective that provides alternatives to established ways of reading and understanding dramatic theatre.

To my mind, Hayles, whose insights will reappear in the chapters to follow, provides a useful and accessible vocabulary for characterizing my project and naming its goals and objects of inquiry. Returning, then, to *Writing Machines*, we find that much of what Hayles has to say about the text-centered impulse of literary scholarship in the mid-to-late twentieth century still applies to scholarship on dramatic theatre. In noting that "literary studies [had] generally been content to treat [...] narrative worlds as if they were entirely products of the imagination" by ignoring materiality and the text's conditions of existence, *Writing Machines* echoes Janet H. Murray's somewhat less nuanced articulation of the same problem five years earlier: "Academic theorists reduce literature to a system of arbitrary symbols that do not point toward anything but other texts."[9] Hayles and Murray alike argue against an approach to literary criticism that sees "literature as immaterial verbal constructions" and "relegat[es] to the specialized fields of bibliography, manuscript culture, and book production the rigorous study of the materiality of literary artifacts."[10] Clear analogs in drama studies present themselves. Just as literary critics have often marginalized considerations of the text-object's materiality, so too does drama studies, particularly as it emphasizes textual drama and tends to de-materialize their objects of inquiry as a species of literary criticism that prizes the immaterial "products of the imagination." Like Foucaultian archaeology and Deleuzo-Guattarian rhizomics, Hayles in particular wants to see representation's various modalities—its materiality, the historical conditions of its existence, its semantics, its narrative, and so on—as "interpenetrating and simultaneous" within a work rather than as delineated from one another, "linear and sequential."[11] With respect to literary study, then, Hayles outlines an approach much more sensitive to the materiality of the text-as-object, an approach she calls "media-specific analysis." She demonstrates her media-specific orientation throughout *Writing Machines* by focusing on works that foreground their own technologically mediated materialities— works she calls "technotexts": "works that strengthen, foreground, and thematize the connections between themselves as material artifacts and the imaginative real of verbal/semiotic signifiers they instantiate." These kinds of works, she says, "open a window on the larger connections that unite literature as a verbal art to its material forms."[12] In addition to having found Hayles's approach a useful model for much of what follows, I also continue to appreciate the clarity and elegance with which she frames her analyses, across the body of her work, refreshing and attractive—a feature of her work that I have tried to make a feature of mine, as well.

Staging Technology is not, I hasten to add, a mere exercise in theory. Attending to the material facts of dramatic theatre and theatre production enriches the reading of particular works for performance, often complicating and deepening them, revealing layers of complexity, particularly with respect to their relationship to their material manifestations in time and space. To the extent, then, that *Staging Technology* wishes to intervene in the practice of representational theatre and drama criticism by rendering theatre's representational technologies visible and available to critical interpretation, it also offers a kind of extended essay on method. Borrowing freely from the work of such historians, philosophers, and theorists of literature and culture as Walter Benjamin, Siegfried Zielinski, Jürgen Habermas, Fredric Jameson, and Anson Rabinbach, in addition to Hayles, Foucault, Derrida, and Deleuze and Guattari, whom I have already cited, *Staging Technology* draws critical attention to the complex interrelationship of performance, text, theatre, and material culture.

The circumscribed practices of drama studies notwithstanding, one way in which theatre and drama have at least partially begun to liberate themselves from the bounded and hermetic unities that post-structural and media-specific analysis wish to reveal and question has to do with the position of the playwright. In contrast to the fixity and finality of most authored texts—poems, essays, stories, novels, monographs, and so on—a dramatic text almost always opens itself to interpretations that exceed what we might imagine to be the playwright's "intention." Reading a play, we imagine voices, settings, bodies, and movements that may be both licensed by the text and yet unimagined by the playwright. Even productions in which the playwright has been involved exceed the text and yet are only provisional—temporary, ephemeral, open to reinterpretation or rejection. We cannot therefore speak of an "authoritative" production of a play as one might speak of authoritative editions of other kinds of literary texts. As a consequence, outside the scholarly context, it is common for performances of plays to be spoken of and advertised with little or no attention to the name of the author—even quite famous or popular pieces. Indeed, there is a strong correlation between a work's textual fixity and its connection to the name of the author and their oeuvre, such that we can imagine a spectrum on one end of which highly fixed texts, such as poems, retain a strong connection to authorial identity, while on the other, radically open, dynamic texts—recipes, for example, but also plays—maintain a weak connection, if any, to their author. To the extent that the collaborative nature of the theatrical enterprise, coupled with the impermanence of any particular production, much less of any particular performance, has somewhat loosened the idea of a play from the idea of literary authorship, drama already shows a susceptibility to innovative, synthetic approaches.

Earlier, I said that the technologies of theatrical performance—including plays, musicals, and opera—tend to recede or disappear *with relatively rare exceptions*. In order to bring these technologies into view, this book focuses on some of those exceptions: fifteen or so works of the twentieth- and twenty-first-century canon of European and American narrative performance that, in one way or another, implicate the technologies of the stage, and by extension, the ideological, political, economic, and social apparatus that make it possible, into the scene of representation. These works are "technotexts" in precisely the way the literary texts Hayles's *Writing Machines* examines are. They include works of the French avant-garde, Brechtian epic theatre, American modernism, European absurdism, postmodern experimental opera, and musical theatre, although within these modes there is considerable variation in the way the apparatus makes itself perceptible and the degrees to which it is literalized on stage.

Thus, *Staging Technology* asks what becomes visible, what interpretive possibilities emerge, when we encounter plays, operas, and musicals that are themselves in one way or another *about* fraught human–machine interfaces with the apparatus of theatre production in mind. What can theatrical production tell us about the way technology functions as an element of ideology and power? About the limits of the human? About the nature of agency and autonomy? About how we conceive of space, time, and movement in real and virtual environments? About big data, information, and cybernetics? Similarly, when we attend to the extratheatrical history of technological development over the past one-hundred years in the areas of industrial production, digital computing, media studies, aerospace engineering, and elsewhere, what can we learn about the possibilities and limits of theatrical representation? About its implication into nontheatrical flows of knowledge, power, and capital? And, not least, what new ways of reading and interpreting theatrical works become available to us? What sorts of critical understanding do they yield?

In addressing such questions, *Staging Technology* offers one way of bridging the divide that frequently separates theatre studies, which often focuses attention on the technical deployment of theatre technology, on the one hand, and drama studies' critical, analytical reading of performance texts, which privileges the literary text over the exigencies of performance, on the other. *Staging Technology* thus weaves together threads spun from theatre history, theatre practice, dramaturgy, drama criticism, and technology and media studies to read theatre technologies as bearers of meaning and to read performance texts as articulated to technologies not just of production, but of spectation, ideology, and commodity production and consumption more broadly.

In some of the pieces under discussion, the technology is staged quite literally and quite explicitly: Beckett's *Krapp's Last Tape* (1958) gives far more discourse to its reel-to-reel tape recorder, central in the mise-en-scène, than to the human actor playing the title character. Similarly, Tod Machover's operatic setting of Robert Pinsky's libretto for *Death and the Powers: A Robot Opera* (2010), imagines a post-organic world in which robotic modules perform again and again a now ancient, seemingly prehistoric saga of a billionaire inventor who succeeds in uploading his consciousness to a digital computing network and leaving his organic body behind, shuffling off his mortal coil. In others, the technologies in question are less central, more attenuated in their representation: In Act One of John Adams and Alice Goodman's *Nixon in China*, Nixon, who has arrived *ex machina* from the flies on a nearly full-size replica of the presidential airplane, sings of the heroic human quest to reach the moon and of the wonders of media broadcast. In Cocteau's *Eiffel Tower Wedding Party* (1921), styled as a "ballet," characters struggle to act in a world where photography, sound recording, communications, and transportation technologies enter a state of flux, always on the verge of becoming other. And in still other plays, the machine emerges as a trace, a logic, or a remainder of mechanical processes of articulation and assembly, as when the human head in Tzara's *The Gas Heart* (1921) is rendered as its several features, each of which performs its role separately, or when Heiner Müller's *Hamletmachine* (1977) enacts the emerging logic of digitality, recursivity, and hyperspace. In these examples, technology operates at several registers, sometimes simultaneously: as a literal object of representation; as a process or logic according to which the world is ordered and flows of force and information are managed; and as a metaphor for the workings of ideological apparatus, financial and economic systems, and modes of social control.

The fact that theatre technologies and their relationship to staged representation have not more often been the objects of sustained reading and reflection is attributable, in part, to the way theatre, drama, and performance studies get distributed across academic disciplines and to the disconnect between the concerns that animate the academic study of theatre and drama from the goals and exigencies that motivate theatrical production. Drama studies, more than other approaches to performance works, sometimes deploys post-structuralist and continental critical methods common to English, Comparative Literature, Rhetoric, Cultural Studies, and to some extent, History departments, at least in the United States. Theatre and Drama programs, by contrast, have largely focused on methods for realizing plays and other performance pieces in a particular way, in a particular place, at a particular time. In these programs, textual interpretation, production history, and script analysis are oriented not toward critical interpretation for its own sake but rather toward eventually mounting a show. The production-oriented posture of the usual theatre-and-drama approach is little abetted by the ambiguities and plays of meaning that multiply in the text subjected to post-structural analysis. A performance, after all, is the result of innumerable interpretive choices; while opening up interpretive possibilities and discovering thematic and motific resonances across diverse modes and moments of theatrical production may be a salutary preliminary exercise, the work of production—design, staging, characterization—requires and enacts at least temporary fixities that demand bracketing off interpretive possibility and imposing provisional constraints on the play of meaning.

Moreover, the persistence of a linear, causal mode of imagining theatre and drama history and the predominance of author-centered approaches in drama studies as they are pursued outside theatre departments constrain the kind of semiotic play, interpretive ambiguity, and material complexity that grow out of more open interpretive methods. While theatre practice—and particularly, publicity for theatrical productions—often elide the name of the author, it is not uncommon for drama scholars to identify themselves as interested in the works of one or a few particular playwrights. John Willett's association with Bertolt Brecht, Christopher Bigsby's with Arthur Miller, and James Knowlson's with Samuel Beckett are only three of the highest profile examples of well-established playwright–scholar dyads in twentieth-century drama studies. Single-playwright societies, such as the Harold Pinter Society, over which I presided for three years, and single-playwright journals, such as *Shaw*, often serve to reinforce the idea of the individual author-genius whose "life and times" get deployed to authorize readings of their works. Other modes of organizing theatre and drama studies mirror those in studies of other literatures, as well: a focus on a particular national tradition (Irish drama, East German theatre), ethnic tradition (Black theatre, Latino drama), historical period (early modern, restoration, modernist), or genre (realism, absurdism, epic drama, environmental theatre, New Brutalism).

Finally, the predominance of phenomenology (as a way for the analysis of literary drama to imagine performance), cultural anthropology (particularly in performance studies), and New Historicism (particularly in studies of historically distant drama) resist a media-specific approach to theatre and drama studies. Each of these modes seeks to organize knowledge about plays, performance, theatre production according to modalities established around one or a few settled truths. New Historicism, for instance, frequently circumscribes the understanding of a text by limiting it to what was thinkable at the historical moment of its creation; phenomenology, likewise, typically limits itself to what is perceptible and legible at the moment of performance and privileges the perceiving body as the site of meaning-making. This limiting function is not, I want to emphasize, a failure of these approaches; or, rather, it is not a failure particular to these approaches. Rather, it enacts the very conditions of existence for something like a discipline or a methodology in the first place.

These ideas about disciplinarity, too, derive from Foucault. In *The Discourse on Language* (1970), Foucault describes disciplinarity as "a relative, mobile principle" that "enables us to construct" statements "within a narrow framework."[13] Foucault goes on to explain that

> disciplines are defined by groups of objects, methods, their corpus of propositions considered to be true, the interplay of rules and definitions, of techniques and tools: all these constitute a sort of anonymous system. [...] In a discipline [...], what is supposed at the point of departure is not some meaning which must be rediscovered, nor an identity to be reiterated; it is that which is required for the construction of new statements. For a discipline to exist, there must be the possibility of formulating [...] fresh propositions.[14]

As a consequence, "[d]isciplines constitute a system of control in the production of discourse [...] taking the form of a permanent reactivation of the rules" for the construction and validation of propositions. Delimited by their objects of study, their methods of analysis, their criteria for validating interpretive or truth-claims, and the ends they seek to advance beyond mere self-perpetuation, disciplines such as drama studies, or subdisciplines, like those that focus on a particular genre, period, national or ethnic origin, or author's oeuvre, are reinforced in their disciplinarity by the organization of knowledge as it manifests in colleges and universities, academic and trade presses, institutional accreditation and licensing criteria, and, above all, historical and ideological exigencies.

In attempting to work across these disciplinary divides, *Staging Technology* considers text, performance, media, and materiality alike as, themselves, effects of larger systems—sign systems, value systems, political systems, and economic systems. Theatre technologies are not, according to this approach, ideologically neutral tools or autonomous systems independent of the meanings they bear and the constraints they impose or the possibilities they liberate. Rather, they activate meanings, sometimes resisting deployment, sometimes amplifying a production's themes, and sometimes doing both at once. Thus, while *Staging Technology* relies extensively on historical and technical examinations of theatre's technologies, it does not reproduce the linear, developmental narratives or utilitarian purposes such works often offer. Likewise, my focus on materiality and mediation render the metaphysics of actorly and spectatorial experience mostly irrelevant to the work *Staging Technology* wishes to carry out. I do not mean to say that phenomenology, as a critical approach to understanding some aspects of the theatre event, does not account for much of what happens when performance takes place before an audience. Rather, I wish to note the distinction between my project, which takes the actorly and spectatorial sensorium as part of the theatrical sign system and techne, from one that focuses on affect, presence, and the experience of being that, together, resist or exceed signification.[15]

At the same time that *Staging Technology* pursues a method distinct from those that animate much of theatre and performance studies, it also goes beyond critical approaches to textuality and literary interpretation often deployed in drama studies. My adherence to rigorously theorized, analytical, and interpretive close reading notwithstanding, *Staging Technology* treats the text as only one component of the complete scene of signification. Moreover, just as it attempts to read the theatrical margins as signifying in their own right, this book attends carefully to the non- and extra-diegetic elements of the performance text, including stage directions; descriptions of setting, spectacle, and sound effects; and the musical score, components of the text often seen as marginal—paratextual—to the main business of characterization, dialogue, and action. Finally, while *Staging Technology* attends to the historical conditions within which a given performance took place and often uses historical documents and historiographical accounts to support its readings, it is not a work of historicism, new or otherwise. Rather, material, cultural, and aesthetic history is one component of a complex assemblage of signs and systems that enable this book's critical project.

I do not wish to suggest that questions of technology and the scene of theatrical representation have never been raised before in the critical literature. Indeed, the chapters that compose *Staging Technology* rely from time to time on essays, articles, book chapters, and books that consider the representation of technology on the stage or the use of technology in production. However, these works often focus on a particular play, the work of a particular author, or a consideration of a narrowly defined class of technology. A relatively recent case in point is Dennis Jerz's *Technology in American Drama: 1920–1950: Soul and Society in the Age of the Machine*.[16] As the kitchen-sink title suggests, it is an uneasy blend of theatre history, formalist criticism, and linear historicism concerned with the grand metanarratives of individual, aesthetic, and cultural progress. While it takes technology as a recurring theme in three decades of American drama, it uncritically maintains such age-old structuring binaries as human/machine and theatre/society and hews to a progressivist, linear account of aesthetic development. Similarly, *Technology in American Drama* repeatedly allows itself to be drawn into theatre and drama's representational illusions, for instance, by reading characters not as signs but rather as fully self-conscious human agents. Their actions, in Jerz's readings, follow upon their willful decisions and intentions, despite the ways technology repeatedly attenuates that foundational concept of human subjectivity to begin with.

By contrast, *Staging Technology* views the theatre apparatus and staged representations of human–technology interfaces as extensions of and elaborations upon a complex and contradictory cultural logic: Theatre, drama, and performance do not merely reflect their cultural moments; they also process, critique, rework, and resist them in ways that go beyond their explicit theses or surface readings of character and action. By maintaining its focus primarily on the internal literary dynamics of the works it examines, Jerz's book does not account for how the theatre apparatus complicates the very notions of the human, the actor, and the character, not just in techno-plays, but in all performed representation. So, while *Technology in American Drama* offers occasional insights and findings useful to my project—especially to Chapter 2—its reliance on expressions of authorial intention, formalist criticism, and aesthetic judgment and on an explicatory rather than dialectical critical perspective is more typical of the strain of drama criticism into which *Staging Technology* wishes to intervene.

Still, in enumerating the ways *Staging Technology* departs from more standard approaches to theatre and drama studies, I do not mean to reject the relevance of these approaches to my project. One of the most concise and compelling articulations of the critical possibilities of an approach that attends to the materialities and technologies of dramatic theatre production comes in Christopher Baugh's introduction to *Theatre, Performance and Technology* (2005). His opening remarks to this comprehensive examination of the development of stage technologies in the twentieth century summarizes centuries of technological innovation in theatre, from the ancient Greeks' painted sceneries and famous crane-like machine, through the increasingly sophisticated staging of opera and stage spectacles in the seventeenth and eighteenth centuries, on to the sensational melodrama and the box-set naturalism that predominated at the end of the nineteenth century. In providing this overview, Baugh rightly notes that "[t]echnologies may have meanings in and of themselves, and are not simple servants to the mechanistic needs of scenic representation. They are an expression of a relationship with the world and reflect complex human values and beliefs"[17]:

> Complex technologies in performance [...] serve as symbols of power and authority, at the simplest where the stage knows or "owns" something that the spectator does not. More subtly, in the knowledge and ownership of technology there may also dwell the colonial power of the nation, the patriarchal power of the monarch, duke and state, the power of the owner of the theatre and its means of presentation. Dramaturgical power and efficacy may also reside in technology; the theatre of Greek antiquity used a *mêchanê*—a mechanized lifting arm or crane to suspend gods over the concluding action of its tragedy. Their suitably elevated status illustrated their ability to provide dramatic resolution to the drama—hence the *deus ex machina*, "god out of a machine."[18]

Baugh is right in directing us to the way theatre technologies do not just enable effects but convey ideological, political, and social meanings as well. Implicit in his remarks is the way technologies of the stage can function both as signs—a bearer of meaning—and tools for the production of effects at the same time. Stage technology thus inhabits a double ontology: As a sign, it can be read for its signifying potential, analyzed in order to read out of it encoded or implicit messages about power, value, and belief; but it can also be understood as an apparatus that produces other effects, themselves open to critical interpretation. Throughout this book, I have tried to remain mindful of both qualities and not to let the effects occlude the machine, on the one hand, or the facticity of the machine as such to detract attention from its representational outputs. Rather, I see the theatre apparatus as such and its effects as part of a continuum of meaning-making, a process for producing meanings and for producing other processes at the same time. In short, stage technology emerges in *Staging Technology* as part of a dynamic system of production, interpretation, ideology, and self-reproduction.

Baugh raises these questions in passing, gesturing toward analytical concerns that go beyond the purview of his book, which enacts a relatively straightforward form of theatre history more in line with the historical narratives of teleology and causality that Foucault critiques. The bounded, linear unity of Baugh's project is signaled by the word "development" in his title and by the book's overall thesis that a modernist aesthetic of rejection was the primary motivating force of theatre's technological innovations. Still, the kind of detailed recapitulation of modern theatre's technology Baugh provides is essential to the media-specific analyses *Staging Technology* offers, and I have made use of Baugh's perspective, along with those of other theatre and design historians, to enable a rhizomic, analytical, and interpretive reading of staged and stage machineries.

And so, the point of *Staging Technology* here is not to denigrate more standard approaches to theatre and drama studies. My own work as a critic, scholar, performer, director, and teacher has benefited from New Historicism, phenomenology, theatre history, and single-author, single-genre, and nation-of-origin perspectives on theatre and drama, and I have contributed articles and essays to journals and volumes organized around these kinds of inquiry. In the pages that follow, I have drawn freely and often deeply from such works. Depending on the uses to which I wish to put a reading, I have knowingly adopted this or that set of limitations, finding them occasionally salutary and necessary. After all, one must somehow draw boundaries, however provisional, around the field of inquiry or risk becoming a kind of mad Casaubon seeking a universal and unconstructed—and thus, precisely impossible—point of view on all knowledge. In what follows, however, thematic, motific, or formal consonances take clear precedence over national, ethnic, linguistic, historical, and generic boundaries. Thus, the reader will find utterances by US presidents, for example, in conversation with those of literary critics, theatre practitioners, historians, computer programmers, mathematicians, media theorists, inventors, and social scientists. The analytical and interpretive moves this book makes emerge from my view of theatre and drama as a radically interdisciplinary, synthetic, and ever-changing set of practices and approaches. Again, the theatre space itself, with its blend of old and new, of organic bodies and inorganic materials, of music, rhythm, speech, and text, of experiment, invention, and method, of play and rigor, stands as a metaphor for the permeability of boundaries and conventions that typically separate fields of study, modes of inquiry, and arenas of endeavor, and for the methodological and disciplinary disruption this work attempts.

Readers already well versed in theatre history, generally, and the history of theatre technologies more specifically, will note that some of the most celebrated and influential individuals in the history of innovative theatre production—recent as well as more historically distant—go unnamed or barely mentioned in this book. For example, this paragraph will mark the first and last mention of innovators like Josef Svoboda, Dion Boucicault, Inigo Jones, and Bernardo Buontalenti. Walter Gropius's designs for Erwin Piscator's theatre, likewise, remain undiscussed because they were never put into action; for a similar reason, Adolphe Appia's designs, which remained as sketches or manifested only as brief experiments in Dalcroze's studio, do not appear in what follows—this, despite the fact that Svoboda, Appia, Piscator, Gropius, Jones, and Boucicault are mainstays of traditional histories of theatre design. Others, like Gordon Craig and Vsevolod Meyerhold, get relatively short shrift. While their designs and dramaturgy evince a high degree of technical sophistication and technological innovation, the fact that their work, like that of Svoboda, was typically deployed in the service of productions of otherwise nontechnological pieces—standards of the theatrical and operatic canon—means that they fall mostly outside the purview of the present project. Similarly, insights into technologically mediated avant-garde, postmodern, nondramatic, and postdramatic manifest themselves mostly in footnotes or asides; for this book's focus on textual and, for the most part, narrative drama leaves these approaches beyond its scope.

However, the approach I have taken to examining technology in and of the theatre may be usefully extended beyond the fifteen or so principal works examined here, as I have tried to demonstrate in a brief epilogue. As technotexts, the plays, operas, and performance pieces I have chosen for consideration especially heighten the salience of stage technologies by staging technology; nevertheless, what they show us about the relationship of the human agent (however it might be construed) and technology pertains no less to Svoboda's highly technologically inflected production of *Hedda Gabler*, the fact that Ibsen's play does not concern itself with technological innovation as such notwithstanding. Likewise, plays that do take as a central concern scientific and technological innovation—for instance, Brecht's *Galileo* (1943), Michael Frayn's *Copenhagen* (1998), David Auburn's *Proof* (2000)—even though their staging may call for relatively simple, unobtrusive deployments of advanced technology—also have much to say about how we conceive of the human in relationship to the scientific, technological, cybernetic, or quantum worlds. Without wishing to apologize for the exclusion of these individuals and works from consideration, I do want to acknowledge them and to confess that their exclusion is in large part due to the not exactly arbitrary, but by no means inevitable boundaries I have drawn around my project, boundaries that are as permeable and provisional as the generic, methodological, historical, national, and linguistic boundaries I have intentionally troubled in what is to come.

One such boundary that will become readily apparent to the reader who makes their way through the five main chapters of *Staging Technology* is cultural: The works under consideration and the productions in question would seem to point to a distinctly Euro-American bias: they have been written by white Europeans and Americans, performed by white European and American actors, and produced for mostly white European and American audiences. This circumscription, which might be seen as a limitation to my project, emerges from the fact that the technotextual interplay *Staging the Machine* examines occurs only in works written in and produced for cultures where technological advancement both in society and large and in theatre production more narrowly has reached a high degree of sophistication and where the interplay of the human with the technological has become a salient cultural concern. For a variety of causes, the cultures of Africa, the Middle East, South America, and South and East Asia have not experienced the technological saturation of everyday life and the techno-rationalist orientation of broad cultural ideologies. Not least of these causes is the ongoing colonial and neocolonial American and European deployment of military power, technological innovation, capitalist economics, and (pseudo-)scientific knowledge and the cultural logic that subtends them for subjugating denizens of the Global South and Middle and Far East. Partly as a consequence of these historical dynamics, theatre and drama outside the American and European contexts have not concerned themselves centrally with representing advanced technology or the effects of their cultural saturation. However, as I will show, my approach to reading the dramatic stage as a technological space in these explicitly technologically oriented plays can be usefully extended to making sense of medium and materiality in less technologically complex works outside the European and American canon.

As I have already suggested, certain accidents of circumstance and initially idle musings have led to this book. They were, and remain, rhizomic and playful, serious and rigorous though my analyses are. I have not tried to provide definitive or authoritative readings of the works under consideration, although I have offered detailed analyses that do, on their own, offer insights into these works singly. At times, what I have to offer may serve the needs of designers, directors, or actors engaged in productions of these pieces. At others, this book follows lines of flight and modes of inquiry that would seem to speak to a more abstract, theoretical, or academic motivation. Some of the following investigations may be seen as experiments in what we might find when we follow the machine and the vectors of force it exerts; elsewhere, this work satisfies itself simply to raise questions; and, from time to time, the analysis will take on aspects of performance itself, amusing or engaging (I hope) without making claims to practicality or applicability.

In retrospect, I attribute the radical contingencies that structure the chapters in *Staging Technology* and the surprising adjacencies that coalesce among the themes, texts, and productions examined, in large part, to the book's pre-genesis in the virtual classroom where

I first offered an undergraduate course titled "Staging the Machine." I took my appointment as a tenure-track specialist in modern drama in the English department at Drake University, a mid-sized American comprehensive university, just at the time the humanities in higher education were beginning to look toward online education as one way of brightening the then bleak outlook for nonprofessional academic disciplines at colleges and universities heavily reliant on student demand and tuition. Consequently, for a few summers thereafter, I taught a lower-division introductory course in modern drama as an online class, one in which students engaged with the texts, with me, and with one another exclusively through an online learning management system and email.

Since the online environment was new and, I confess, disorienting to me, I decided to design the class in a way that would allow for some consonance between the plays and concepts we would discuss, on the one hand, and the digital environment in which our learning and discussions would take place, on the other. I hoped, thereby, to create a teaching and learning experience that in some measure accounted for digital mediation rather than resisting it. To do so, I selected six plays that centered on fraught human–machine interfaces: Elmer Rice's *The Adding Machine* (1923), Sophie Treadwell's *Machinal* (1928), Samuel Beckett's *Krapp's Last Tape* (1958), Harold Pinter's *The Dumb Waiter* (1960), Eugène Ionesco's *The Future Is in Eggs* (1957), and Don DeLillo's *Valparaiso* (1999). Throughout the course, I asked students not only to conduct a close, critical analysis of the plays as literary texts but also to situate their reading and interpretation in the context of late industrialism and the digital age, generally, and of online learning in particular. The technologically mediated interface my students and I contended with over the term made us increasingly aware of dynamics often considered merely supportive of or peripheral to teaching, learning, reading, and analysis: If scheduled maintenance or unscheduled disruptions brought the system offline, for instance, we needed to adjust our schedule of readings and assignments; students and I, alike, became sensitive to the danger of losing whole posts or lines of thought by "clicking" the wrong "button." Cluttered and user-hostile as these kinds of interfaces were twenty years ago, we needed to learn to read differently, scanning toolbars, sidebars, top and lateral menus, and embedded links to navigate the site successfully. I recall lots and lots of aimless navigation, meandering through an endless series of pages before discovering a sought-after menu or application. Eventually, each summer, usually during a discussion of *The Adding Machine*, one student would remark that in order to successfully turn in an assignment or post a comment, one repeatedly had to click "Submit," always one of two options, the other being "Cancel." By (forced) choice, we were all submitting to the technology in both literal and metaphorical ways.

This heightened awareness of the digital periphery and of the constraints our content management system imposed, even as it liberated us from a number of the traditional constraints of the college classroom, accounted in part for some of my students' closer attention to the periphery of the dramatic texts as well. While students in my in-person drama classes are wont to read quickly through the stage directions, if not ignore them altogether, in the online environment, stage directions became much more central to our understanding of how particular plays worked and how, as texts, they simultaneously invoked and elided the scene of production. Stage directions often feel like constraints, anyway—theatre students taking my drama classes frequently tell me with enviable confidence that stage directions are optional in production. Even while I disagree that stage directions invite us to overlook them as readers, as if they were written in a kind of disappearing ink that fades as soon as the student's gaze falls upon them, I do recognize that they can often seem micromanagerial, obtruding on the otherwise organic unfolding of plot and dialogue and obstructing the mind's-eye-view of the imagined action. Being inside the machine as readers and discussants during those summer online versions of "Staging the Machine" brought the salience of the stage directions and their liberating/constraining duality into sharper focus.

While I no longer teach that course online, I credit that experience with awakening my interest in plays that take the machine as a central concern in addition to relying on advanced or sophisticated technology to enable their production onstage. As that interest has grown over the years, and as I revised that course into a more expansive, in-person upper-division version that included more and more challenging theory, criticism, and history in its reading list, the concept for this book began to take shape. For, while articles, essays, and book chapters here and there address in focused ways the appearance of machineries and other technologies in plays, and much has been written about the development of advanced technology in production practices, no sustained investigation into the interrelationship among staged technologies, theatre technology, historical and critical analyses of technological innovation, and close reading of dramatic representations of technologies exists.

To the extent this book is, in some ways, an outgrowth of that earlier teaching experience, the carnivalesque, rhizomic, multivalent, and ambiguous dynamics of the classroom remain as traces in the approach I have taken, the arguments I've offered, and the form this work takes overall. Still, one wishes to conform to at least some minimal expectations about bookness, for the sake of navigability and legibility, if for no other reason. And so, in deference to those expectations, *Staging Technology* presents itself in five chapters of roughly the same length and an epilogue, each dealing centrally with a few works that may be seen as more or less closely related.

Before providing brief summaries of those chapters, another concession to the conventions of the academic monograph, I want to make clear that this arrangement of elements, like the methods, connections, and interpretive claims I have chosen to advance, might—and probably should—be read as provisional, as the manifestation of one among many possibilities for putting these works and these interpretations in relationship to one another. Returning, now, to early notes and drafts of these chapters, and to the conference papers, talks, and essays on which I have built in bringing forward *Staging Technology*, I am reminded of the many books this book will not prove to have become. In some of those versions, the book is more rigidly chronological in its arrangement. In others, the chapters seem to want to coalesce around generic similarities; and in still others, similarities and differences among these plays' social or political truth-claims, whether implicit or explicit, seem to have suggested the organizational rubric. In some ways, what follows is only one more in a potentially endless series of arrangements and rearrangements, each of which bears its own potential advantages and drawbacks. Traces of those earlier, but finally rejected, organizations remain as cross-references, embedded throughout, indicating connections between material or lines of thought in one chapter and those to be found elsewhere. Accordingly, I invite readers finally to find their own ways into and through the text, following whatever lines of flight seem most compelling, interesting, or even useful. The very adventuresome reader may wish to let the alphabetic arbitrariness of the index suggest a way through the text. Others may take scissors and glue to the whole thing, reassembling it as they wish. (In doing so, they will come very close indeed to the process of writing the book.)

This caveat notwithstanding, something like an arc or architecture emerges when one considers the chapters in the order I have presented them. The earliest two chapters, in which I examine European and American modernist plays, give their attention to performance pieces in which technology and the logic of technological innovation takes a mostly linear, objective, teleological, analog and Newtonian form: trains, elevators, automobiles, engines, broadcast and sound recording devices, home appliances, and an assembly-line logic of industrial production animate these pieces and speak to the ideologies of late industrialism as it manifested itself between 1920 and 1960. Chapter 3, with its focus on the emerging technologies of network broadcast and transoceanic flight, can be seen as a transitional or bridge chapter that presages the later two chapters' increasingly central focus on recursivity, digitality, and virtuality as they characterize both the staged environment and action and also the theatre technologies that enable such staging. Admittedly, my characterization of this arc presents the book itself as more linear, historically bounded, and progressivist than it is, and the reader will

Introduction 27

begin fairly early to note ways such a narrative gets disrupted—lines of flight, rhizomes, flows, and connections that circumvent or short-circuit this overall structure. Still, if bearing this overarching structure in mind makes navigating *Staging Technology* a more straightforward enterprise than it might otherwise be, I invite readers to do so.

Chapter 1, "Avant-Garde Assemblages," examines four pieces from the French modernist theatre: Jean Cocteau's ballet *The Eiffel Tower Wedding Party* (1921); Tristan Tzara's play *The Gas Heart* (1921); and two companion pieces by Eugène Ionesco: *Jack, or the Submission* (1955) and *The Future Is in Eggs* (1957). I read these pieces as subverting, through enactive satire, wordplay, fragmentation, and wry self-referentiality, the logic of the capitalist and military–industrial machine, both literal and metaphorical. Through fragmentation, articulation, and rearrangement, they send up the modularity and linear logic of the machineries of industry, figured as stage settings, human–machine hybrids, typography, and Aristotelian causality, and evidenced both in the staged representation and also in the apparatus of theatrical production. Borrowing insights from Anson Rabinbach's archaeology of the human/machine metaphor in *The Human Motor*, Marshall McLuhan's mid-century reflections on media in *Understanding Media*, and Deleuze and Guattari's concept of the "assemblage" discussed in *A Thousand Plateaus*, I argue that these works' rhizomic narratives at the level of plot, their linguistic slippage and wordplay at the level of the utterance, and their deployment of stage machineries at the level of the material practices of theatre invite audiences to question causality, teleology, and productivity as the structuring values of everyday life.

Chapter 2, "Machineries of Nostalgia and American Modernity," examines the relationship between the machineries that regulate capitalist enterprise in Elmer Rice's *Adding Machine* (1921), Sophie Treadwell's *Machinal* (1928), and Arthur Miller's *Death of a Salesman* (1948), on the one hand, and these works' construction of a freer, more natural and unconstrained ideal of American individual identity captured in Herbert Hoover's notion of "rugged individualism," itself a product of Emersonian, Toquevillian, and Jeffersonian ideals of

Americanness. In all three plays, the main characters find themselves burdened by the machineries of everyday life, including in their professional and domestic identities, and long for freedom, figured as the frontier, the exotic, the open road, or an Elysian paradise. In evoking this freedom/constraint binary, these works reinforce a nostalgia for an impossible fantasy-ideal of an American past, one that echoes both Marxian aspirations of liberation and the kind of longing Raymond Williams deconstructs in *The Country and the City*. The machine, in these plays, then, becomes a foil for unconstructed, unfettered human agency, an ideal Miller's, Rice's, and Treadwell's works do not subject to critique. The chapter closes with a brief consideration of Isaac Gomez's *La Ruta* (2018), an American play that, in examining the human–system dynamics of post-NAFTA (North American Free Trade Agreement) Mexico, uses a manifestly nonwhite, non-American, working-class perspective to reveal the limitations of the fantasy-nostalgia at work in these earlier plays.

Chapter 3, "Alienating Devices," takes up the question of stage technologies and staged representations of technology in the context of Bertolt Brecht's views on the relationship among theatrical production, advanced aviation and communication technology, and capitalist subjectivity, especially as his views were realized in Caspar Neher's scenic designs and through Kurt Weill's music. In examining Brecht and Weill's collaboration *Lindbergh's Flight* as it was produced in 1929, at the Baden-Baden Chamber Music Festival and at the Stadttheater in Breslau (Wrocław), and by the Opéra National de Lyon in 2006, I argue that these productions demonstrate the susceptibility of Brecht's alienation "devices" to appropriation by an ideologically affirmative technical apparatus that prizes absorption and spectacle over critical distance and pedagogical dramaturgy. By contrast, John Adams and Alice Goodman's *Nixon in China*, in its 1987 premiere and in two early twenty-first-century revivals, and Don DeLillo's straight play *Valparaiso* (1999) offer a post-Brechtian critique of telecommunications and aerospace technologies. That critique, from the vantage point of our contemporary moment, anatomizes the way the collapse of time and space, on the one hand, and the appropriation and attenuation of human subjectivity by new media abet capitalist ideological hegemony, on the other. At the same time, the influence of Brecht is apparent in these later works; the complex interplay of stage technologies with staged representation and alienated, gestic acting in both works, as well as Adams's post-minimalist musical setting of Goodman's libretto in *Nixon*, rework epic dramaturgy well after it had become a mainstay of Western theatre. In the chapter's final pages, Athol Fugard's devised play *The Island* (1973) provides an example how the complex interplay between theatrical and extra-theatrical systems can emerge as an object of analysis even in a technologically fairly simple performance context. In addition to Brecht's theoretical writings, Walter Benjamin's perspective on technologies of representation and Stuart Ewen's analysis of the way human–machine interfaces structure leisure and the literal creation of the human in the last two decades of the previous century inform my reading of these works.

Chapter 4, "Machineries of Constraint," focuses principally on two plays of the early absurdist tradition (if it may be termed a tradition): Samuel Beckett's *Krapp's Last Tape* (1958) and Harold Pinter's *The Dumb Waiter* (1960). These two plays, written at the same time and premiered in London within two years of each other, explicitly name their central machineries in their titles: Krapp's reel-to-reel tape recorder and the dumb waiter that will dictate Ben's and Gus's fates. Importantly, in naming staged machineries—the one quite advanced in its time, the other quite simple—the titles of these plays also focus our attention on the theatrical apparatus by means of which productions create their machine effects. On the one hand, the tape recorder's function on stage in *Krapp's Last Tape* depends on the availability of audio technology in the theatre, while the dumb waiter—although we do not presume that an actual dumb waiter is in service—functions as a mise en abîme, its system of cues, pulleys, and cables creating a microcosm of the theatre itself. Moreover, these machineries effect a transformation in the humans who interact with them, transforming Krapp, Ben, and Gus alike into human–machine hybrids whose interior states of mind, desires, fears, and thoughts must conform to the machine's logic just as their physical actions begin to take on the rhythms and operational principles of the machines they engage with. Emerging from this dynamic is a sense of constraint, of the attenuation of human agency and the contraction of the sphere within which it might be exercised. Drawing on Hayles's work on cybernetics and the post-human, as well as upon Habermas's and Louis Althusser's theories of ideology in late capitalism, this chapter uses *Krapp's Last Tape* and *The Dumb Waiter* to establish the sense of constraint and forced choice that will come to characterize Beckett's shorter works, including *What Where* (1983) and *Play* (1964), examined in some detail in the final pages of the chapter. In these plays, the staged machine disappears almost entirely, elided into the machineries of the stage: the sound or lighting system. This collapse of staged and staging machines in Beckett's later works, like that of *Krapp's Last Tape* and Pinter's *The Dumb Waiter*, gives rise not simply to postmodern meta-theatricality, but rather to an examination of the theatre as a machine where ideological constraint gets reproduced, reified in the very practices of theatrical production and performance.

Chapter 5, "Post-Human Recursivity," examines three examples of what has been termed post-human theatre: Heiner Müller's *Hamletmachine* (1977); Julie Taymor's monumental production of *Spider-Man: Turn off the Dark* (2010), with music by U2's Bono and The Edge; and Tod Machover's *Death and the Powers* (2010), a "robot opera" with libretto by former US poet laureate Robert Pinsky. By invoking, enacting, and representing scientific and technological innovation, these three works push against the idea of the human as a unified, self-identical, embodied entity and thereby disrupt traditional notions of portrayal, characterization, and setting. In doing so, they also question the limits of the stage as a material site of performance and theatre as a coherent set of representational practices. The transformations suggested by these three very distinct works—a non-narrative play, a Broadway musical, and an opera—are enabled by advances in information theory, cybernetics, digital computation, and mathematics as well as by innovations in nondramatic performance, such as dance and performance art. They refocus the machine-critique of the plays by Rice, Treadwell, and Miller, discussed in Chapter 2, and by Pinter and Beckett, examined in Chapter 4, on the limits of the human as such, suggesting an analog between the disintegration of the human into sign systems, biological phenomena, and encoded data and a radical rupture of the stage as place and as apparatus. This chapter also attempts to connect these recent works with what is perhaps the earliest manifestation of the post-human on the Western stage, Karel Čapek's *Rossum's Universal Robots* (1921) and with countervailing tendencies in contemporary stage practice, such as Handspring's manual puppetry in Nick Stafford's stage adaptation of Michael Malpurgo's novel *War Horse* at London's Royal National Theatre (2007).[19] In doing so, I hope to demonstrate again how the most recent technological innovations in theatre production and the question of the human in relation to technology and performance have been embedded in modern drama since the 1920s, and that a simple, linear chronology of technological development cannot account for the reemergence of these concerns simultaneously with a return to less technologically sophisticated production values in the second decade of the twenty-first century.

Readers familiar with Una Chaudhuri's 1995 book *Staging Place* will recognize in the title of the present volume, *Staging Technology*, an echo of her title.[20] In the preface to *Staging Place*, Chaudhuri describes space as "that essential element of all theatrical presentation." In the course of researching and writing her book, she says she

> discovered [...] that an intricate and often contradictory circuitry links the various spaces, places, and representations of place that the theatrical apparatus makes possible. So complex and so fundamental is this network of relationships that I have come to believe its full articulation [...] can yield a new methodology for drama and theatre studies, a "geography" of theatre capable of replacing—or at least significantly supplementing—its familiar "history."[21]

Staging Technology shares some of the goals and methods evident in *Staging Place*: to theorize structures of meaning, structures pervasive across the history of staged performance in the West and, in the twentieth and twenty-first centuries, at work in almost every identifiable stage aesthetic, including realism, absurdism, epic, performance art, opera, and the avant-garde. For Chaudhuri, the element structuring the questions that most concerned her and the interpretive possibilities she pursues is the implicit and explicit evocation of spatiality and placeness on stage. This element is so constitutive of staged performance, so *obvious*, that the unasked but underlying question of Chaudhuri's book is *how could place have gone so long unnoticed and untheorized?* Staging Technology pursues a similar line of questioning about the intersection of real-world technologies, technologies of the theatre, and the representation of technologies in performance texts and productions: *How might drama studies advance when we begin systematically to notice and account for technology as a constitutive element of meaning-making in production?*

Without question, Chaudhuri's book changed the course of theatre and drama studies less because of the specific claims it advanced about the way space was represented on the Western stage, and more because in asking those questions and advancing those claims, *Staging Place* made spatiality visible and offered practitioners and critics alike a set of lenses through which to view it and a vocabulary to report on what we saw. Its salience as a pivotal moment in the scholarship of theatre and drama may be seen in the fact that numerous books on the "staging" of this or that element of theatre or drama have emerged since Chaudhuri's study: Katherine Burkman and Judith Roof's collection *Staging the Rage* (1998); Greg Geikekam's *Staging the Screen* (2007); Magdalena Kasubowski-Houston's *Staging Strife* (2010); and Barry Freeman's *Staging Strangers* (2017). My hope is that *Staging Technology* will do for the technologies in and of dramatic theatre what Chaudhuri's volume did for representations of place and space: That is, to make them legible as objects of interpretation subject to critical analysis and rigorous theorization. If it moves the study of theatre and drama only incrementally toward a new way of seeing and theorizing technologies of the stage, it will, in my view, have achieved its goal.

Tellingly, the importance of theatre technology and its relationship to other technologies, both real and represented, was already latent in Chaudhuri's articulation of her own project vis-à-vis space and place. For she describes the links among staged and stage spaces as an "intricate [...] circuitry," a "network" that the "theatre apparatus makes possible." So, while Chaudhuri claims that space and place compose an "essential element" of theatrical representation, her formulation of the critical questions that animate her work simultaneously gestures fleetingly toward and brackets off another equally "essential" factor at play: the "apparatus." And so, with the opening chorus of Brecht and Weill's *Lindbergh's Flight*, I offer this invitation: "Here is the machine. Step in!"

1

Avant-Garde Assemblages: Tristan Tzara, Jean Cocteau, and Eugène Ionesco

We begin in Paris, because Paris is the nexus of many of the economic, social, historical, technological, and artistic concerns that will continue to inform this book's work here and in subsequent chapters. It is "the city of light," both because it was the seat of the European enlightenment, whose measured rationality echoes in Haussmann's comprehensively designed, open plan, with its gardens and wide boulevards, and because it was among the first cities to adopt gas lighting. The city of Voltaire, D'Alembert, Diderot, and Descartes (for a time), and the adopted home of Rousseau during the Enlightenment, Paris also nurtured the American expatriate and European avant-garde in the early twentieth century: There, an international gallimaufry of artists, writers, and composers, including Gertrude Stein, Wassily Kandinsky, Sergei Diaghilev, Igor Stravinsky, Francis Picabia, Marcel Duchamp, Pablo Picasso, Tristan Tzara, Jean Cocteau, James Joyce, Georges Auric, Louis Durey, Arthur Honneger, Darius Milhaud, Francis Poulenc, and Germaine Tailleferre, laid siege to the Enlightenment traditions of rationality, cool reflection, and aesthetic balance and coherence, on the one hand, and occupied modernism's barricades built against the romantic ideals of individualism, agrarianism, and self-expression, on the other. No artifact symbolizes Paris' fraught hybridity of classicism, romanticism, and disruptive experimentalism so well as the Eiffel Tower.

So pervasive a symbol of *rive gauche* Paris is the Eiffel Tower that those of us who do not live in Paris can easily forget that it is, in fact, invisible from most quarters of the city. Moreover, its ubiquity in film and advertising suggests permanence, as if the tower were a somehow autochthonic feature of prehuman geography, when it is, in fact, among the newer landmarks in that ancient city; only a few decades into its still relatively brief existence, it lost its subversive edge and shed the aura of the shockingly new. Popular belief has it that Guy de Maupassant took to lunching in the restaurant at its base because it was one of the few places in the seventh arrondissement from which the tower itself was not visible, so monstrous did it seem to his aesthetic sensibilities, steeped as they were in romanticism's more bucolic, sentimental mists. In fact, Maupassant opens his 1890 memoir *La Vie Errante*, with this claim: "I left Paris and, indeed, France because the Eiffel Tower succeeded in bothering me too much."[1] By 1921, thirty-two years after its opening as the gateway to the 1889 World's Fair, when Jean Cocteau set his surrealist "ballet" *The Eiffel Tower Wedding Party* [*Les Mariés de la Tour Eiffel*] on its first platform, it had become a tenacious symbol of modernity.

Although the Eiffel Tower itself has been fully woven into the texture of the city, *The Eiffel Tower Wedding Party* still retains the power to amuse and disorient its audience. Produced at the beginning of what would become a decade of diverse and bold experimentation in every artistic mode, Cocteau's piece already looked forward to the absurd, non sequitur logic of Eugène Ionesco's plays—in particular, *Jack, or The Submission* and its sequel *The Future Is in Eggs, or It Takes All Sorts to Make a World*—and echoes the contemporary fragmentation and tangential texture of Tristan Tzara's *The Gas Heart*. In what follows, the Eiffel Tower will provide a starting point—a gateway—for understanding the interrelationship among these four plays and their concerns with the machineries of late industrialism and with the formal experimentations of high modernism in the French theatre. Apart from its cultural symbolism and the alienating effect it had on the Committee of 300—writers, painters, and thinkers who, like Maupassant, saw the encroachment of modernity as an almost unbearable outrage against good taste and order—the Eiffel Tower condenses a number of motifs and themes that will continue to emerge throughout the discussion of

Cocteau, Tzara, and Ionesco that follows. We will see that, despite the apparent randomness and senselessness of these plays, they do, in fact, offer a critique of late-industrial advances in technology, especially the technologies of capitalist production, communication, and warfare, foreseeing the hegemony of the military–industrial complex US president Dwight D. Eisenhower would name explicitly in his farewell address, some forty years after the premiere of Cocteau's and Tzara's plays considered here, on January 17, 1961.[2] Cocteau, Tzara, and Ionesco use enactment and form to suggest, often through satire and exaggeration, their works' minatory orientation toward these technologies and their effects. That is to say, they frequently mimic the rhythms, flows, and logics of the machine, creating an analogy whereby the breakdown of the performance and its mechanisms marks the limits of a more general machine logic. They thus invite their audiences to imagine dysfunctional worlds in which machine logic and machine power have become the determinants for even the smallest details of everyday life. Indeed, the range of registers in which these plays speak—from the world-historical to the everyday individual in an everyday moment—help explain their often collage-like quality.

Cocteau's *Eiffel Tower Wedding Party* first appeared at the Theatre Champs-Élysées on June 1, 1921, as part of a triple bill featuring Jean Börlin and Rolf de Maré's ballet company, with choreography by Cocteau himself and music by members of the Parisian collective *Les Six*: Tailleferre, Auric, Honneger, Milhaud, and Poulenc.[3] The Théâtre des Champs-Élysées was, by that time, known for its avant-garde bill of fare, having opened in 1913 with the premiere of Stravinsky's *Rite of Spring*. Given its surrealist aesthetic—including often seemingly tangential or non sequitur dialogue, abstract sets, and exaggerated costumes, masks, and gesture—*The Eiffel Tower Wedding Party*'s plotline is deceptively simple. A photographer on the Eiffel Tower, hired to photograph a wedding celebration to be held on the tower's first platform, is beset with camera malfunctions, so that he must continually delay the photo-taking. During the delay, several other characters intrude on the party, often complicating (and nearly derailing) the celebrations, but sometimes merely commenting upon the action. However, once the photographer sets his camera to rights—a process that takes the entire play—and can take the photograph, order is restored and the wedding party departs.

The nature of the malfunction the photographer must contend with is bizarre, however: In place of the little mechanical birdie that should have popped out from the camera to attract his subjects' gaze, other animals emerge instead: an ostrich and a lion. Attracted by the presence of the lion, a hunter appears, only to discover that his good luck has doubled with the availability of an ostrich. Indeed, the malfunctioning camera becomes the site of the entrances of all the characters as well. And so, the middle part of the play is taken up with accidents, misunderstandings, tangents, and divagations of all kinds as the photographer attempts to get the ostrich back into the camera (which, it seems, would return it to working order) before the hunter shoots it. He succeeds and is finally able to arrange the wedding-party tableau; however, before the picture can be taken, an art dealer and a collector arrive on the scene and mistake the motionless wedding party for a piece of abstract modern art. The collector buys it, even though he remains unsure what it means. As the photographer finally takes the photo, a dove of peace appears and the subjects one by one reenter the camera, which, at the end of the play, converts itself into a train to take all the guests—except the hunter, who has missed the scheduled departure—away.

The Eiffel Tower, both as a setting and as historical artifact, proves especially significant in terms of the piece's technological motifs. It is as much a spectacle of its own conditions of possibility as it is a building. The fact that visitors can, for a few hours, explore its complex of platforms and trellises and take their déjeuner among its girders is incidental to its formal homage to the very means of its construction. The occasion for which it was built, the 1889 Paris World's Fair, itself offered a backdrop of technical invention, often exorbitant. Moreover, the tower was intended as a temporary, rather than permanent monument, designed to be easily dismantled, making it one of the first explicitly disposable structures of the modern world.[4] Its history and form, then, considered together suggest its aspirations to a technical aesthetic pure and disconnected from history and functionality.

The Eiffel Tower Wedding Party explicitly invites comparison of the tower to a nearby structure much more grounded in history and function: The Cathedral of Notre Dame: "The Eiffel Tower is a world unto itself, like Notre Dame. It is the Notre Dame of the left bank."[5] The Cathedral's artisanal virtuosity, engrained religiosity, and seeming timelessness—recent major fire damage notwithstanding—challenge the tower's modernity. Dedicated to a quite specific and local function, as the seat of a bishopric, Notre Dame's symbolic value is secondary to its functional value. Or, to put it a different way, its symbolism is almost entirely exhausted by its function. What falls outside its functional realm—its attraction to tourists, its title role in Hugo's novel—is surplus, a supplemental value without which the Cathedral would lose none of its cathedrality.

By contrast, the Eiffel Tower stands as a monument to modernity, simultaneously the avatar, index, and harbinger of the cultural logic of high modernism. Partly functional, its elevator and steps giving access to increasingly rarified views of the city and its height enabling it to serve as a telecommunications antenna, the Eiffel Tower *seems* useful. The austerity of its reticulated girders, joists, and braces gesture formally to the verticalization of functional architecture that would, in time, geometrically increase the capacity of urban spaces. And yet the spaces it contains and the zones it delimits are, effectively, empty and mostly useless: Nothing happens there. And, because of that, the tower refuses to become a cathedral despite the occasional wedding party. Indeed, it embodies a new theory of the aesthetic, not as distinct from functionality, but as an almost Platonic attenuation of functionality. The modern sculpture, in the tower's idiom, offers us the formal impression of functionality without end: both purposeless and ceaseless.[6]

The sense of ceaseless movement detached from practical ends is captured in what is perhaps the most obvious formal feature of the staging of *The Eiffel Tower Wedding Party*: All of the action is mimed or indicated through stylized gesture and dance, and all the speech is either delivered by two oversized phonographs inhabited by human actors on stage right and left or is represented musically by the orchestra. The phonographs, we learn, "speak very loudly and very quickly and distinctly articulate each syllable,"[7] emphasizing the mechanical reproduction of speech. In fact, this separation of characters' (and actors') voices from their bodies points to four features of the Technological Revolution's machine logic: modularity, mechanical reproduction, routinization, and the division of labor.

The machineries of sound reproduction to which the oversized phonographs refer dislocate the voice, taking it out of the body and relocating it in the mechanism and, more precisely, in the grooves of the wax cylinder. The fact that phonograph designs typically featured amplifying horns in the shape of flowers suggests the degree to which manufacturers found themselves at pains to emphasize the natural, rather than unnaturally produced, quality of the sound. The actors' bodies on stage are no longer the source of the voiced sounds. They simply gesture and move more or less in sync with the speech voiced through the simulacral phonographs.

This dislocation of the voice—an effect I will return to in discussing Arthur Miller's *Death of a Salesman* in Chapter 2, Don DeLillo's *Valparaiso* in Chapter 3, and Samuel Beckett's *Krapp's Last Tape* in Chapter 4—presents several interpretive possibilities. One is that the bodies on stage have taken on a further level of representational mediation. In conventional realist theatre, the bodies of actors stand as iconic representations of the bodies of the characters the actors portray, as is especially apparent in plays where one actor is required to play more than one role. In those cases, we understand that the actor's body serves as a sign of something different—a different body—at different times; but more important, the conventional actor's body serves as a sign of only one thing—*only one character's body*—at any given time.[8] Certainly, the actors' bodies in *Eiffel Tower Wedding Party* signify, in part, according to that convention: The body of the actor playing the role of the General is meant to represent the General's body.

My point is that, in *The Eiffel Tower Wedding Party*, the body on stage, while not entirely evacuated of characterological significance, is a body manqué. The voice that normally goes with it, as one of the functions of the human physiological apparatus, is produced elsewhere: by another body, costumed as a machine. Further, as the stage direction cited above indicates, the actors/machines voicing the characters are not expected to differentiate their voices to suggest distinctions among the characters they speak for. Rather, each of the voices gets condensed and mechanically reproduced as one of just two voices. So, in dislocating the voice, the gramophones will have split the bodily function and thus have compromised the integrity of the body—and the body as sign—on stage. The body has become an articulated, rather than organic sign-entity, whose functions have become modular and can be distributed across a system of representational mechanisms. And thus a second representational ambiguity emerges. Does the modularity of the voice represent an aesthetic, technical production value—that is, a stylistic choice? Is it *just* aesthetic? Or, on the contrary, does it point toward something essential about the characters as such: that they are to be understood as split subjects, for instance, or unself-conscious?

Examples of unvoiced acting as an aesthetic or generic choice abound: Mime, for instance, uses voicelessness as the constraint that conditions its form. We are not meant to imagine that the characters in mime suffer a debility, that we are watching a show about aphasiacs or otherwise speech-impaired or cognitively compromised people. Rather, we understand that some of the gestures are the formal representation of some speech that, in the world of the show, is occurring. Our access to that speech is made available, however, according to a nonvocal sign system. The dumb show that precedes *The Mousetrap*, the "play" with which Hamlet will "catch the conscience of the king," is another example of voicelessness as a primarily formal feature: It offers a synopsis of the voiced play to follow.[9] Brechtian drama, as we shall see in Chapter 3, also at times complicates the voice/body/character relationship as a formal alienation technique.

A nearer analog to *The Eiffel Tower Wedding Party* occurs in Julie Taymor's 1992 production of Stravinsky's oratorio *Oedipus Rex* (1927), for which Cocteau wrote the libretto. In this highly stylized performance, influenced by Japanese *kabuki* and *bunraku*, the singers—including Jessye Norman, Philip Langridge, and Bryn Terfel—do not engage in the action, even as they voice the characters. Rather, a combination of puppetry and shadow play composes the gestural element of the action.[10] By employing actors costumed as gramophones to provide the voiced elements of the play—dialogue and narration alike—*The Eiffel Tower Wedding Party* could be understood to engage in a related aesthetic tradition of vocal dislocation.

At the same time, we are invited to consider the possibility that the bodies of characters themselves lack the vocal apparatus necessary for producing speech, or even the cognitive development necessary for imagining the world in signs. Thus, the phonographs would operate to encode the characters' thoughts and desires in a spoken language that is inaccessible to them. This interpretation would explain how it is that an infant (from the Latin *infans*: speechless), in Cocteau's play, expresses demands of its parents: its prelinguistic impulses are translated by and related through the gramophones. A version of this possibility—namely, that the world of this piece is one in which human agents have ceded to the machines their capacity for speech altogether—fits with the conceit of the play, in which a group of live people is mistaken for an artwork because they are silent and, since they are about to be photographed, still.

And here, the ambiguity presented by the dislocation of voices from bodies to enacted machines points toward the ambiguities of still life: Is the still life *still* because it does not move? Or is it a still life because it does not make a sound? Or both?[11] Either way, it is *still life*, the play seems to suggest, but it is a life that, like the actors' bodies, is missing something: language. We can, of course, understand these possibilities as simultaneously activated: They are not mutually exclusive, after all, given that it is a stage representation and not real life. So, such features can be taken as both formal and representational at the same time.

It remains for us to ask, however, how we can understand the relation of bodies to the vocalizing mechanisms in terms of autonomy and authority. At times, the phonographs ask each other questions about what is taking place; they engage in a hermeneutic enterprise, attempting, it seems, to discover the code or logic according to which the action and gestures unfold. In the opening minutes of the play, Phonograph Two narrates an entrance: "Here is the Photographer of the Eiffel Tower. He speaks." But having announced that "he speaks," the phonograph asks, "What does he say?" Phonograph One answers the question by saying the Photographer's words: "You haven't seen an ostrich go by?"[12]

At other moments, the phonographs seem to react with surprise at what they have witnessed in the action. For instance, they have difficulty in keeping up with the newborn's bad behavior:

Phono One He runs away [from the adults]. He screams! He stomps! He wants "to live his own life."
Phono Two I want to live my own life! I want to live my own life![13]

In this exchange, Phonograph Two voices the infant's words after they have been summarized and quoted by Phonograph One, suggesting not that the phonographs are voicing the characters' speech as it is spoken, but rather have fallen somewhat behind the unheard stage speech, more like translation than substitution; alternately, perhaps Phonograph One is cuing Phonograph Two, the relationship of the time of their speech to the time of the action being of no consequence. Having regained purchase on the speech and action and on the alignment between them, however, the phonographs are distracted again, and again seem to fall behind:

Phono One But what is this other sound?
Phono Two The director of the Eiffel Tower. What does he say?
Phono One A little silence, everyone, please. Do not frighten the dispatches.
Phono Two Daddy! Daddy! Dispatches![14]

In exchanges such as these, which occur throughout the piece, a rhythm is established: Having fallen behind, the phonographs hurry to catch up to the action, at which point they are able to channel and thereby to voice the dialogue without pausing to question the means by which they are able to do so. Thus, a kind of irony emerges: Machines meant to replay recordings of past events are put in the position of having to interpret and then to translate gestures and actions into speech nearly simultaneously. Their objectivity, as recording devices, has given way to subjectivity: judgment, conjecture, and questioning. The *re* of *recording*, suggesting repetition and again-ness, has given way to a vocal *cording*, speech ex nihilo. They must, in other words, produce instead of reproduce speech. In this analysis, the machines—which we must constantly remind ourselves, as readers, are not machines but characters (or rather, are both machines/not-machines and characters)—follow the action and dictate it at the same time.

Inasmuch as they both dictate the action and are dictated by it, the phonographs are truly dictation machines. They speak the already spoken, the *on-dit* of the script as well as the unspoken truths about live theatre's mimetic conventions. In so doing, they both disperse the speaking subject, dislocating the agency conveyed through the voice from the actor's body, and also signal the integration of the human (actor and character) into the machinery of the stage and staged machineries alike. Further, this "integration into" the machine is a disintegration. In this way, the phonographs enact a central component of machine logic: the intermingling of human consciousness with machine technology. While the concepts of the cybernetic and cyborg as we understand them today would have been unthinkable in 1921, from the present perspective, it is impossible not to think of Cocteau's play as presaging the dynamics of a post-human subjectivity, which will form a central concern in Chapter 5.

This dislocation of voice from the bodies of actors and characters and the consolidation and centralization of the voice function of *The Eiffel Tower Wedding Party* can be understood according to what would have been, at the play's inception, a relatively recent development in the organization of labor in factories in France: namely, the introduction of the science of work to manage labor, including industrial labor. Initiated in France in 1905, an empirical approach to measuring productivity against time-on-task and fatigue introduced to French agrarian and industrial labor the notion that efficiency, profit, and workers' cooperation could be secured by objective measurement, analysis, and redesign of labor processes.[15] These efforts to introduce scientific rationalism into labor practices culminated, in the wake of the 1913 Renault labor strike, in a years-long debate over the effectiveness of Taylorism in French factories and small shops alike.[16] As Anson Rabinbach explains in *The Human Motor* (1990), the introduction of rationalist "state social policies" alongside the "post-war socialization of the industrial sphere and the rationalization movement in both Germany and France" brought about "a new role for science in the resolution of social"—that is, class—"conflict":

> In the debates on the productivity of the worker, the length of the working day, the military and education question, the working body was subject to a new energetic calculation that placed fatigue at the center of a politics of energy conservation.[17]

These debates over labor and the socioeconomic factors that impinged upon efficiency in the factory system, by 1921, resulted in even the most vocal critic of Taylorist methods, Jean-Marie Lahy, "conced[ing] that the Taylor system 'partially addressed the problems of the organization of work,'" although it would still need to be "modified and accompanied by methods of 'preserving the individual and the race.'"[18] Rabinbach usefully summarizes Taylorism and the scientific approach to labor and production management:

> Broadly conceived, "scientific management" [...] rationalizes the component parts and the general functioning of the enterprise in a series of stages in order to increase productivity and eliminate the waste of labor power and materials. These stages included (1) the division of all shop-floor tasks into their fundamental parts; (2) the analysis and design of each task to achieve maximum efficiency and ease of

imitation; (3) the redesign of tools and machines as standardized models; (4) the linking of wages to output; and (5) rational coordination and administration of production. [...] More narrowly conceived, the Taylor system was concerned with determining the most efficient method of accomplishing each task in the labor process and with the division of all tasks on the shop floor into replicable units.[19]

Salient in the socioeconomic background of *The Eiffel Tower Wedding Party*, and reified in the Eiffel Tower's design and construction itself, the scientific management of labor enables a politically inflected reading of Cocteau's piece.

Particularly relevant to this discussion are four stages enumerated by Rabinbach: division of labor; efficiency and ease of imitation; standardization; and rational production management, as well as the scalability enabled by replicability. For *Eiffel Tower Wedding Party* divides the representational labor onstage between the gesturing, dancing actors, and the speaking ones. In fact, because of some of the speech is conveyed instrumentally, not vocally, such as the oration of the General, whose "speech is orchestral" while "he only gestures,"[20] the work of representing characters is manifestly divided in at least three ways. Division of labor is nothing new in theatrical production and was quite an established practice even in 1921, when the play was first produced. All along, theatre has been made possible by the work of discrete units, each responsible for one or more aspects of the production: properties, costuming, character portrayal, music, set design, and so on. But until the advent of theatrical modernism, the apparent unity of effect produced by these separate organs of production masked the variety of techniques used to produce that unity. Cocteau's modernism, like Bertolt Brecht's, calls attention to the articulated mechanisms of theatrical production, its division of labor. In other words, the division of representational labor as such becomes one of several new objects of representation in European modernist theatre. *The Eiffel Tower Wedding Party* offers us, as spectators, a view of the mechanistic logic of theatrical production, even if that view is itself one of the effects produced by the representational apparatus itself. Thus, *Eiffel Tower Wedding Party* seems to expose its own representation logic. But it does so as a formal or aesthetic feature—the exposure is, itself, an effect of the theatre-as-machine: The actual mechanisms of production—notably, the actors' bodies, themselves encased in exaggerated and deforming costumes, their faces covered by grotesque masks—lie hidden behind the machine effects apparent in performance.

A dynamic central to the piece will make clear the distinction between the apparatus whose functions get represented in production and the apparatus whose functions enable that representation in the first place: namely, the one between the *functioning theatre apparatus* and the constantly *malfunctioning staged apparatus*. For, time and again, the technologies represented in *Eiffel Tower Wedding Party* fail. At times they fail in quite literal ways, as when the camera repeatedly malfunctions. But the more suggestive, and prescient, failures are also more attenuated. The same camera that will not take photographs also begins to take on functions quite alien to its purpose: Worth mentioning again is the way the camera continually emits animals and secondary characters. Indeed, the lion that emerges from it will eventually devour the general, and the newborn will shoot the assembled using the bullets [*balles*] that he has carried from the camera in a little basket.

This latter malfunction—resulting in a temporary carnage—suggests an implicit play on words. For, while the stage direction indicates that the newborn "bombards" the wedding party—"*L'enfant bombarde la noce*"—the fact that he has deployed bullets [*balles*] to do so, and that Phonograph One uses the sound effects of gunfire, "Bang! Bang!" [*Pan! Pan!*], invites us to imagine gunfire: The unspoken verb "shoots" [*tire*] lingers as a trace in the dialogue.[21] However, it returns explicitly later in the play, again in connection with the child, who "want[s] nothing more than to have a picture taken with the general."[22] Notably, Phonograph One uses the French idiomatic "*me tire en photographie*," that is, "to *shoot* my photo." This usage allows us to see that the camera's recent malfunction has been due not to a mechanical malfunction, but to a slippage in language, a play on words: instead of metaphorically shooting the assembled, as in photography, the camera has allowed for the assembled to be literally shot with a gun. In fact, this slippage from the metaphorical to the literal has already been suggested by the fact that the child's basket carries *balles*: balls or bullets, or both. While the *balles*/bullets/balls pun does not translate well into English, the *tire*/shoot one does.

The piece ends with an elaborate series of plays on words that, again, involve slippage from metaphorical to literal renderings of the camera's mechanical function. Repeatedly referred to as the "apparatus" [*l'appareil*], it begins to work, to function properly [*il marche*] when the photographer has counted to five, literally "taking" the picture as the members of the wedding party two by two enter the camera's oversized shutter. Only the general seems reluctant to depart, but the child drags [*traîn*] him by the hand. Just as he does so, the scene on the Eiffel Tower's platform [*plate-forme*] transforms to become a scene of departure on a train platform: For the hunter rushes on, too late to "catch the last train" [*prendre le dernier train*]. But, since the child's pulling the general along [*{Il} le traîne par le main*] is indicated only by the stage directions, and the bridal train only by association, the three-way *traîn*/*train*/*train* pun, again, emerges only as a trace, a suggestion. Having become a train, the apparatus, no longer a camera but a machine in the more general sense of the French *appareil*, is set in motion [*se met en marche*] while its "bellows" [*son soufflet*] that extends from the lens plate to the film plate has become the train cars—*les wagons*: But, again, the slippage of the words *appareil* [camera/machine], *marche* [functions/moves], and *soufflet* [camera bellows/furnace bellows] emerges in the printed stage directions.[23]

Whereas the human engages with connotation, metaphor, symbol, synecdoche and metonymy, condensation and repression, and wordplay, the machine operates according to the literal and the manifest; indeed, we lack the precise terms for how what the machine does can be understood as signification in the first place, since actual machines, outside of representation, are incapable of generating, on their own, signs as such. The closest this engagement comes to representation, however, is literality, which itself stands as a metaphor for actuality. So, the implicit punning of the last scene of the play, and the more explicit punning of the massacre scene, offer an alternative to machine logic, even as each of these episodes develop around the function/malfunction of the photographer's apparatus.

By way of concluding this discussion of *The Eiffel Tower Wedding Party*, I want to look very closely at an even more elaborate series of plays on words that structures much of the middle section of the play, all of which are interconnected, beginning with some seemingly bizarre business involving some telegraph dispatches that are roosting in the upper reaches of the tower. The wordplay at work in these episodes signals the piece's entanglement in and resistance to technologies of communication and transportation. In one of their more choric exchanges, the two phonographs offer the following insights into the workings of the tower.

Phono One You may well ask yourselves where the ostrich hunter and the manager of the Eiffel Tower have gone. The hunter is searching every level for the ostrich. The manager is searching for the hunter and managing the Eiffel Tower. It is not a sinecure. The Tower is a world unto itself, like Notre Dame. She is the Notre Dame of the left bank.
Phono Two She is the Queen of Paris.
Phono One She *was* Queen of Paris. Now, she's a receptionist.
Phono Two One has to survive, after all.[24]

The Eiffel Tower, we learn, is complicated environment—no "sinecure"—requiring the constant attention of the manager: While it had served a symbolic function as the gateway to the Paris World's Fair of 1889—at which American inventor Thomas Edison, a champion of Gustave Eiffel's innovative engineering and design work, introduced the phonograph—since then, the tower had become host to scientific apparatus and innovative technologies of all kinds, including a laboratory, wind tunnel, and radio transmission site. Indeed, its function as a radio antenna for two-way communication during the First World War is credited with saving it from eventual dismantling.²⁵

So, when Phonograph One insists that the tower is no longer the "Queen of Paris," but instead is merely its "receptionist"—literally, a "telegraph girl," one of a the women hired to monitor incoming and outgoing communications for an organization—our attention is drawn to the tower's function as a center of communications. (Even after 1921, its communications function would continue to expand to include radio and television broadcast and digital communications.) This explicit reference to telegraphy connects to the ongoing business with the dispatches [*les dépêches*], the telegrams received and transcribed at the tower. Three lines into the play, "a large, blue dispatch falls from the girders" after having been shot inadvertently by the hunter chasing the photographer's escaped ostrich. We soon discover that the "dead letter" [*dépeche {...} morte*]—the first pun in the piece—is meant to inform the manager that a wedding party is on its way. Here, the tower's function as a radio transmitter and receiver is literalized in the suggestion that telegrams roost like pigeons in its upper reaches.

Later in the play, after the tower manager asks for silence in order not to frighten the dispatches roosting above, several more dispatches make their appearance:

Phono Two   Incoming dispatches fall onto the stage and flutter around. The whole wedding party chases after them and leaps onto them. [...] The dispatches calm down. They form into a line. The most beautiful one steps forward and gives a military salute.

Phono One   (*in the voice of a vaudeville emcee*) And where are you from?

Phono Two   I am a radio dispatch, and, like my sister, the stork, I come from New York.

Phono One   (*in the voice of a vaudeville emcee*) New York! City of lovers and silhouette lighting.²⁶

This brief segment, apart from making starkly apparent the tangential and associative nature of the narrative, also demonstrates the technological layering that characterizes the play's motifs and form. At once, this passage invokes radio technology and telegraphy, gesturing again to the tower's role as a communications apparatus. References to recently achieved trans-Atlantic flight and, in a wry comment on ersatz American urbanity, *contre-jour* or backlighting (in contrast to Paris, "city of lights") add to the layering, making the tower a nexus for technologies of communication, aviation, scientific inquiry, and the conduct of warfare. Together with its functionalist and mechanized architecture, the tower has itself become a military–industrial complex.

In short, by 1921, Paris, and more particularly the Eiffel Tower as a symbol of both Parisian modernity and modernism, had served as metonymic sites for a particularly dense entanglement of industrialization, technological advancement, functionalized architecture and design, and mechanized militarization for nearly three decades. Conceptually, it had become what Gilles Deleuze and Felix Guattari, in *A Thousand Plateaus*, would term an *assemblage*, a quasi-machinic metaphor naming a dynamic complex of movement, meaning, and functionality, often internally inconsistent or contradictory:

> [T]here are lines of articulation and segmentarity, strata and territories; but also lines of flight, movements of deterritorialization and destratification. Comparative rates of flow on these lines produce phenomena of relative slowness and viscosity, or, on the contrary, acceleration and rupture.[27]

An assemblage, like the Eiffel Tower and European modernity, more generally, combines the ordered, mechanical, teleological, hierarchical, and managed activity, a Taylorist hive of activity, with the freer flowing, uneven, aimless, and organic dynamic of resistance, escape, and excess. A feature of the assemblage of particular interest here is the liability of one element, one trajectory, or one substance within it to transform itself, to change direction or function, to exceed what appeared to be its boundaries or limits, or to double back on itself and undermine the teleologies it had formerly served. Deleuze and Guattari call this transformational tendency *rhizomatic*, taking their metaphor from plant biology. They distinguish the rhizome from the more differentiated and hierarchical root structure and root logic often imposed on language, thought, culture, and custom, noting that the "rhizome itself assumes very diverse forms, from ramified surface extension in all directions to concretion [...]. A rhizome ceaselessly establishes connections between semiotic chains, organizations of power, and circumstances relative to the arts, sciences, and social struggles":[28]

> [T]he rhizome connects any point to any other point, and its traits are not necessarily linked to traits of the same nature; it brings into play very different regimes of signs, and even nonsign states. The rhizome is reducible neither to the One nor the multiple. [...] It is composed not of units but of dimensions, or rather directions in motion. It has neither beginning nor end, but always a middle (*milieu*) from which it grows and which it overspills.[29]

Furthermore, these rhizomatic flows and transformations coalesce into "plateaus": nodes of meaning or object formations, more or less temporary "region[s] of intensities whose development avoids any orientation toward a culmination point or external end."[30] Indeed, in the context of *The Eiffel Tower Wedding Party*, we may usefully substitute "platform" for "plateau" to emphasize the way the tower's first platform serves as the nexus of rhizomatic flows and transformation.

With its ceaseless movement up and down, punctuated by platforms, Cocteau's tower might have been the very object of Deleuze and Guattari's characterization, except for their tendency to ignore drama—a tendency they share in common with most of what is now called "high theory." Still, these passages from *A Thousand Plateaus* certainly describe *The Eiffel Tower Wedding Party*: Mirages, ostriches, lions, bathing beauties, a camera become a train to Nice, and dispatches become pigeons become chorus girls all attest to the rhizomatic nature of the piece. Each character, prop, and element of design may, at any moment, become something else by means of transformations whose logic is always of the moment. The wedding party becomes an artwork because the narrative demands a closure, a slowing down, and therefore, in the tradition of melodrama and medieval drama alike, a *tableau vivant*. The bicyclist becomes a mirage because the tower collapses distance. The general's discourse is orchestral because his bombast must finally be evacuated of content, like the speech of the orator at the end of Ionesco's *The Chairs* (1952). The camera becomes a train because the narrative demands a way out; in this case, it is not a *deus ex machina*—a god from a machine—that saves the day, but *un train de l'appareil*: a train from the camera. And, in becoming train, the camera reconfigures the observation platform into a train platform.

The machine becoming machine, the *machina ex machina*, is perhaps less radical than the machine becoming animal or human. The latter is the apparent "line of flight," to borrow Deleuze and Guattari's formulation, taken by the dispatches that enter the scene from the girders.[31] I want to suggest that this particular offshoot of the play's associative rhizomics leads us to a quite literal machine-rhizome: the Parisian pneumatic post. First put into service in 1886, the pneumatic post became, over the course of its 108 years of operation, a widespread network of pneumatic tubes branching all over Paris, from bureau to bureau. Telegrams received in Paris would be transcribed on the service's signature blue paper—hence the *dépêche bleue* that appears at the beginning of *The Eiffel Tower Wedding Party*—and then bundled with others en route to the same arrondissement, placed in a narrow cylindrical capsule, and sent through pneumatic tubes to its next destination. On arrival, the dispatches would be sorted and sent further on, until they reached the point of having to be delivered to individual addresses by courier.[32] This quite literally rhizomic network of pneumatic tubes branches out just below the surface of streets from bureau to bureau, connecting with and diverging from one another, animated by differential air pressures and valves to regulate the flow of tubes from place to place.

This pneumatic post, of course, did not include dispatches perched in the highest levels of the Eiffel Tower, more like pigeons than telegrams.

However, when we consider that carrier pigeons made up the corps of what might be considered the beta-prototype for a pneumatic—that is, air-driven—postal system, an associative logic begins to appear: as a zoological adjective, *pneumatic* characterizes the porous, air-filled bones of birds, which allows them to be light enough to fly and yet strong enough to support their body structure. Moreover, according to the rhizomic connectivity by which such a logic operates, this description recursively refers back to the tower's structure of girders and joists, as much air as iron, which allows the structure to withstand heavy winds. In this case, even Deleuze and Guattari's theoretical terminology becomes peculiarly literal, too: The metaphorical "lines of flight" they use to characterize non-teleological, nonhierarchical narrative flows, have come, in this analysis, to be quite literal "lines"—that is, communiques—of "flight."

Having fallen and spent some time fluttering around on stage, *les petits bleues*, as the pneumatics were often called, stop behaving like either pigeons or dispatches, and start to behave like showgirls, arranging themselves in a line and responding to a vaudeville emcee's cues. Here, the associative chain continues to combine literal and metaphorical modes: the showgirls are pneumatic women, "women with [...] well-rounded figure[s], esp[ecially] a large bosom," a meaning invoked in the use of the term in English at least as early as 1919, according to *The Oxford English Dictionary*, in F. Scott Fitzgerald's *The Great Gatsby*.

Establishing these intensities and networks of connections does more than historicize *The Eiffel Tower Wedding Party*. It also shows the extent to which the play, seemingly random on its surface, is in fact structured according to complex connotations, associations, and wordplays, both explicit and implicit, depending on the instability of its signs and the slippage in its language. If a Taylorist logic of productivity and labor emphasizes division of processes into discrete and separable units or steps, standardization, efficiency, rational coordination, and linearity, *The Eiffel Tower Wedding Party* deploys the machineries of communication, production, reproduction, and transportation to trouble binaries and to destabilize the logic of the late-industrial age, of which the Eiffel Tower stands as a symbol. In place of industrial machine logic, the piece offers a rhizomatic resistance to reification and stratification. Despite its literally highly structured setting, *The Eiffel Tower Wedding Party* finally evinces a sensibility much more playful than mechanistic. Associative, rhizomatic, punning, a-teleological, senseless and surreal, the play suggests ways of experiencing and interpreting the world that would, if widely adopted, derail industrial production and rationalist ideology.

Cocteau's critique of the formal logic and ideology of the machine between the wars stands in contrast to the work of other avant-garde groups and practitioners. For instance, Italian Futurists, with their proto-fascist celebration of industry and warfare as the dynamos of nationalist resurgence, produced the highly mechanized Futurist Ballet and compressed, articulated *sintesi*, brief episodes each of which was meant to inspire a single, strong sensation. In England, Edward Gordon Craig, in 1911, called for a theatre that would dispense with human actors altogether and rely, instead, on giant mechanized puppets: *Übermarionettes*.[33] In Russia and the Soviet Union, avant-garde practitioners such as the cubo-futurists, the machinist, theatre director, and apparatchik Aleksej Kapitanovich Gastev, and theatre director Vsevolod Meyerhold would look to Taylorist techno-rationalism as the basis for a new aesthetic[34]: Meyerhold's acting method, biomechanics, borrowed the formal aesthetic of constructivism and futurism, a move which, by the 1930s, had doomed his theatre and, indeed, himself, under the Soviet system.

Cocteau's theatre, by contrast, sought to "deterritorialize" the theatre, turning its mechanisms of representation against the mechanistic logic of late industrialism, not only in *Eiffel Tower Wedding Party*, but perhaps more famously in his retelling of the Oedipus story, *The Infernal Machine* (1934), whose opening narration introduces the action thus:

> Watch now, spectator. Before you is a fully wound machine. Slowly, its spring will unwind the entire span of a human life. It is one of the most perfect machines devised by the infernal gods for the mathematical annihilation of a mortal.[35]

Here, the literal mechanics of the theatre and the metaphorical mechanics of narrative replace Sophocles' mythopoetic conception of fate and conspire together against human agency.

Only eight days before *The Eiffel Tower Wedding Party* had its premiere at the Théâtre Champs-Élysées in Paris, Tristan Tzara's *The Gas Heart* [*Le Coeur à Gaz*][36] had its first performance at the nearby Galerie Montaigne. In comparison to Tzara's play, Cocteau's ballet may well have seemed almost realist: for, unlike *The Eiffel Tower Wedding Party*, *The Gas Heart* rarely sustains cogent sense even for as long as a complete sentence. Of the two plays, it is the much more highly fractured and tangential, both formally and at the level of the dramatis personae, which are not even whole personae to begin with: Rather, they are each a facial feature—Eye, Nose, Mouth, Eyebrow, Ear, and Neck. So, from the very beginning of Tzara's "play"—a term I use for want of a better one—any hope for unified, coherent emplotment or characterization is lost. The very opening speech, spoken by Eye, typifies the seemingly endless repetition of nonsense phrases:

Statues jewels roasts
statues jewels roasts
statues jewels roasts
statues jewels roasts
statues jewels roasts
and the wind open to mathematical allusions

cigar pimple [*bouton*] nose
cigar pimple nose
cigar pimple nose
cigar pimple nose
cigar pimple nose
cigar pimple nose
he was in love with a stenographer

eyes replaced by motionless navels
mister mygod is an excellent journalist
inflexible yet aquatic a good morning was drifting in the air
what a sad season[37]

While it is possible, within even this brief opening monologue, to detect perhaps some patterns—the recurrence of bodily images ("pimple," "nose," "eyes," "navels"), for instance—and to group, as Robert A. Varisco has attempted, the motific elements into recognizable themes,[38] by far the dominant effect of *The Gas Heart* is one of profound disorientation. Almost every pattern that might occasionally emerge proves too ephemeral to provide the ground for critical interpretation, either by a reader or a spectator. Its plateaus, to borrow again from Deleuze and Guattari, are too fragile, its rhizomatic transformations too swift.

The play's protean quality notwithstanding, Stanton B. Garner, Jr., offers a view of *The Gas Heart* that enables a reading of it as resistant to mechanical processes. Instead of approaching the play as a stand-alone text capable of a formalist understanding, Garner reads the text's very fragmentation—particularly of the human face—as suggestive of its own historical moment. In other words, his is an oblique, historicist investigation that, without saying so explicitly, finds a way of tracing its rhizomatics through the First World War and its aftermath. In "*The Gas Heart*: Disfigurement and the Dada Body," Garner argues that Tzara's play "draws upon wider historical, cultural, and aesthetic preoccupations of a Europe traumatized by World War I," and identifies as especially salient in that regard, "issues of disfigurement, defacement, and fragmentation."[39] While Garner is careful to situate his reading of *The Gas Heart* within the context of avant-garde performances, which even before the war had experimented with fragmentation, narrative disorientation, and the distortion of speech, language, and meaning, these features of Tzara's play resist being reduced to nonsense because they "acquired particular urgency" after the brutalities of "the battlefields of France and Belgium, where disfigurement achieved a corporeal severity unimaginable in the context of earlier European warfare."[40] Because the "number and severity of facial injuries," in particular, because "trench warfare [...] exposed the head and face to machine guns, mortars, and other weapons from the war's technologically advanced armory," Tzara's focus on the dismemberment of facial features offers an all but explicit link to mechanized warfare. (Even the "gas" of the title is suggestive of poison mustard gas first used as a weapon in the First World War.) Garner, however, notes that in addition to the facial features and the silent heart, numerous other body parts are named throughout the play, which becomes a way of "fragmenting the body onstage and in language" and thus "call[ing] into question such notions as identity, the body–mind continuum, and the human itself": In short, the piece offers "a general revaluation of the human in relation to the non-human world of metal and other substances."[41]

In providing such a reading, Garner argues for an understanding of *The Gas Heart* that we might term *performative*, in the strict linguistic sense, instead of *constative*. That is, instead of *saying* something, at the level of either individual utterances or overall themes, it replays—performs—in an exaggerated and sometimes puerile way the pervasive sense of bodily and cultural fragmentation that lasted for years, even after the end of the First World War. Perhaps, in doing so, it elevates it as a formal aesthetic; perhaps, however, it debases it as the object of childish ridicule; or perhaps it does neither, offering no comment upon it except to frame it in a particular way. And, although Garner intends primarily to speak to the way *The Gas Heart* offers an enactive representation of the fragmentation of the human body as a phenomenon of its historical moment, his reading speaks to the current project as well. For, it brings forward the relationship of mechanized military conflict and the technologies of facial reconstruction and prosthetics to the kind of fragmentation apparent not just in *The Gas Heart*, but also in *The Eiffel Tower Wedding Party*. Garner notes, in passing, that "[l]ike the phonograph horns of Jean Cocteau's *Wedding on the Eiffel Tower* […], Tzara's body parts recite lines that, fundamentally, they do not own."[42] Likewise, while warfare did appear, in an attenuated way, in Cocteau's piece—in the person of the general and in the brief episode during which the child massacres his family after having been christened "another pretty little death for the next war"[43]—Garner's consideration of the widespread use of prosthetics and facial reconstruction to ameliorate the grave wounds of returning soldiers, not to mention the scarified landscapes of Western Europe, reminds us that the kind of fragmentation both pieces enact would have resonated with French theatregoers in 1921.

In fact, however, Tzara's title is the only explicit indication of a specifically technological orientation to his piece. While the French *Le Coeur à Gaz* is typically rendered *The Gas Heart* (as I have done here, following Michael Benedikt's translation), idiomatically, the phrase *à gaz* typically denotes "gas-powered" or "gas-operated." Indeed, the stage directions in French make this idiomatic sense of the phrase clear, explaining that "the heart, heated by gas, walks slowly, circulating widely about," and calling the play "the greatest fraud of the century in three acts" perpetrated upon "industrialized idiots."[44] However, because the heart remains silent throughout the performance and is assigned no specific action, it is impossible to judge what effect its presence may have had on stage, or even to accurately imagine how its gas-operated mechanism might have been represented visually or gesturally.

On the page, however, Tzara's play offers a more complex, if nearly unstageable, moment of resistance to machine imperatives. Interpolated into the middle of the piece is a bizarre and confounding textual performance, the "*DANCE of the gentleman who falls from a funnel in the ceiling onto the table.*" This "dance" is rendered typographically and goes entirely unmentioned in the dialogue. In the 1922 edition, it appears as six lines of seemingly arbitrary type, made up of random capital letters alone or in clusters of two or three. Sometimes, in this version, the letters are inverted. While it invites reading, it also repels interpretation: as a code or syntagm, it fails. In later published versions of the play, including the 1946 standard edition, the dance features only three letters from the Roman alphabet: A capital V, a capital Y (repeated in different sizes), and a lower-case, italic *r*. While the capital V appears fixed on the page, the Ys and *r*s seem to tumble about, suggesting movement through three dimensions, despite the fixity of type. The choice of these letters points perhaps back to the traditions of classical Greek theatre. Depending on how one orients the page, the V may appear as a capital *lambda*, and the Ys and *r*s as *upsilons*, making the dancing letters into a kind of Greek chorus—from *choros*, "dancer"— whose mute choreography (literally, "dance-writing") fails to serve its traditional choric functions. The French name for the letter Y—*i-grec* (the Greek *I*)—underscores this reading.

Sarah Bay-Cheng persuasively reads this configuration as textually enactive, performing the falling gentleman's dance typographically and thus underscoring Dada's frequently anti-embodiment stance toward performance. While Bay-Cheng overstates the impossibility of staging such a textual dance, claiming that "[t]o perform the play, one must destroy these text-based figures, replacing them with inadequate human representations"[45] because they are "at odds with the essential nature of performance,"[46] she is right in seeing the "text as a performer without a body,"[47] which highlights the way the European avant-garde conceived of the "printed word [and] the page as a theatrical venue."[48] Indeed, Bay-Cheng suggests that the dance is to be performed by rotating the page, so that the figures seem to move through space; the fact that *y*, in French, is an adverb that means both *here* and *there* lends credence to Bay-Cheng's reading of this textual figure as moving through space.

Bay-Cheng's focus on the typographical "dance" and the way it "complicate[s] the viewing position of its reader/spectator/viewer"[49] enables us to see a how Tzara's play undermines machine logic to a degree further than that suggested by Garner's contextualization of it within the aftermath of the First World War alone. Namely, in drawing readerly attention to textuality as such, *The Gas Heart* articulates to the technological aspects of typography. Indeed, the etymologies of *text* and *tech* already indicate a fundamental link between the two concepts: Both derive, through Greek and Latin, from the reconstructed Proto-Indo-European root **teks-nā*, meaning "craft": From it, we get *architecture*, *tectonics*, *texture*, and *textile*, as well as *text* and *technology*. These words share the idea of craft, the application of knowledge and skill to artificial production. And so, at a very basic level, a text is always a technological artifact. But, as Marshall McLuhan notes, the technological nature of the typographic text gets intensified by moveable type, which he sees as the prototype for all machine technology that followed it:

Perhaps the supreme quality of the print is [...] that it is a pictorial statement that can be repeated precisely and indefinitely [...]. Repeatability is the core of the mechanical principle that has dominated our world, especially since the Gutenberg technology. The message of the print and of typography is primarily that of repeatability. With typography, the principle of movable type introduced the means of mechanizing any handicraft by the process of segmenting and fragmenting an integral action. What had begun with the alphabet [...] reached a new level of intensity [...] with typography.[50]

So, not only is typography the result of technological innovation, its linearity, articulation, and repeatability establish the paradigm for mechanical processes of all kinds—processes that would have become starkly visible in the context of industrialization and mechanized warfare in the early twentieth century.

Typography, according to McLuhan, changed the relationship of reader to text: "[T]he printed book [...] intensified perspective and fixed point of view. Associated with the visual stress on point of view and the vanishing point that provides the illusion of perspective" in Renaissance painting, "there comes another illusion that space is visual, uniform and continuous" in the typeset text.[51] This shift in readerly perspective allowed for what McLuhan calls "detachment and noninvolvement," the maintenance of the critical distance necessary to the Enlightenment's foundational philosophical contemplation.[52] By the middle of the twentieth century, McLuhan was able to imagine it "easy to document the processes by which the principles of continuity, uniformity, and repeatability have become the basis [...] of industrial production, entertainment, and science," noting that the printed book became the first "uniformly priced commodity" and therefore served as the material basis of "price systems" in European economic exchange.[53]

And so, when Tzara's typographical performance "complicate[s] the viewing position of its reader/spectator/viewer," as Bay-Cheng rightly claims, it also imagines the text as a theatre whose machineries work against the logic of mechanization and destabilizes the consumer–commodity relationship. Moreover, the very repeatability that enabled

Europe's technological advancement becomes an obstacle both to reading and performing Tzara's play: Its so-called dance "enabl[es] the textual performance and thwart[s] the progress of the embodied play" to such a degree that "the reader/performer unwittingly [...] becomes trapped in the perpetual repetition of the performing text."[54] In doing so, it enacts not just an "anti-corporeal" logic[55] but an anti-machine logic in line with much of European avant-garde's experiments with typography and textuality.

What is striking about Tzara's piece, however, is that he situates it the context of a play-script, a technology that points to theatre as itself a human–machine hybrid, as Tzara's title implies. In quoting Beatrice Warde on the subject of dancing type, McLuhan allows us to see that Tzara's conception of typographic characters as theatrical ones was not unique to his imagination: "I saw two club-footed Egyptian A's...walking off arm-in-arm with the unmistakable swagger of a music-hall comedy team."[56] McLuhan informs us that Warde's vision of literally moveable type came in the form of a "Norman McLaren movie advertisement."[57]

Despite the textual nature of the dance and its critique of linear machine logic, we can see an alignment of concerns between *The Gas Heart* and *The Eiffel Tower Wedding Party*. And, although the former understates its critique of the mechanization, almost to the point of muting it by embedding it in an unperformable typographic "dance" or in the opening stage directions, the latter is somewhat clearer in its deprecation, if not outright condemnation, of techno-rationalism in its exaggerated send-up of late-industrial logic. Still, true to the avant-garde impulses that animated both authors, these pieces rely to a greater or lesser degree on attenuation and obliqueness in articulating their views of industrialized capital and mechanized warfare. Eugène Ionesco's two short companion plays *Jack, or The Submission* (composed 1950; premiered 1955) and *The Future Is in Eggs, or It Takes All Sorts to Make a World* (composed 1951; premiered 1957) are much more obvious in their satire of industrial modernity. Appearing over three decades after *The Gas Heart* and *The Eiffel Tower Wedding Party*, at the height of the French economic boom that would eventually be called "The Glorious

Thirty Years," they echo many of these earlier play's formal aesthetics. For instance, exaggerated costuming and masks, disorienting and tangential narrative lines, stylized speech, and seemingly nonsensical dialogue connect these three plays in a clear lineage of avant-garde drama in France. At the same time, Ionesco's plays are marked by their particular delight in overtly deflating the optimism that followed the defeat of German Nazism and the attendant celebration of French economic resurgence.[58]

My interest here has primarily to do with the way machine logic and industrial technology inform not just the overt content of these pieces, but also their formal manifestation. In this regard, *The Future Is in Eggs* is the more relevant piece; however, because it serves as a sequel to *Jack, or The Submission*, it is useful to treat the two plays together at the outset. Like that of *The Eiffel Tower Wedding Party*, the plot that connects these two plays is seemingly straightforward. The Jacques[59] and Robert families are eager for their children to marry. However, first introduced to Roberta, in *Jack, or The Submission*, Jacques refuses to marry her, supposedly the Roberts' only daughter. And so, the Roberts introduce Jacques and his family to their second daughter, Roberta II, who is identical to Roberta—indeed, she is played by the same actress— except that she has three noses and nine fingers on her left hand. Left alone, Jacques and Roberta hit it off, finding a shared fascination with the word "cat" (*chat*). They confess their love of anything that has the syllable *chat* in its name—castles [*châteaux*], housekeepers [*chatelaines*], and vaginas [*chattes*].[60] By the end of the play, they have decided that they will simply substitute any word they wish to use in conversation of any kind with the word *chat*, so that, for instance, "[i]n order to say: bring me some cold noodles, some warm lemonade, and no coffee," one must simply say "Cat, cat, cat, cat, cat, cat, cat, cat."[61] The close of the play finds them, along with their families, squatting together, uttering "vague miaows while turning around, bizarre moans, croakings."[62]

The opening of *The Future Is in Eggs* alerts us to the passage of time: For now, Grandfather Jacques, quite alive in *Jack*, is memorialized in a (living) portrait on the upstage wall, while a large "hatching apparatus" now takes up much of the stage, set up, apparently, in anticipation of the eventual birth of Jacques and Roberta's offspring. The now-married couple seem, however, not to have moved since the end of *Jack*, and remain in their squatting position whispering cat sounds to one another. The two families must now encourage their children to reproduce, which they finally do, once Jacques is brought out of his reverie by the news that his Grandfather has died. His grief fuels his determination to reproduce, and so he is set up on the hatching apparatus while Roberta, having been ushered offstage by the women, begins laying innumerable eggs. In a frenzy of activity, the remaining characters carry basket after basket of eggs to the apparatus for Jacques to hatch, and amid this chaos, accompanied now by noises of industrial machineries, voiced by the characters, the play ends: "A trap door may or may not open," the final stage directions read, "or perhaps the stage may or may not slowly collapse, and the characters—all unwittingly—gently sink and disappear without interrupting their actions—or just quite simply carry on, according to the technical facilities available."[63]

While the closing exchange between Roberta and Jacques in *Jack, or the Submission*, suggests the Taylorist logic of modularity, standardization, and simplification, with the substitution of a single, repeated word for all verbal discourse between the two lovers, it is during *The Future Is in Eggs* that these play's machinic aspects become central, as does the rhizomatic nature of their resistance to the machine's imperatives. Early in the play, when Jacques is confronted with the news of his Grandfather's death, he is unable at first to react emotionally, until his parents remind him that the emotion appropriate to the news is grief:

Father-Jacques   Your grandfather is dead.

(*She gives him another nudge.* **Jacques** *still makes no reaction.* [...])

Don't you understand your grandfather is dead?

Jacques   No. I don't understand that grandfather is dead.

Mother-Jacques   (*whining*) Poor child. Your reflexes must have stopped working. We must get them going again.

(**Jacques** *falls into* **Jacqueline**'s *arms, who stands him up again. For a few moments his face remains expressionless. The parents, the grandmother and the sister search for a sign on their son's face. They appear to be very worried.* **Mother-Jacques** *says:*)

Mother-Jacques   (*to her son*) Cry! Let yourself go, my boy, and cry! (*Silence*) Cry! Come on then! (*Silence. Suddenly* **Jacques** *starts to sob.*)
Father-Jacques   There we are, at last! That's done it.[64]

Once started, however, Jacques's weeping becomes so intense and prolonged that it continues right through a rhythmic round of condolences, in which Grandfather, from his portrait, takes part. Father-Jacques surmises that they've "made his reflexes too sensitive," while Jacqueline attempts to shame Jacques into silence: "Shut up, you're upsetting everyone." Only when Jacques's father insists, "That's enough!" do Jacques and everyone else fall silent.[65]

Far from an authentic emotional reaction, which stage convention dictates should present itself as verbal outpourings, self-recriminations, expressions of conflictedness, and so forth, Jacques's expression of grief is entirely phatic and entirely in one register. His repeated "Hiii! Hiii! Hiii!" soon takes on a machinic cadence, inhuman in its inarticulacy, emphasizing the degree to which Jacques's emotions need kick-starting, like an engine, in order to run, but then will continue to run ceaselessly.[66] Here, we see a vivid, if absurd, example of the human-become-machine, the literalization of the "human motor" of Rabinbach's study. The mechanized, rhythmic weeping early in the play foreshadows the way Jacques, hatching Roberta's eggs, will begin *"puffing noisily like a steam engine,"* emitting a constant "Tuff! Tuff! Tuff!" in counterpoint to Roberta's offstage chicken squawking.[67] These noises set the rhythm for the other characters who begin to call out their hopes for what the eggs, once hatched and grown up, will become, beginning with "sausage meat," "cannon fodder," "athletes," "modelling paste," "pastry paste," through "opportunists," "nationalists," "industrialists," "revolutionaries," "anti-revolutionaries," "radishes," and "radicals," and culminating, finally, with commercial products: "stairs and shoes," "pencils and pen-holders," "aspirins," and "matches." Throughout this chanted list of possible products, the two grandmothers continually take up the chant "Production! Production!"—notably, not *re*production—eliding the processes of human and animal reproduction, on the one hand, and commercial production, on the other.[68] Only when Jacques expresses a desire to produce "pessimists," "anarchists," and "nihilists"—in other words, elements who do not contribute to society's well-oiled functioning—does the momentum of the action and speech lag for a moment before the rest of the family, reminding Jacques of his "obligations" and crying, "long live production! Long live the white race! Keep it up! Keep it up!" manage to restart the process of egg-laying and hatching that will continue as the play winds to its ambiguous conclusion.[69]

Ionesco's play, adopting and perverting the rhythms, patterns, and sounds of mechanical production, satirizes the intersection of European white nationalism, middle-class commodity consumption, and capitalist industrial technologies. In echoing them in its formal aesthetic, they also indicate the elevation of these processes and beliefs to the ideological level: that of a naturalized, socially unconstructed given. By doing so, *Jack, or the Submission* and *The Future Is in Eggs* make explicit the more understated satire of modern industrial technology and techno-rationalist ideologies enacted in Cocteau's *Eiffel Tower Wedding Party* and their even more attenuated enactive representation in Tzara's *The Gas Heart*. Given that *The Future Is in Eggs* premiered only three years before Eisenhower's farewell speech-cum-warning quoted at the beginning of this chapter, Ionesco's plays bring us full circle, to a moment when an American president, having overseen the period of most rapid economic, industrial, and infrastructural expansion in modern history, could find it appropriate to express his gratitude to the very technologies that, as we will see in the Chapter 3, come to dominate Western politics and society, particularly after 1970. Eisenhower began his address thus:

> First, I should like to express my gratitude to the radio and television networks for the opportunities they have given me, over the years, to bring reports and messages to our nation. My special thanks go to them for the privilege of addressing you this evening.[70]

That the head of state of the world's most powerful liberal democracy would see the exercise of his prerogative, indeed the fulfillment of an obligation, as a "privilege" "given" to him by "television networks," for which he feels "gratitude," precisely demonstrates the degree to which these and other advanced technologies had taken on an ideological cast. As we shall see in Chapter 3's discussion of Bertolt Brecht and Kurt Weill's oratorio *Lindbergh's Flight* (1928), particularly its later revivals, John Adams and Alice Goodman's opera *Nixon in China* (1987), and Don DeLillo's play *Valparaiso* (1999), the mechanisms of mass communication and mass media engage in complex and suggestive ways with the mechanisms of live theatrical production, raising questions about subjectivity, authority, and ideology in the contemporary world. In the meantime, Chapter 2 will focus our attention on American plays more or less contemporary in their creation and first productions to those discussed above, plays whose expressivist, rather than surrealist orientation toward modernist stage aesthetics enable a kind of humanist nostalgia in the face of the technologization of everyday life, a nostalgia absent from the works of Tzara, Cocteau, and Ionesco.

2

Machineries of Nostalgia and American Modernity: Sophie Treadwell, Elmer Rice, Arthur Miller, and Isaac Gomez

In Chapter 1, we saw several ways machineries manifested themselves in theatre traditions that emerged from a primarily—although not exclusively—European ideological, aesthetic, economic, and technological context. They share much in common with the American expressivist strain of drama concerned with the machine, three examples of which form the basis of this chapter: Elmer Rice's *Adding Machine* (1923), Sophie Treadwell's *Machinal* (1928), and Arthur Miller's *Death of a Salesman* (1949). Like Cocteau's *Eiffel Tower Wedding Party* and Ionesco's *Jacques* plays, Treadwell's play uses sound and rhythm to suggest machine effects, both in scenes where literal machineries play central roles and in those where they are either ancillary or absent altogether. Similarly, *The Adding Machine* presages Krapp's obsessive interaction with his recorder (discussed in Chapter 4), which, itself, echoes Willie Loman's unfortunate encounter with a dictation machine in *Death of a Salesman*. We will also notice resonances between these modernist works for the American stage and Brecht's episodic, alienating formal innovations, their relatively brief, articulated scenes echoing the division and intensification of labor during the technological revolution relied on to maximize productivity and efficiency, in Chapter 3. What sets *The Adding Machine*, *Machinal*, and *Death of a Salesman* apart from the plays we have seen so far and will examine later, however, is the degree to which, as expressionist works, they make the problem of human subjectivity, complicated by human–machine interfaces, explicit in dialogue, and especially so in the utterances of their respective central characters: Mr. Zero, The Young Woman, and Willy Loman, all of whose monikers call attention to their marginalized social position.

This focus on the individual is also what makes these plays stand out among the others this book considers, as particularly American; for, they explicitly critique the American myth of "rugged individualism," an idea made famous by American president Herbert Hoover and associated with the doctrine of Manifest Destiny and with theories of laissez-faire capitalism and self-sufficiency especially dominant in American political and economic thought.[1] Rice's, Treadwell's, and Miller's protagonists suffer from the keen tension that arises between belief in these deep-seated American mythologies, on the one hand, and firsthand experience of the way advanced capitalism renders these ideals impossible, on the other. Unable to resolve this tension, however, these plays instead foreground the impossible position of the everyday working person. Indeed, that the plays all feature their protagonist's death both emphasizes and individualizes this impossibility.

These are not subtle works, by any means: One does not leave the theatre wondering what their social message has been. In production, each of them calls for technical and scenic innovations that make what is already explicit in the dialogue and plot even more so. And yet, beneath their explicit condemnation of capitalist exploitation of the everyday middle-class Americans and their depiction of the impossible bind they find themselves in because of the incommensurability of ideology and lived experience, a more subtle tension emerges under analysis. For, while these plays apparently recognize the vacuity and contemporary irrelevance, if not impossibility of the mythologies of rugged individualism, Jeffersonian agrarianism, Toquevillian self-interest, and Emersonian self-reliance,[2] they nevertheless evince a strong sense of nostalgia for these ideals, inviting audiences and readers to imagine and long for a preindustrial, prelapsarian, extra-ideological period during which these individualist aspirations were widely achievable—a period, one needs hardly add, that never existed. As this chapter concludes, it will consider Mexican-American playwright Isaac Gomez's recent play *La Ruta* (2018), which recapitulates many of the modernist themes elaborated in Rice's, Treadwell's, and Miller's plays but also works against the nostalgic fantasy of individualism and frontiersmanship that remains as a trace in those earlier plays.

Elmer Rice's *The Adding Machine* is among the earliest, if not the earliest American play explicitly to link technological advancement to capitalist exploitation and individual disempowerment. Famous more because of its early experiments with expressivist aesthetics, formally fragmented narrative, and its agit-prop-style discourse in the final scene than with the nuance and complexity of either its plot or its overall social message, Rice's play deserves our attention because it establishes the benchmark for Treadwell's and Miller's later expressionist critiques of techno-modernity. The play follows the final days of Mr. Zero, a bookkeeper in a department store who, after twenty-five years of service, is fired, made redundant by the adding machine. Before its introduction, the work of bookkeeping, as *The Adding Machine* depicts it, is nearly mindless drudgery. Much of the dialogue between Daisy, who reads out numbers, and Zero, who copies them into a ledger, consists of monetary figures. Indeed, with the exception of a few barbed insults across the counter and an occasional request to repeat a number, to speed up, or to slow down, we are to understand that the moments when Daisy or Zero express something like an inner thought or feeling as representing their state of mind, are inaudible to all but the audience. Thus, a sharp distinction delineates these characters' outward manifestations and the content of their thoughts, beliefs, and desires. Already inherent in this representational mode, then, is the divisibility of the human subject and the dissociation of speech from ideation. The subject, in other words, of Rice's play is modular and articulated, made up of pieces that, if they are not strictly separable, can be imagined as such.

At key moments, however, the outer world and inner worlds collapse, as when the Boss invokes an explicitly Taylorist logic, discussed in Chapter 1, in explaining his decision to terminate Zero:

Boss [...] The fact is that my efficiency experts have recommended the installation of adding machines.
Zero (*staring at him*) Addin' machines?
Boss Yes, you've probably seen them. A mechanical device that adds automatically.
Zero Sure. I've seen them. Keys—and a handle that you pull. (*He goes through the motions in the air.*)
Boss That's it. They do the work in half the time and a high-school girl can operate them. Now, of course, I'm sorry to lose an old and faithful employee—[3]

So shaken is Zero by the news of his dismissal, contrasting so sharply with his expectations of a promotion and a raise, that soon all he— and the audience—can hear of what his Boss says are fragments: "I'm sorry—no other alternative—greatly regret—old employee— efficiency—economy—business—*business*—BUSINESS—."[4] Finally, the Boss's "voice is drowned out by the music" of "the mechanical player of a distant merry-go-round."[5] At the same time, the stage itself begins to rotate more and more rapidly as the music's volume increases, signaling the increased confusion and rage Zero experiences.

A number of observations relevant to the question of the human–machine interface, both in the context of the theatrical production as such and as it is represented in the production, suggest themselves in this passage. First, soon after mentioning time savings and ease of labor, the Boss's language becomes fragmented, as if the invocation of mechanized efficiency had had a mechanical effect on his utterance, dividing it, preserving only its most significant terms, and condensing his words into the most efficient conveyers of meaning, without prepositions, verbs, particles, or rhetorical niceties. The machine, in other words, seems to have processed speech. At the same time, as is common in expressionist works of all genres, the whole atmosphere of the piece begins to enact the dynamics of the inner mind of its main figure: Thus, music, light, and stage mechanisms begin to operate in an increasingly intense and overbearing way. The result is that Zero's disorientation at being replaced by a machine is represented, itself, as a mechanically produced impression, as if Zero conceives of his experiences of himself as a kind of clockwork mechanism. The stage directions, at the end of the scene, when in a blind rage Zero kills his Boss, emphasize the highly mechanized effects to be seen and heard and their reliance on the technical apparatus of the theatre for their legibility:

> His voice is drowned out by the music. The platform is revolving rapidly now. **Zero** and the **Boss** face each other. They are entirely motionless save for the **Boss**'s jaws, which open and close incessantly. But the words are inaudible. The music swells and swells. To it is added every offstage effect of the theatre: the wind, the waves, the galloping horses, the locomotive whistle, the sleigh bells, the automobile siren, the glass-crash. New Year's Eve, Election Night, Armistice Day, and Mardi Gras. The noise is deafening, maddening, unendurable. Suddenly it culminates in a terrific peal of thunder. For an instant there is a flash of red and then everything is plunged into blackness.[6]

The deployment of the technologies of the stage not only to express Zero's reaction to his dismissal, but also to foreclose upon the traditional registers through which drama expresses itself—speech and gesture—point toward a theatre technology at odds with the conventions of naturalist or realist theatre, an apparatus on the verge of complete overload, an effect also suggested by the final stage directions of Ionesco's *The Future Is in Eggs*, discussed in Chapter 1.

Expressionism, as an aesthetic mode, already embeds the logic of the modern machine of capitalist productivity. Whereas naturalism and realism rely on the suggestion of inward psychological states through the reproduction of only minimally heightened dialogue, gesture, and action deployed as mimesis, expressionism, as the moniker suggests, deploys a much more symbolic repertoire of representational practices. As Anthony F. R. Palmieri notes, in his study of Rice's work, the term *expressionism* is "not easy to describe in brief simple terms."[7] Nevertheless, the brief summary Palmieri provides aptly captures Rice's use of expressionist tropes:

> In a nutshell, expressionism is a form of artistic expression that seeks to externalize inner experience. It aims to objectify the concrete. For the expressionistic artist, outward impressions have significance only insofar as they symbolize, signify, or suggest inward meanings, emotional or thematic implications.[8]

To do so, the production "will employ clever mechanical devices, strange effects and weirdly distorted settings."[9] The necessity of such "devices," coupled with a drive for explication—for making the implicit explicit, the abstract concrete, and the ephemeral and invisible visible—requires that theatre production reproduce the logic of industrial production, which transforms unrefined materials and human ingenuity and desire into concrete, discrete objects whose meaning and value are legible in their form and function. Expressionism, as much as it attempts to heighten the psychological, the emotional, and the ineffable, does so through an industrial logic of concretization, explication, and analog representational legibility.

Thus, unlike in the surrealist theatre of Cocteau, Tzara, and Ionesco, in Rice's play, the deployment of the theatre apparatus to produce an explosion of sound, light, and movement do not signal the end of representation and the limits of the representational capacity of theatre, but rather express the moment of crisis from which the remainder of the plot will develop. This crisis, expressed through an overwhelming experience of light and sound, is uncannily echoed in Rice's description of the moment the idea for the play struck him:

> Suddenly, as though a switch had been turned or a curtain raised, a new play flashed into my mind, wholly unrelated to anything I had ever consciously thought. When I say "flashed into my mind," I mean that quite literally, for in that sudden instant I saw everything complete: characters, plot, incidents, even the titles and some of the dialogue. [....] I was actually possessed, my brain in a whirl, my whole

being alive. I sat for a while trembling with excitement, almost gasping for a breath. Then, hardly knowing what I was doing, I went to my study and began to write.[10]

Whereas Palmieri sees this account as "preternatural,"[11] it is, quite obviously, mechanical and theatrical. Rice imagines both a "switch" and a "curtain"; the instant of inspiration is illuminated with electrical lighting effects, a "flash" he claims to have "literally" experienced, and, like the spectator at a theatrical production, he "saw everything complete" in an "instant." As a consequence, Rice begins to operate as an automaton, writing without "knowing what [he] was doing," and producing in a mere seventeen days a complete, finished draft of the play that, according to Palmieri, "Rice never changed" again.[12] Rice, as a writer, seems already to have conceived himself as a human machine and the moment of inspiration, as having been mechanically produced by a theatre apparatus.

Rice's "flash" of inspiration and the subsequent, almost automatic writing he claims to have engaged in, formally resembles the rage and loss of self-control Zero experiences that lead to the Boss's murder, which, in turn, lead to Zero's arrest, conviction, and execution. But Zero's plight continues in the afterlife as well. For so engrained in his soul are the imperatives of drudge labor that he rejects the promise of eternal happiness, symbolized by the pastoral ease of the Elysian Fields characterized by free love, leisure, idleness, and artistic creation in contrast to the purposive-rational constraints of earthly life and labor.

Instead, Zero opts to spend the next twenty-five years of his afterlife incessantly and pointlessly operating an adding machine, producing a "strip of white paper-tape" that "flows steadily from the machine. [...] The room is filled with this tape—streamers, festoons, billows of it everywhere. It covers the floor and the furniture, it climbs the walls and chokes the doorways."[13] When his guardians inform him that, now that his soul has been cleaned and refreshed, he must return to earth to continue his subservience, Zero is aghast, refusing to relinquish his hold on the machine until forced to do so and not wishing to believe that, over the many thousands of years of reincarnation, his soul has devolved, becoming fit only for more and more menial labor on earth. As his chief overseer in the afterlife explains:

> I'll tell you what you were the first time—if you want to know so much—a monkey. [...]—just a hairy, chattering, long-tailed monkey. [....] You weren't so bad as a monkey. Of course, you did just what all the other monkeys did, but still it kept you out in the open air. And you weren't woman-shy—there was one little red-headed monkey—well never mind. Yes, sir, you weren't so bad then. But even in those days there must have been some bigger and brainier monkey that you kowtowed to. The mark of the slave was on you from the start.[14]

Rice's play thus reinforces the association of freedom and happiness with unadulterated nature, innocent of modernity and the technological advances that have led to the increasing subjugation of men like Zero. Here, also, the play introduces its social message; namely, that capitalists of all kinds—those in control of the mechanisms of production—wish for the underclass to believe that their subservience, their miserable lot in life, is "mark[ed]" upon their souls and that an unalterable fate has determined their social position. Zero, of course, resists this revelation, and all too eagerly indulges in the fantasy-mirage of "Hope," a female figure his afterlife taskmaster invites him to follow as he returns to earth for another lifetime of emptiness.[15] For Rice, then, ideology is simply false consciousness, a belief in outright lies and distortions foisted upon the underclass by a masterful, knowing class of overlords. There is, in other words, a manifest *outside* to ideology, one free of the illusions created and sustained by capital and its reliance on techno-rationalist modes of thought and the advanced technologies of production and constraint that sustain them.

Lee Simonson's set designs for the 1923 production at the Garrick Theatre in New York City emphasize *The Adding Machine*'s expressionism through the exaggerated verticality of the space by deploying high-angle lighting and gobos to suggest long, high-set windows and narrow doorframes of the accounting department, the shadowy menace of the courtroom, and the invasion of mathematics into the Zero home.[16] In addition to underscoring the expressionist aesthetic by creating stage pictures whose sharp angles and sense of height highlight Zero's increasing sense of disorientation and helplessness, Simonson's design also relies on relatively recent innovations in stage lighting. So enamored was Simonson of the capabilities of lighting to set the tone for a stage production that his writings on set design and the history of scenography, he treats lighting effects as almost magical, the most important of the scenographer's tools.[17] Confident that lighting design, above all else, could determine the success or failure of a play, he issued the following dare to American playwrights in the New York *World*:

> Let me go on record as offering a standing challenge to [...] any [...] American playwright who dares to accept it: Namely, Let one of them write a play in which lines and business are so independent of scenery that it can be played on a bare stage. [...] I'll gladly offer my services free to light the show. But I am making a safe offer. It won't be taken up. If it is, what you will see will be, not a new school of stage setting, but a new school of play writing.[18]

Simonson saw the mastery of new lighting techniques and apparatus as "extending [the designer's] technical control" and called for the "reconstruct[ion of] our crammed and cluttered playhouses so that they can be ready to meet, with the speed and precision of modern machines, the constantly changing demands of modern plays."[19] The discourse of "technical control" and the call for "speed and precision" precisely recapitulates the discourse of Taylorism and the intensification of labor through industrial technologies against which Rice's plays and, as we shall see, those of Treadwell and Miller react.

Treadwell's *Machinal* follows the Young Woman, its protagonist, through nine brief episodes over a period of perhaps a few years, from her employment as a stenographer and her unhappy marriage to her boss, Mr. Jones, including the birth of their daughter, through a year-long love affair with an unmarried adventurer, to her conviction and execution for her husband's murder. Throughout, the contrasting themes of confinement and freedom structure the narrative, while machineries of all kinds create a motif through the play, connecting the Young Woman's unhappiness with the constraints and pressures of urban, industrial modernity. Marriage and motherhood, the play suggests, have become subject to the same kind of intensification and division industrial labor has undergone, the Taylorist logic of efficiency and productivity extending from the factory to the office and into the domestic sphere. This intensification, we are given to understand, is primarily responsible for the Young Woman's disaffection; her desire for freedom does not, for instance, extend so far as freedom from men or the desiring male gaze, as her idealized affair with Richard Roe demonstrates. Rather, her disgust with her husband and with the conditions of her existence have to do more with their modernity, which is emphasized by the play's highly machinic first and final episodes.

The play opens in the outer offices of the George H. Jones company, where various clerks, telephone operators, and typists are more or less busy, interleaving the rhythms of their workaday routines with idle chatter and gossip. The hectic rhythm is established at the outset by sounds called for in the opening stage directions: "office machines: typewriters, adding machine, manifold, telephone bells, buzzers."[20] The rhythm and cacophony created by these machines is echoed in the staccato dialogue, fragmented and rapid:

Adding Clerk	(*in the monotonous voice of his monotonous thoughts; at his adding machine*) 2490, 28, 76, 123, 36842, 1, 1/4, 37, 804, 23, 1/2, 982.
Filing Clerk	(*in the same way—at his filing desk*) Accounts—A. Bonds—B. Contracts—C. Data—D. Earnings—E.
Stenographer	(*in the same way—left*) Dear Sir—in re—your letter—recent date—will state—
Telephone Girl	Hello—Hello—George H. Jones Company good morning—hello hello—George H. Jones Company good morning—hello.
Filing Clerk	Market—M. Notes—N. Output—O. Profits—P.—! (*Suddenly*) What's the matter with Q?

Telephone Girl	Matter with it—Mr. J.—Mr. K. wants you—What you mean matter? Matter with what?
Filing Clerk	Matter with Q.
Telephone	Well—what is? Spring 1726?
Filing Clerk	I'm asking yuh—
Telephone Girl	WELL?
Filing Clerk	Nothing filed with it.
Telephone Girl	Well?
Filing Clerk	Look at A. Look at B. What's the matter with Q?
Telephone Girl	Ain't popular. Hello—Hello—George H. Jones Company.
Filing Clerk	Hot dog! Why ain't it?
Adding Clerk	Has it personality?
Stenographer	Has it Halitosis?[21]

This brief exchange, setting the tone for the whole play before any of the principal characters has entered, compresses several of the motifs we have seen and will: non sequitur dialogue; the use of nonsense speech to establish rhythm and tempo; denaturalized dialogue; and the attribution of human qualities to machines and vice versa. Moreover, the appearance of the adding machine in the first scene, with its ungainly operation and clicking buttons and gears, along with the deployment of numbers as speech, recalls Rice's play, perhaps even as an homage to its critique of clerical modernity.[22] We might recall, as well, that clerical subservience appears in Cocteau's *Eiffel Tower Wedding Party* when the Eiffel Tower is called "*une demoiselle du telégraphe*" and in Tzara's *The Gas Heart*, when Eye mentions that "he was in love with a stenographer."[23]

Upon her entrance, the Young Woman, one of the office clerks, appears out of place. Her coworkers at once shame her, pointing out that she has arrived late to work for several consecutive days and reminding her that she is liable to lose her job; when she replies "I can't," they demand an excuse, in response to which she tentatively offers, "The subway?"[24] She explains haltingly that she needed to "get out," away from "[a]ll those bodies pressing": "I thought I would faint!

I had to get out in the air!"[25] Feeling trapped in the subway, that most modern of urban conveyances, the Young Woman has chosen to walk to work instead, which, in turn, puts her at odds with the principles of timeliness and efficiency according to which the office runs. Her boss, Jones, has already asked for her by the time she arrives. And so, her lateness has come to the attention of one of the firm's executives—the very man who will soon ask her to marry him. Because she cannot risk losing her job, and because her aging mother is in need of financial support, she accepts: the pressures of modernity, densely enacted and represented by machineries and the techno-rationalist logic of big business and economic survival, force her choice.

These pressures surface when, at the end of the scene, she is heard "thinking her thoughts aloud—to the subdued accompaniment of the office sounds and voices":

> Marry me—wants to marry me—George H. Jones—George H. Jones and Company—Mrs. George H. Jones—Mrs. George H. Jones—Dear Madame—marry—do you take this man to be your wedded husband—I do—to love honor and to love—kisses—no—I can't—George H. Jones—How would you like to marry me—What do you say—Why Mr. Jones I—let me look at your little hands—you have such pretty little hands—let me hold your pretty little hands—George H. Jones—Fat hands—flabby hands—don't touch me—please—fat hands are never weary—please don't—married—all girls—most girls—married—babies—a baby—curls—little curls all over its head—George H. Jones—straight—thin—bald—don't touch me—please—no—can't—must—somebody—something—no rest—must rest—no rest—must rest—no rest—late today—yesterday—before—late—subway—air—pressing—bodies pressing[26]

And so on for quite some time. This expressionist moment—one of several in the play—is notable for its highly articulated representation of thought as fragmented, associative, and disoriented. The form her thoughts take in speech show that the Young Woman, in her anxiety, has also internalized the rhythm and logic of the machines that accompany her. Tellingly, however, in expressing her reservations about the proposal she has accepted, the organic body becomes a site of her fixation: his flabby hands, thin frame, and bald head inspire repugnance in her. This repugnance will emerge in Episode 2: "At Home," when the Young Woman laments to her mother that she is not in love with the man she will marry and in Episode 3: "Honeymoon," when she resists her husband's sexual advances, recoiling and wincing under his touch.

Throughout, Jones is linked not only with wealth, but mechanical technology. For instance, in the Honeymoon episode, Jones—styled "Husband" in the script—imagines a trip to Europe he will someday take with his new wife, where she will "buy a lot of that French underwear" and he will finally get the "Swiss watch" he's "wanted all [his] life": "All my life I've wanted a Swiss watch that I bought right there. All my life I've counted on having that some day."[27] His having "counted on" owning a Swiss watch becomes menacingly literal a few lines later when, impatient with her delays, he gives her "[j]ust a minute" to prepare to go to bed with him: "(*laughs and takes out watch*): 13-14—I'm counting the seconds on you—that's what you said, didn't you—just a minute!—49-50-51-52-53-."[28] Here, Jones's predatory sexual desire, his longing for a Swiss watch, and timekeeping itself condense into an image of Jones as a clockwork mechanism of which business, courtship, marriage, and intimacy are all functional elements; like the watch, the Young Woman is expected to function as an instrument fulfilling his desires. Moreover, Jones's timekeeping recalls the image of Frederic Taylor himself, measuring the efficiency of the industrial laborer, as we saw in *The Adding Machine*, and connects the domestic sphere of the Jones household to whole enterprise not just of industrial efficiency, but to what Charles Tung has neatly summarized as the "new pace of railways, automobiles, the telegraph and wireless communication, mass production, and urbanization" in the late nineteenth and early twentieth centuries.[29]

Jones's association with modern technology extends to the couple's home-life as well. In Episode Seven: "Domestic," the Joneses are at home, "seated on opposite ends of the divan" reading newspapers.

Although they are reading "to themselves," they speak aloud snatches of what they come upon:

Husband	Record production
Young Woman	Girl turns on gas.
Husband	Sale hits a million—
Young Woman	Woman leaves all for love—
Husband	Market trend steady—
Young Woman	Young wife disappears—[30]

A clear pattern emerges: While Jones takes an interest in business and economic news, the Young Woman notices news about women's exercise of agency, presumably in a domestic context. Taken as a whole, the conversation echoes both Gus and Ben's exchanges over the newspaper in Pinter's *The Dumb Waiter*: Far from creating a shared sense of home, the nightly ritual of reading the paper has become one of almost complete separation.

This pattern is broken only when Jones receives the first of four phone calls during the scene, during which he discusses his stake in a real-estate transaction, expressing self-regard for his business acumen. As these phone calls come in, they set the tone for much of the rest of the Joneses' conversation, with her asking rote, cliché questions about his business dealings and him responding in kind:

Husband	[...] Well, it's all settled. They signed!—aren't you interested? Aren't you going to ask me?
Young Woman	(*by rote*) Did you put it over?
Husband	Sure I put it over.
Young Woman	Did you swing it?
Husband	Sure I swung it.
Young Woman	Did they come through?
Husband	Sure they came through.
Young Woman	Did they sign?
Husband	I'll say they signed.[31]

This exchange is clearly a version of one they have had before, for the Young Woman's mechanical questions and his pat answers indicate a routine very much like a pre-scripted performance (which, of course, in one sense it is). Here again, *The Dumb Waiter* comes to mind, with Ben and Gus's rehearsal of their hit late in the play; but, here it is the telephone, not a dumb waiter, that brings the demands of the larger social system into the space of the domestic, transforming husband and wife alike into dictation machines.

Helen's sense of confinement, literalized in the spaces of the office, the apartment building, the hotel, the maternity, ward, and the home, finds relief only in marginal places—the speakeasy of Episode 5: "Liberated," where she meets Richard Roe, newly returned from life-threatening adventures in Mexico, coded as lawless and liberating, and in Episode 6: "Intimate," where she has had apparently deeply satisfying sex with him in his street-level apartment. Roe woos the Young Woman with a tale of derring-do, which includes his escape from Mexican bandits who, for reasons unexplained, had taken him hostage. In making his getaway, he says, he used a bottle to bludgeon one and the broken neck of the same bottle to slit the throat of the other. When the Young Woman registers mild surprise at his account, he repeats his motive: "I had to get free, didn't I?"[32] This account will suggest the means and motive for her killing Jones later in the play, but also serves to arouse her interest in Roe, whose personal history allures her because of his association with brinksmanship and the will-to-freedom. Roe's gift of a lily in a vase of pebbles, symbolic of her own dreams of freedom from stony confinement, at the end of Scene 6, will become the weapon of the unstaged murder.

The allure of the untamed wilds of Roe's adventured become central to their pillow talk in the Episode 6, when he regales the Young Woman with his impressions of San Francisco, which he styles "Frisco":

> The bay and the hills! Jeez, that's the life! Every Saturday we use to cross the Bay—get a couple nags and just ride—over the hills. [...] At night, we'd make a little fire and eat—and then roll up in the old blanket and—[...] Jeez, that dry old grass out there smells good at night—full of tar weed—[....] it's a good smell![33]

Roe's stories of freedom and adventure in the west and south of the border, which, as we shall soon see, closely resemble Biff's reminiscences about his years in Nebraska and Texas in *Death of a Salesman*, are enough to convince the Young Woman to risk everything, including a murder conviction and execution, to secure her own freedom from the mechanized routines of domestic life and the modern city.

If freedom is figured as a geography untouched by modernity's sophistications, female agency in *Machinal* is symbolized by the Young Woman's hands and the lavish care she takes of them both before her marriage and once her affair with Roe has begun. In fact, her attention to the appearance and texture of her hands will be a key piece of circumstantial evidence leading to her conviction, because it will indicate to the jury that she has taken on a lover and also will explain why she would have had rubber gloves available with which to mask her fingerprints in committing the murder.[34] The hands as symbols of agency and self-respect, in fact, recur throughout the play, established as a motif as early as Episode 2: "At Home," and connect the play's expressivist aesthetic with that of German expressionist painting of the previous decade, especially of artist Egon Schiele, which often exaggerated the prominence of their figures' hands. The expressive emphasis on the body as the site of meaning and experience reinforces the binary regime that sets urbanity, modernity, machinery, and confinement in opposition to frontier wilds and the organic freedom of self-reliance and rugged individualism.

The play culminates in the moment of the Young Woman's execution by electrocution at the end of Episode 9: "A Machine." During the scene, she must submit to the rote prayers of the priest, rough handling by guards and barbers, and the gaze of reporters. All the machineries of the play—office machines, a rivet gun, a hand organ, an electric piano, a garbage chute—and the everyday machinic noise and pace of the city, now coalesce into this one lethal, literal machine, itself never to appear onstage. The point of this industrial mode of execution could not be clearer: For the electric chair condenses, in its inhuman singularity of purpose, every other machine indexed or represented in the play up to this point; they are all, we are given to understand, mechanisms of death. Modern technology and modernity, of which it is an extension, have forced the Young Woman's choices from the very beginning, so that, like Cocteau's infernal machine, whose "spring will unwind the entire span of a human life,"[35] they have essentially become the "ultimately determining factor" in shaping the course of life, to borrow from Marxian conceptions of technology.[36]

And yet, outside the determining power of the machine, beyond its reach, the play offers us the possibility that some kernel of essential personhood inheres in the Young Woman, figured as her longing for freedom and agency. Even without the ability to pursue that freedom or exercise that agency, her humanity is evidenced by the expression of the desire to do so, however thwarted. This fantasy of a desire unconstructed by the constraints of modernity, technology, and ideology is precisely what safeguards *Machinal* from having been seen as a radical or subversive play. The offstage cri de coeur with which the play ends—"Somebody! Somebod—"—alerts us to the persistence of that desire to engage authentically and freely with another human being in an nonideological space, a kind of imagined Mexico, where human interactions are uncorrupted and unmediated by the technologies of urban modernity.[37] The Young Woman's dreams of freedom, leading up to her final cry, contrast sharply with Beckett's *Krapp's Last Tape*, in which the recorded voice of the 39-year-old Krapp recalls listening to an older recorded version of himself giving a "yelp to Providence," a cry that the theatre audiences only hears about at two removes. Krapp's "[p]*rolonged laugh*" in response signals his dismissal of such expressions of epiphany and longing as futile.[38]

Machinal thus recoils from Krapp's cynicism; it does not entertain the possibility that even the Young Woman's desires—particularly her desire for unconstrained romance—are themselves ephemeral and ideological, already constructed by capital and patriarchy. This recuperative move allows the play to pin the blame for the Young Woman's alienation and despair, and that of young women generally, on urbanity and mechanization: The play's French title, which combines the sense of "mechanical" with "unconscious" and "involuntary," says as much. Thus, it can leave intact the fantasy of freedom, figured here as an untamed territory, in much the same way that Rice's *The Adding Machine* postulates an immortal soul and the promise of Elysian paradise as the alternative to mechanized subservience. Miller's *Death of a Salesman*, I hope to show, while it is the most nuanced in its reflections on capital, machinery, and ideology, also expresses a similar fantasy-ideal of the American frontier as the site of authentic, unconstructed, masculine freedom, one undistorted and uncorrupted by the imposition of advanced technology on the organic movements, desires, and rhythms of the a priori human.

The human in question in Miller's *Death of a Salesman* is, principally, Willy Loman, the title character, whose name itself suggests his social position: low. Willy's nostalgia for a simpler, freer, more hopeful and, on the whole, more humane world is signaled throughout the play in three main ways: In the play's present, Willy speaks about his own past as a salesman, when he was more energetic and successful, which he links to a period when his neighborhood, now overshadowed by a soaring urban skyline, was more suburban and pastoral; he also recalls his own brother Ben's success as an explorer and businessman, a testament to the triumph of the human will; and, finally, the play occasionally slips into sepia-toned flashbacks, filtered through Willy's distorted memory, of days when Willy, Biff, and Happy seem to have led more carefree lives and to have interacted in a more authentic way, familial and familiar.[39]

Biff, of Willy's two sons the one more frequently at odds with his father, is also the one whose aspirations take their contours from this idealized past; for he has only recently returned from out west, where he has tried his hand at manual labor in an attempt to free himself from what he and his father both see as the constraints of modern urbanity. Like his father, Biff is "mixed up," gripped by a longing for the open frontier in fulfillment of his own manifest destiny and yet anxious to prove himself a financial success:

I've had twenty or thirty different kinds of jobs since I left home before the war, and it always turns out the same. I just realized it lately. In Nebraska when I herded cattle, and the Dakotas, and Arizona, and now in Texas. It's why I came home now, I guess, because I realized it. [...] Texas is cool now, and it's spring. And whenever spring comes to where I am, I suddenly get the feeling, my God, I'm not gettin' anywhere! What the hell am I doing, playing around with horses, twenty-eight dollars a week! I'm thirty-four years old, I oughta be makin' my future. That's when I come running home. And now, I get here, and I don't know what to do with myself.[40]

As Michael J. Meyer observes, "Biff's return to a deteriorating suburb in New York suggests he is still confused, unable to understand how his personality traits continue to be [influenced] by his heritage from his father although he has struggled to distance himself from it."[41] Imagining Biff as a "revived Adonis," Meyer sees him as transformed at the end of the play, free of the constraining ties that bind him to his father's failures:

> The Biff of The Requiem does not desire possessions and can do without "things"; instead, he retains his childlike passion for wonder and nature, for animals and weather changes. As the play closes, Biff has discovered that to be an adult means only one thing: refusing inherited traits that are imposed from without and redefining the word "success" in terms of self-knowledge.[42]

In reading the end of the play as an endorsement of Biff's epiphany and aspirations, in contrast to Happy's determination to succeed "in this city" where his father failed, "to lick this racket," Meyers's essay highlights the play's transcendentalist bent.[43]

Biff's ambivalent longing for the open country of the west is echoed, a few moments later, by Willy who, caught in a flashback of happier times with his two teenage sons, promises Biff that the three of them will drive north through New England together when "summer comes":

> America is full of beautiful towns and fine, upstanding people. And they know me, boys, they know me up and down New England. The

finest people. And when I bring you fellas up, there'll be open sesame for all of us,' cause one thing, boys: I have friends. I can park my car in any street in New England, and the cops protect it like their own. This summer, heh?⁴⁴

Here, Willy's fantasy of driving his boys through "all the towns [...] up and down New England," a synecdoche for the whole nation, itself "full of beautiful towns and fine, upstanding people," is combined with the privileges of professional success, not least of which is that freedom to "park [...] in any street." Combined with Willy's idealized memories of Ben's exploits in Africa and Alaska, Willy's characterization of his own travels in New England creates a vision of success as a combination of frontier freedom and salesmanship. This combination of mobility and financial success characterizes both Willy and Biff's ideal of complete agency and self-determination.

The idea of subjectivity and agency as constitutive of a unified, self-evident and self-willed individual, we should remember, is inherent in what would come to be known as "The Method," based on Konstantin Stanislavsky's theories at the Moscow Art Theatre in the 1890s and further developed in the Group Theatre in the 1930s, of which Elia Kazan, the director of the premiere of *Death of a Salesman*, was a member. Matthew C. Roudané explains that "Miller's stage directions provide insight into what Kazan (and Stanislavsky before him) calls the characters' spines, or their fundamental nature."⁴⁵ The very idea of a "fundamental nature" of a character elides the fact of representation from the field of representation; like the machineries that disappear behind their own effects in realist drama, discussed in Chapter 3, the constructedness of the individual character is meant to give way, through the deployment of The Method, to a perception of an authentic, whole, unified, and coherent individual. Roudané perceptively notes that this effect is created repeatedly through the way the actor playing Willy is to embody the character as frequently stooping or slouched, noting that "Miller presents no fewer than twenty-five scenes in which Willy's body language and dialogue create images of the fall, the falling, or the fallen."⁴⁶ In so doing, the abstract idea of Willy as a fully formed individual composed of a "fundamental nature" is further unified with his and the actor's bodily facticity. This coherence of body and individual subjectivity, and of subjectivity with fundamental nature, is echoed in the unified effect of the stage itself, which through "shifts in lighting [...] register[s] through direct"—that is, not mediated or constructed—"sensory experience the cohering of social, psychic, and actual time."[47]

While Willy himself does not go so far as to express a desire to leave the city and salesmanship altogether, his own remarks on the decline of the neighborhood demonstrate his nostalgia for what he remembers as a freer, more natural time: "The street is lined with cars. There's not a breath of fresh air in the neighborhood. The grass don't grow any more, you can't raise a carrot in the back yard. [...] Remember those two beautiful elm trees out there?"[48] This nostalgia remains untouched throughout the play; Biff's heroic quest to return to the west, to unburden himself of "the wrong dreams" his father harbored, we are given to understand, represents a liberating epiphany, a moment of self-discovery and truth, belying Happy's "*hopeless*" determination to "win" the battle his father "fought."[49] This validation of Biff's longing for freedom, unfettered by the demands of modern city life, is reinforced in Linda's final soliloquy over Willy's grave, in which she laments that, even though she has "made the last payment on the house today [....] there'll be nobody home": "We're free and clear [....] We're free. *Biff comes slowly toward her.* We're free...We're free..."[50]

Throughout the play, this desire for an authentic, liberated, organic experience of oneself repeatedly runs up against quite literal technologies of the modern city. *Death of a Salesman* stages these machines as foils for Biff's and Willy's agrarian dreams much as Treadwell's and Rice's plays do. In fact, *Death of a Salesman* presents itself in key ways as a hybrid of *The Adding Machine*, with its focus on the drudgery of dead-end professional employment, and *Machinal*, which connects its fantasies of freedom to unencumbered masculinity in rugged geographies innocent of modernity.

A telling episode occurs late in the play when Willy's boss, Howard, shows Willy his new dictation recorder, which, like Rice's eponymous adding machine, serves as a harbinger of dismissal:

> **Howard** I bought it for dictation, but you can do anything with it. Listen to this. I had it home last night. Listen to what I picked up. The first one is my daughter. Get this. *He flicks the switch and "Roll out the Barrel" is heard being whistled.* Listen to that kid whistle.
> **Willy** That is lifelike, isn't it?
> **Howard** Seven years old. Get that tone.[51]

In showing off his new machine, Howard employs language that suggests an unproblematic human–machine interface. For instance, he uses the colloquial "picked up" to mean *recorded* and "get" to mean *listen to*, eliding these terms' more literal meanings, which would suggest human action, grasping or taking hold of something and keeping it. Howard's proud remark, "Seven years old. Get that tone," switches referents without signaling that switch. He apparently means that his daughter, not the machine, is seven years old, while the "tone" is the machine's, not the daughter's. Howard's unmarked segue from talking about a human to talking about a machine shows that, in his mind, humans and machines are not so distinct as they might appear. The 7-year-old daughter is presented onstage by means of the machine, a machine that neither embodies her nor gives her voice (yet), while the machine's "tone" seems almost human. Willy, in this exchange, is the one whose remark shows an awareness of the human/machine distinction. Instead of commenting on the daughter's skill at whistling, Willy confines his remarks to the quality of the machine's reproduction of her whistling: It's not life; it's "life*like*."

The machine seems to speak, as well, in the voice of Howard's son:

> **Howard** Sh! Get this now, this is my son.
> **His Son** "The capital of Alabama is Montgomery; the capital of Arizona is Phoenix; the capital of Arkansas is Little Rock; the capital of California is Sacramento..." *on, and on.*
> **Howard** *(holding up five fingers)* Five years old, Willy!
> **Willy** He'll make an announcer some day.

The layout and typography of this passage alert us, again, to the fraught nature of the human–machine interface. On the one hand, the text signals the voice of Howard's son as if he were an onstage character: The line is labeled "His Son." On the other hand, what his son says is set off by quotation marks, as if to remind the reader that Howard's son—a budding young "capital"-ist—is not saying these things, present onstage, but rather that the machine is quoting him. Moreover, the italicized direction that the machine/son's recitation of state capitals is meant to go "on, and on" points out that the words will have been prerecorded, that they need not be scripted, because it is just an alphabetized list of states and capitals.

Again, Willy's response to Howard's pride about his son's age—which, we imagine, is pride that a boy so young can memorize state capitals, not that he can speak into a microphone—demonstrates Willy's refusal or inability to conflate the human with the machine. By focusing on the son's potential as an announcer, and not, say, as a geographer or cartographer, Willy's comment reminds us that the voice is coming out of a machine, that it has been subjected to mechanical processes, and that the human remains behind.

So, although the scene between Howard and Willy progresses to Willy's desperate plea for better working conditions and Howard's increasing determination to fire Willy, a larger thematic tension emerges between two fundamentally different worldviews. Willy understands the world as a place where American values of hard work, ingenuity, and personal magnetism assert themselves against the encroachment of mechanized, routinized, urbanized anti-individualism. Howard, by contrast, is permitted his view of the machine as less fixed and less hostile to his own interests, something you "can do anything" with, because of his status as the machine's owner and operator. Howard's easy assumption that the machine is benign because he remains in control of it is of a piece with Rebecca Rey's view of the human–technology relationship in DeLillo's *Valparaiso*—mistaken, in my view—which I will discuss in Chapter 3. Howard's verbal slippage, the pride with which he speaks both of his children and of his machine, and his ability to shrug off Willy's pleas when the exigencies of business demand, attest to the ease with which he accepts the displacement of the human by the machine. Willy's position vis-à-vis the machine is indicated by the confusion into which his encounter with Howard's dictaphone a few minutes later throws him. Willy has just invoked his relationship with Howard's father and the "promises made across this desk," speaking in apparent anger and frustration, prompting Howard to leave the office so Willy can "pull [him]self together." Alone, Willy muses: "Pull myself together! What the hell did I say to him. My God, I was yelling at him. How could I!" At which point, he "breaks off, staring at the light, which occupies the chair, animating it. He approaches this chair, standing across the desk from it," imagining Howard's deceased father, his former boss. Willy begins to speak to the imagined ghost, "Frank, don't you remember what you told me that time? How you put your hand on my shoulder, and Frank…" But before he can complete his reminiscence, "[h]e leans on the desk and as he speaks the dead man's name he accidentally switches on the recorder and instantly":

> **Howard's Son:** "…of New York is Albany. The capital of Ohio is Cincinnati,[52] the capital of Rhode Island is…"
>
> *The recitation continues.*
>
> **Willy**   (*leaping away with fright, shouting*) Ha! Howard! Howard! Howard!
> **Howard**   (*rushing in*) What happened?
> **Willy**   (*pointing at the machine, which continues nasally, childishly, with the capital cities*) Shut it off! Shut it off![53]

This moment provides perhaps the most condensed example of the uneasy way nostalgia, the human, and the machine interrelate in *Death of a Salesman*. For in the course of only a few moments, the dialogue and action have moved from Willy's speaking about Howard's father to Willy imagining, analeptically, Howard's father's presence, to, finally, the recorded voice on the machine usurping the place of that imagined father. The movement from memory to flashback to technology, and the fear and dismay this development creates, captures the play's overall implication that the injustices Willy faces are primarily the injustices of technological modernity, not the larger system of capitalism as such.

Willy's encounter with the recorder connects to his difficult interactions with other technologies, including the family car, which, in a moment of inattention (the family believe), he recently "smashed up"[54]; the refrigerator, which "consumes belts like a goddamned maniac"[55]; the home's heater, which literally "glow[s]" with significance and from which he has periodically used a tube to inhale natural gas in so-far unconsummated attempts to commit suicide.[56] The heater's glow recapitulates, in miniature, the "angry glow of orange" that surrounds the Loman house, indicating that the hostility of the industrial city has infiltrated the home, as well.[57] Jo Mielziner's set for the 1949 premiere, a faithful realization of his drawings for the play, hearkens back to Rice and Treadwell's expressionism.[58] Although as a unit set it remains static and does not rely heavily on the mechanical capacity of the theatre to effect rapid changes, it nevertheless externalizes and concretizes Willy's inner, psychological dimensions: The permeability of its playing spaces, the collage-like arrangement of rooms and levels, and the fragile outline of its roofline and chimney set against a backdrop of looming apartment buildings, rendered as recognizable but by no means realistic, represent Willy's own sense of smallness, vulnerability, and defeat. Despite the relative naturalism of Miller's dialogue in *Death of a Salesman*, the expressionist qualities of the set, the reliance on lighting cues and music to establish the play's emotive tonalities, and the enactment of memory and hallucination throughout the play continues to engage in the same kind of explication that, in *The Adding Machine* and *Machinal*, articulate to the productive function of capitalist machineries.

Death of a Salesman is not Miller's first play to link exploitative capital with machinic failure. His second play, and his first successful one, *All My Sons* (1947), which preceded *Death of a Salesman* and shares major themes with it, including fraught father–son relationships, concerns the lingering guilt and shame Joe Keller experiences after having authorized the delivery of defective airplane engine components from his manufacturing company to the US Army for use in the Second World War, engines whose failure cost the lives of young American pilots. Again, the connection between literal machines—in this case, plane engines—and the capitalist machine, which elides ethics in favor of the exigencies of "business," is in play, both of which also inform paternal failure and lead, finally, to the father's suicide. But in *Death*, the interplay of modernity and constraint, throughout associated with mechanization and technological innovation, and a nostalgic notion of organic human freedom is more fully developed, more central to the play's motific structure. Thus, it presents its bias toward that nostalgic fantasy-ideal much more saliently.

Christopher Bigsby's remarks on *Death of a Salesman* in his erudite *Arthur Miller: A Critical Study* crystallize the attraction of conceiving of the play as one primarily concerned with recapturing and reconnecting with a compelling image of authentic human agency and expression. Noting that Miller himself "has offered a number of intriguing interpretations" of the play, including several that emphasize the problem of modern technology, Bigsby notes that "those who saw this play at the time [of its premiere], and in the over fifty years since [...], have connected to it less through its comments on a culture wedded to a myth than through characters whose hopes and illusions seem instantly recognizable and archetypal."[59] Accordingly, despite the centrality of the mechanical and technological to *Death of a Salesman*, Bigsby sees Miller's remark that "*Death of a Salesman*, really, is a love story between a man and his son, and in a crazy way between both of them and America" as the "observation that goes most directly to the heart of the play."[60] Bigsby's view that a love relationship, rather than larger ideological stakes, lies at the "heart" of the play—a remark that highlights the play's organic, human anatomy—implicitly supports my view that *Death of a Salesman*, like *Machinal* and *The Adding Machine*, privileges an atavistic and recuperative notion of the human, even if Bigsby's explicit contention is that this bias toward the human accounts for the play's success.

Like *All My Sons*, *Death of a Salesman* sidesteps the dialectics of ideology critique, preferring to see the human uninflected by industrial modernity as a natural, nonideological given. Emphasizing the simplicity of the play's machine/nature binary, Chaudhuri notes, almost in passing, that "Willy's tragedy *easily boils down to* an alienation from the expansive American dream of ceaseless motion, vigorously exemplified in his brother Ben, and in the sad state of crisis in his son Biff."[61] It thus continues to extend the melancholy posture of Treadwell's *Machinal* and Rice's *The Adding Machine*, which likewise hearken back to and evince a longing for an impossible, nonexistent fantasy ur-state of unconstructed human agency. In all three plays, the contrast between agency and constraint, between the human and the machine, are presented as unambiguous binaries. Agency and liberated desire get coded through expansive geographies: Ben's Alaska and Africa; Richard Roe's Mexico; Zero's Elysium and his simian jungle existence; and even Willy's drives through New England. These images of freedom also take the form of specifically masculine notions of desire and conquest, including physical violence and the specter of death.

Constraint, by contrast, coalesces in machineries, which both dominate and, in the case of Zero and Willy, emasculate. For this reason, the machineries of Rice's, Treadwell's, and Miller's plays are much more literal than figurative or symbolic, in contrast to the attenuated machineries of the plays discussed in the elsewhere in this book: While they may point to a nonideological superstructure, they are more commonly deployed as signs of themselves, mimetic representations of machine power. As such, they are not Deleuze and Guattari's desiring machines, whose multivalence complicates the plays under discussion in Chapter 1, inviting a dialectical critical engagement; on the contrary, the machineries of these American modernist plays are mostly to be seen as inflexible, self-evident, and unmoving bulwarks against idealism, desire, and fantasy, simply evacuating the lives they touch of authenticity and fulfillment.

Thus, the human/machine, organic/technological, natural/constructed, and urban/frontier binaries these plays reinforce appear, on the whole, simple to the point of being reductive, a tendency Raymond Williams analyzes and critiques in his seminal study *The Country and the City* (1973). Noting the way the geographic country/city binary's terms have been "generalised" in literary and other cultural representations of these realms, Williams explains that:

> [o]n the country has gathered the idea of a natural way of life: of peace, innocence, and simple virtue. On the city has gathered the idea of an achieved centre: of learning, communication, light. Powerful hostile associations have also been developed: on the city as a place of noise, worldliness and ambition; on the country as a place of backwardness, ignorance, limitation. A contrast between country and city, as fundamental ways of life, reaches back into classical times.[62]

These broad associations belie a "real history" that, "throughout, has been astonishingly varied," a claim that underscores the simplicity of these three plays' binary configurations.[63]

Ninety years after the first production of Treadwell's *Machinal*, Mexican American playwright Isaac Gomez has returned to many of the themes common to the three plays I have discussed so far in this chapter. His episodic play *La Ruta*, explores the tension between an exploitative techno-rationalist economic and social order, on the one hand, and the aspirations to individual freedom and autonomy, on the other.[64] It has in common with *Machinal* its focus on the particularly oppressive effects of this social order on women; its staging and critique of the dominating logic of capital and the mechanized workplace; and its highly episodic structure. But in shifting the locus of that critique from the urban centers of the American commercial enterprise to post-NAFTA border areas of northern Mexico, Gomez's play brings Treadwell's critique into the twentieth-first century and situates it within a context of arguably even greater psychological and material privation: the communities of women essential to the success of the American maquiladoras who, despite their economic value as resources of labor, nevertheless face the dangers of living in a society indifferent to patriarchal and economic violence alike. It also gives the lie to the fantasy-ideal of Mexico as an antediluvian paradise of personal freedom upon which Treadwell's Young Woman fatally pins her hopes. Featured as part of the 2018–2019 Steppenwolf Theatre series, *La Ruta* deploys a relatively simple array of theatrical technology, its most sophisticated being video projection used to create a documentary-film effect in its mise-en-scène. Despite this simplicity—or perhaps because of it—aesthetically, thematically, and linguistically, *La Ruta*, as it was produced at Steppenwolf, successfully transports itself to the cultural and national margins of the US–Mexico borderlands, freely integrating, as it does, Spanish and particularly Hispanic renderings of English into its dialogue.

In *La Ruta*, the larger systems of exploitation and the infrastructure they depend on are indexed by more local technologies—in this case, those of transportation and textile production; and as in *Machinal*, even these local technologies are materially absent from the mise-en-scène, frequently suggested by reference in the dialogue, the gesture and movement of the actors, and the music and soundscape enveloping the action. The bus that takes young women to and from their low-paying jobs at the denim clothing factory near the border, for instance, is indicated by the sound of its approach and the glare of headlights from offstage; likewise, inside the factory itself, the young women go through the motion of feeding cloth through industrial sewing machines, which are, themselves, invisible. Only the workers' mechanized, repeated movements and a still, hazy projection of a vast, dim room full of sewing machines indicate the machines' dominating presence.

Indeed, whether the scene is the home Yolanda has shared with her recently abducted daughter Brenda, the bus station where she and her friend Marisela wait in vain for Brenda's arrival, the factory floor, a town's central plaza, a memorial park dedicated to young women lost to sex trafficking, or a desert roadway far from town, the set remains mostly unchanged: Framing the space are a high cinder-block wall along stage right and a high unfinished upstage wall, on which images establishing the exterior and interior environments are projected along with captions that mark the dates during plaintive musical interludes sung by the mysterious Desamaya; a small kitchen and its adjoining kitchen garden occupy the down left corner, separated from time to time by a clothesline of blankets. Even the video projections take up a poor aesthetic, often only suggestive of place and out-of-focus.

La Ruta—named for the bus transport line—is not, centrally, about exploitative labor practices and factory conditions; rather, they serve primarily as the menacing backdrop for the story of a young woman's abduction, abetted by a coworker, Ivonne, who herself is attempting to ransom the life of her own abducted sister, Erika, by providing a local gang with new victims. And yet, the way the factory system uses these women, the managers often firing women as they become older and slower, only to replace them with their own daughters, and subjecting them to intense demands for productivity during long shifts at dangerous machines, offers a clear analog to the criminal enterprise that abducts, traffics, and ultimately kills young women in and around Juárez. Further linking these women's everyday lives are the denim jeans they all wear; they are the consumers of the very products they are underpaid to produce, doubly linked to their own exploitation. Finally, as Yolanda becomes increasingly despondent after Brenda's disappearance, she takes to obsessively folding and refolding laundry, including items of clothing long unworn by her abducted daughter. In doing so, she unconsciously replicates many of the same movements the women in the textile factories are forced to repeat.

Again, attention to the interplay of theatre technologies and the technologies of the wider world alert us to *La Ruta*'s critique of techno-rationalist exploitation and the way the ideologies that sustain it articulate to other systems of exploitation and injustice. Yet, unlike Miller's *Death of a Salesman*, the minimal technological sophistication in evidence in *La Ruta* forestalls the possibility that spectators might find themselves fascinated by technical facility on display to a degree that would invite complicity with the systems of capitalist production and commodity consumption that make them possible. And, whereas *Machinal*, *The Adding Machine*, and *Death of a Salesman* all traffic, to differing degrees, in nostalgia for an imagined halcyon past of rugged individualism and frontier freedom and optimism, *La Ruta* does not. Indeed, it explodes those fantasies, emphasizing that its characters' quest for autonomy—whether that is economic autonomy gained through work at the maquiladoras or social and sexual autonomy to be fought for through public protest—is an almost certainly fatal and futile quest.

In doing so, *La Ruta* also eschews the binary logic of these three earlier plays, which Williams elucidates above. And yet, binarity itself, as we will see in Chapter 5, is foundational to cybernetics, with its dream of reducing all experience to information and all information to binary code. And so, in one way, less bold in their indictment of exploitative systems than *La Ruta* is, *Machinal*, *The Adding Machine*, and *Death of a Salesman* mount their resistance to machine logic, to technological domination, and to rationalist ideologies in ways that presage and enact the very logic that will come to mark the ascendancy digital technologies in the second half of the twentieth century.

3

Alienating Devices: Bertolt Brecht & Kurt Weill, John Adams & Alice Goodman, Don DeLillo, and Athol Fugard

Chapter 1 advanced the view that Cocteau's *Eiffel Tower Wedding Party*, Ionesco's *The Future Is in Eggs*, and Tristan Tzara's *The Gas Heart* all reflect, critique, satirize and, to different degrees, imitate the machineries of their production in their articulated, modular, and highly stylized mise-en-scénes and diegetics, through articulation, fragmentation, transposition, intensification, and the management of flows—of human bodies, objects, and messages. What these works may have to say about these machineries comes through primarily as suggestion, formal irony, multivalent slippages, and wry parody rather than explicitly or didactically. Chapter 2, by contrast, considered modernist plays in the American canon that more explicitly implicated the social and ideological function of machineries, deploying the technologies represented onstage or referred to in dialogue as indices pointing toward larger technological systems.

The four pieces under examination in this chapter continue to take on social and political themes quite directly, and in two cases all but explicitly argue for a skeptical, even highly wary view of technological advancement. *Lindbergh's Flight*, Bertolt Brecht and Kurt Weill's 1929 oratorio, dramatizes the first solo transatlantic flight, using it as an occasion to offer a Marxist lesson in class consciousness and social advancement. Lindbergh is to be understood as a kind of everyman, typifying the struggles and achievements of the commoner who makes use of the technologies at hand for social and political advancement. At the same time, Brecht hoped that the radio broadcast of the live performance would encourage listeners to enter into a shared consciousness, identifying with the part of the flier as he battles the elements and his own physical limitations. While Neher's set designs, with their studied crudity and simple stage devices, tempered what might otherwise threaten to become a celebration of capitalism's technical efficacy, a revival of the piece some eighty years later by the Opéra National de Lyon, would offer an unambiguously celebratory display of technical facility. Brecht, Weill, and Neher's approach to creating and staging *Lindbergh's Flight*, and its susceptibility to absorption by the culture industry, will occupy much of what follows and will serve as the theoretical grounding for the examination of two later pieces: John Adams and Alice Goodman's opera *Nixon in China* (1987) and Don DeLillo's play *Valparaiso* (1999). In these two late twentieth-century American pieces, telecommunications and aerospace technologies once again take center stage. In what remains of this chapter, I will argue that they offer a critique of technological advancement that both reveals the limitations of Brecht's view of technology's liberating capacity and situate new media and modes of travel within a matrix of technologies that disperse the subject and diminish, if not eliminate, human agency by appropriating it and representing it as a product of technology itself. And yet, in order to do so, both pieces must deploy the full complement of theatre technologies, themselves the product of global capitalism and of hierarchical cultural and social systems. By contrast, Athol Fugard's *The Island* (1973), a play devised with its two original actors, deploys relatively simple theatre technologies to offer a critique similar to those enacted by the previous three pieces.

While these motifs involving technologies of mass communication and transportation overlap to some degree with the formal elements of the plays examined in Chapter 1—particularly with regard to articulation and fragmentation—here, as in the plays considered in Chapter 2, these technologies are more central to the unfolding of the narratives and stand out more emphatically as objects of consideration and analysis. Still, these works, particularly as they have been mounted in late-twentieth and early-twenty-first-century productions, enter into an uneasy, and potentially self-defeating relationship to the theatre technologies necessary for rendering them onstage, even as some of those theatre technologies are quite ancient in their provenance.

The ancient Greek *mêkanê*, for example, has proven still capable of producing spectacular effects on the contemporary stage: *Nixon in China*, under the direction of Peter Sellars, received only lukewarm reception when it premiered at the Houston Grand Opera. Nevertheless, the arrival of the presidential airplane on stage was met with "spontaneous applause" at the opening.[1] The plane—formerly *Air Force One*, but renamed (temporarily, as it turns out) *The Spirit of 76* for the occasion of Nixon's visit to China in 1972 and in anticipation of the 1976 bicentennial of the US *Declaration of Independence*, but also to suggest a connection to Lindbergh's historic flight—landed more as a helicopter might, gradually drifting straight down out of the flies, its nose and the forward half of its fuselage descending vertically to meet the waiting red-carpeted stairway. In landing vertically, rather than rolling in from right or left as an actual landing plane would have done, the *Spirit of 76* arrives in a way that immediately signals the work's resistance to historical or representational realism and, instead, draws attention to the effect as one produced by fairly simple machineries of the theatre: The guy wires supporting the aircraft are quite visible, even in the PBS broadcast recording of the original production, and the manifestly muslin door slides open, as a pocket door might, rather than swinging outward, to reveal not the plane's interior, but the dimly lit, bare trees that form the backdrop of the whole stage.

These visual effects—the vertical landing, the sliding muslin door, the backdrop visible through the plane—may be understood as representational failures, the inability of the set designer and theatre technicians to get it right. Such an understanding would point toward the limitations of the particular opera house in which the premiere took place; we might imagine that insufficient wing space (no pun intended) and the need to move and store set elements quickly and easily required compromises in verisimilitude. But three factors militate against so easy a dismissal of these effects as shortcomings and instead invite an interpretive engagement with them. First, the opera as a whole continually calls attention to representational and communication technologies, gesturing toward Nixon's "constant surveillance of his image" and the White House's careful staging of his visit, only months before the 1972 presidential election.[2] Constantly referring to the care with which the whole visit was choreographed for public consumption, the opera takes a meta-theatrical orientation toward its own representational practices. Second, while Adams, Goodman, and Sellars consulted an extensive array of historical sources, including photographs, broadcast recordings, primary and secondary historical sources, and journalism, and while the libretto, score, and staging occasionally quote from these materials, the overall representational aesthetic of the entire piece resists realism. Moments of authenticity, such as they are, work less as guarantees of accuracy and more as sutures, from time to time tying the otherwise fanciful fabric of the production to recognizable historical backing, which remains perceptible only as a trace. Finally, the original staging employed manifestly epic-theatrical techniques for disrupting audience identification or absorption, engendering—quite successfully, if some contemporary reviews are to be trusted—alienation in the Brechtian sense of the word rather than the kind of unmediated involvement realistic drama frequently fosters. For the moment, I want to pursue this third line of inquiry first—that is, the resonances between Brechtian theatre and Sellars's staging of Adams and Goodman's opera.

In British and Continental drama studies, Bertolt Brecht's approach to staging social and political critique has, over the course of the past one hundred years, become the standard for thinking about the political in drama. As Anthony Squiers notes, "[s]ince Brecht's death" in 1956, "a whole academic industry has emerged" around Brecht's work "on both sides of the Atlantic which continues to grow steadily."[3] Even as the so-called New Brutalism of Sarah Kane and Mark Ravenhill, the mid-century plays of Edward Bond, the late works of Harold Pinter, and the realist commentaries of David Hare and John Osborne offer non-Brechtian alternatives to staging political themes, Squiers reminds us that "within drama studies, [Brecht] is widely considered to be one of the most important figures of the twentieth century."[4] But the persistence of epic and neo-epic drama and its aesthetic dominance in late-middle and late twentieth century work of Caryl Churchill, Howard Brenton, and others and in critical appraisals of staged politics reinforces the primacy of Brechtian theory and practice.[5] Despite John Willett's early cautionary reminder, in 1963, that "the endless working and re-working" that Brecht's theories "underwent [...], the progress from an embryo to an often very differently formulated final concept, the amendments and the after-thoughts," frequently get "overlooked," it is nevertheless the case that practitioners and critics still generally conceive of epic dramaturgy as effectively oppositional to dominant capitalist aesthetics.[6] The results are that, first, conceptions of political drama by and large exclude absurdist and more subtly enactive plays from consideration, and, second, epic drama has become increasingly susceptible to the very cultural and economic forces it initially confronted.

The question of spectacle, one of several questions that arise in relation to the decreasing relevance of Brechtian dramaturgy as a viable political-theatrical practice, and the way spectacle shapes and responds to the taste for works of art as consumer commodities offer a way into the complex problematic emerging from this susceptibility. Spectacle, in aesthetic production, is what happens when the question "How do they do that?" becomes more significant in defining an audience's various responses than the question "What are they doing?" or "What does it mean?" Spectacle draws the audience's attention—usually admiring—to the sensational effects produced by the theatre's technological capacity;[7] in doing so, it tends to fix audience responses in the emotional, rather than critical or analytical register, precisely the opposite of what Brecht hoped to achieve with his *Verfremdungseffekt*: distantiation or alienation effect.

Here, I should acknowledge that my use of the term *spectacle* differs from two more famous and long-standing deployments of the term, both of which actually militate against the term's critical usefulness to the study of stage technology and theatrical effects. The first is the term as it is often used in translations of Aristotle's *Poetics* to render the Greek *opsis*, which would be more usefully and accurately translated as "visual effects," since spectacle, in common English, always suggests sensory excess; it is not a value-neutral term, as Aristotle's *opsis* is. The second is the more recent critical use of the term spectacle, also as it appears in translation, this time of Guy Debord's French *spectacle*, used throughout his brief epigrammatic volume *Society of the Spectacle*.[8] While Debord's use of the term relies on the sense of excess absent from Aristotle's *opsis*, for Debord, spectacle's visuality is only sometimes sensory; at other times, it is metaphorical or metonymic, standing in for mediated experiences of all kinds—sensory, intellectual, emotional—enabled by nonstop production of the cultural superstructure of late capitalism. While the use of the English *spectacle*, the cognate of Debord's term in French, preserves this metaphoric quality and the sense of excess or surplus production, it also names a process by which its effects are made to seem natural or quotidian. By contrast, in what follows, I want to emphasize theatrical spectacle as representational excess responsible for creating a "wow factor" that resists naturalization, however often repeated or witnessed.

Those of us who inhabit the milieu of early twenty-first-century global capitalism are surrounded by spectacles of all kinds. IMAX film, NASCAR racing, computer-generated imagery (CGI) effects in movies and television, arena rock concerts, virtual reality, and immersive video games, to name a few, all draw our attention to the spectacle of technical facility—that is, to the sophistication of the technological apparatus responsible for the production of their particular effects.[9] But spectacle is not ideologically neutral in these contexts. Rather, they offer us a value system often more compelling than the seemingly ideologically neutral "content" we generally believe we're watching (a race, a musical performance, a penguin migration). These attractions draw to their technical facility a desiring, admiring attention: we are held as much by their mystery as by what is manifest. We are invited—perhaps coerced—into applauding the pyrotechnics of the spectacle, and, by implication, to acquiesce to—indeed, approve—the socio-historical material conditions that make them possible. And, generally, we accept that invitation. In fact, we usually pay for it. This celebratory disposition toward technical sophistication will seem familiar to most readers. At the same time, we are permitted to forget that consumer commodities and the distribution and communications systems their flow relies on, were first developed to facilitate warfare and to enable capitalist ideological hegemony.

These observations are meant to foreground questions about the ethics and aesthetics of avowedly leftist theatre production: If the technical facility with which a production is staged affirms, sub-rosa, a techno-capitalist status quo even as its staged utterances question or denounce it, then we might wonder about how this paradox gets negotiated. It is precisely the development, deployment, and finally, impossibility of just such a negotiation I want to consider in three productions of Bertolt Brecht and Kurt Weill's oratorio *Lindbergh's Flight*, first performed at the Baden-Baden Chamber Music Festival in 1929 (with some music by Paul Hindemith); then fully staged later that year (with music composed entirely by Weill) at Breslau's Stadttheater; finally, in 2006, the Opéra National de Lyon in 2006 mounted a lavish production featured at the Edinburgh Festival. Apart from its usefulness as an example of the way Brechtian theatrical practice has evolved over the past century, the centrality of an historic intercontinental, transoceanic flight by an American hero after whose plane Nixon explicitly renamed *Air Force One* makes it a resonant companion piece for examination alongside *Nixon in China*.

Brecht, as a political and dramaturgical theorist, is perhaps most famous for his invention of the *Verfremdungseffekt*, translated variously as the "alienation effect," "A-effect," "V-effect," "distantiation," and "estrangement." Inasmuch as this effect attempted to counter the prevailing realist, sentimental, broadly comic, or spectacular aesthetic of 1920s German opera and popular performance, Brecht's dramaturgy serves as a case of high modernism's refutation of traditional genres, modes, and forms. However, unlike the avant-garde modernism of Cocteau, Ionesco, and Tzara, on the one hand, or a formalist notion of defamiliarization or estrangement, Brecht's drama also propounded explicit leftist political commentaries on class and power, and occasionally even gender. So, while his alienation effect, by itself, offered an implicit critique of the formal aesthetics of popular performance, the dialogue and action offered explicit critique of what he saw as capitalism's moral corruption.

The alienation effect, meant to contravene an audience's identification with characters and events on stage was, for Brecht, a means to engage audiences in analytical-critical reflection and debate about the social, political, and economic questions his productions tried to raise. Importantly, Brechtian aesthetics were never merely formal, on the one hand—a set of decorative choices and stylistic gestures that could be made in the staging of just any play—nor ends in themselves, able to stand alone and speak the resistance unsupplemented by the text, characterization, and other dramatic elements. Rather, Brecht attempted to alienate his audience's usual responses as a means toward a more fundamental goal: to teach them a moral or political lesson. To disrupt an audience's absorption, conditioned by realist drama, opera, and the music hall, Brecht introduced what are now somewhat problematically called alienation "devices" (echoing Viktor Shklovksy's formalist notion of the artistic "device"[10] and suggesting that they were merely mechanisms for producing effects): Actors occasionally sing songs set to Kurt Weill's angular, metrically difficult, and dissonant music; they fall out of character when they are not speaking and inhabit character ironically or approximately; they enact gesture in mechanical, ironic, rote, and unconvincing ways; auditorium lights remain on; smoking and conversation are encouraged during performance; plots are episodic, rather than linear and causal; and placards, supertitles, and banners textualize the production, often announcing the political and historical contexts for the play and labeling the scenes, even as the characters, such are they are, are sometimes themselves apparently ignorant of the ideological stakes of their actions. The deployment of such formal features results in a performance that can seem uneven, disunified, and jagged: alienating. Such performances can also seem crude, bordering on amateurish. But Brechtian crudity is also a studied, rehearsed crudity. Audiences are meant never to lose sight of the fact that they are watching a play, and the acting, lighting, design, and direction are to be understood as both political acts and forms of labor. Neher's intentional, studied crudity in set and technical designs for Brecht's works in the 1920s and 1930s show that Brecht and his production team were aware of spectacle's dangerous excesses: namely, that the technology enabling production might threaten to overwhelm the didactic intent of the works themselves. According to Christopher Baugh, Neher "tried to find the theatrical equivalent of the sketch, [...] ways of giving timber canvas and stage paint a softness of definition similar to the tentative and suggestive effects achieved by drawing and writing with ink upon damp watercolour paper; a medium that Neher particularly favored."[11]

In his theoretical notes, Brecht emphasizes the need to reveal the means by which conventional theatre maintains its artifice in order to demonstrate how theatrical realism and spectacle conspires with capitalist hegemony. Accordingly, in his designs for Brecht's plays, Neher sought "true theatrical reality," according to Baugh, by "consistently reveal[ing] the mechanics of stage construction" instead of attempting "to create a credible spectacle of another world, a transport into a coherent, harmoniously designed past where the very considerable technologies that the theatres utilized would be hidden from the immediate consciousness of the audience," as the great European theatres of the nineteenth century did.[12] Characterizing these retrograde forms as "culinary,"[13] Brecht expounds on the dangers of traditional theatrical and operatic forms:

> Great apparati [*sic*[14]] like the opera, the stage, the press, etc., impose their views as it were incognito. For a long time now they have taken the handiwork (music, writing, criticism, etc.) of intellectuals who share in their profits—that is, of men who are economically committed to the prevailing system but are socially near-proletarian—and processed it

to make fodder for their public entertainment machine, judging it by their own standards and guiding it into their own channels.[15]

"Society," Brecht argues, taking his terminology from Marx, "absorbs via the apparatus whatever it needs in order to reproduce itself"—that is, whatever ideological and representational effects tend toward the advancement of capital. Accordingly, as Baugh explains, Neher wished to

> extend the metaphor of the scene as machine and to suggest that we should conceive of the making of theatre (the rehearsal process) as the constructing of a machine for performance: a machine that naturally includes the physical elements of scenography—setting, costumes, wigs, make-up, properties, furniture—but also a machine that includes movement, light, sound and time. Since all these elements and more operate variously and concurrently during a performance, the *processes* of their creation must surely reflect this.[16]

So, to clarify the paradox that neo-Brechtian dramaturgy must continually negotiate: on the one hand, to avoid complicity with wider social mechanisms by which authoritarian, totalitarian, and capitalist regimes are produced and maintained, and to do so by continuously calling critical attention to the technological means and labor power by which stage effects are produced; on the other hand, in calling attention to those technologies and that labor, to avoid making them into objects of fascination or desire, since doing so risks allowing the production to celebrate them, and implicitly, to reaffirm the very ideological mechanisms that enable the scientific and technological processes and the social organizational regimes by which capital maintains its power.

The studied crudity in Neher's designs, then, was a measured, restrained crudity. The measure and restraint mark the means by which Brecht's aesthetic attempted to run the straits of amateurism, on the one shore, and spectacle, on the other. They are, in any case, unrefined and simple enough to forestall the spectacle's question, "How did they do that?" because the means by which the stage effects are produced—wires, pulleys, pipes, projection screens, and so forth—remain visible even when the effects they produce appear: the means of production do not disappear behind their own effects as they did, for example, at the Richard Wagner Festspielhaus in Bayreuth, where optical illusion and a shrouded orchestra created what Wagner described as a "mystic gulf" between the audience and the performance.[17] At the same time, the effects do not inspire the kind of awe that might distract from the recognition of the artifice *as artifice*. The Brechtian stage presents its effects quite transparently as the products of human labor and simple machine force.

With *Lindbergh's Flight*—the libretto for which Brecht retitled *The Ocean Flight* (*Der Ozeanflug*) in 1950 because of Lindbergh's failure to oppose the rise of Nazism after 1935[18]—the paradox described earlier is not so easily negotiated. The piece, with music by Weill and Paul Hindemith,[19] premiered at the Baden-Baden Chamber Music Festival in July 1929 and fully staged later that year with music by Weill alone, is an oratorio for male soloist, chorus, speaker, and orchestra, and dramatizes the first solo transatlantic flight. It is divided into many small segments: the chorus sings the roles of well-wishers in New York before the flight, of jubilant Parisians at the landing, of two fisherman who briefly witness the flight, and of the fog, rain, wind, and sleepiness that jeopardize the crossing. Between these choral segments, the soloist reflects on the dangers of his journey, rejoices at surmounting obstacles, considers his self-conception and his place in history, and acknowledges the intimate relationship between his machine (*der Apparat* of the Introduction's epigraph) and himself. At intervals, a narrator provides commentary, summary, and historical context. As a whole, the piece is structured as a kind of recitation lesson or school exercise—a *Lehrstucke*: The soloist, sometimes called "the listener" (*der Hörer*) finds himself under examination, tested by the chorus, while early listeners to the Baden-Baden radio broadcast and in attendance at the 1929 festival were given instructions for how to follow along with the listener's part, explaining that

[t]o avoid these distractions (of "free-roaming feelings") the individual shares in the music, thus obeying the principle that doing is better than feeling, by following the music with his eyes as printed, and contributing the parts and places reserved for him by singing them for himself in conjunction with others.[20]

The chorus and the music serve as primers or promptbooks for the soloist, whose performance is meant to enact and echo the audience's engagement with the text and music. By the end of the piece, then, the audience, like the soloist, was meant to understand that achieving a fully Marxist socialism depended on redeploying capitalism's technological advances—radio broadcast technology and mechanized flight—as means for social transformation through self- and class-consciousness.

The semi-staged oratorio at the Baden-Baden festival enacted Brecht's aesthetic by avoiding technical sophistication beyond what was just necessary to perform the piece.[21] Placards name the place of the two main components of the performance-cum-lesson: *Der Hörer* (the listener and soloist singing the flier's part) sits stage left, his music stand before him, slouching in his seat as if to emphasize the degree to which the singer is not "in character" and has not internalized Lindbergh's state of mind; and, because the audience in the auditorium is obviously not also listening to the broadcast, the placard on stage right identifies *Das Radio* (the radio orchestra and chorus who represent the voice of the social apparatus, the elements, and their demands upon the flier) as if even the live performance were, in fact, somehow mediated by the broadcast apparatus. Finally, the text of the instructions quoted above dominates the backdrop. The textualization of the performance space by means of placards, signs, and supertitles, the antiphonal orientation of singer to apparatus, and the mechanical, articulated, halting manner in which Brecht instructed the performers to sing their roles, all were intended to heighten the sense that the audience members were experiencing a lesson rather than a show.

The fully staged production that soon followed the Baden-Baden broadcast at the Stadttheater Breslau was the first of its kind, even though there had already been a "large number of performances of *Der Lindberghflug* in concerts and in schools."[22] The uncredited photo of the presentation that accompanies Josef Heinzelmann's liner notes to the 1990 Capriccio recording shows a more finished set design, but it is by no means realist or grand. Rather, borrowing a highly modernist, formal, abstract style reminiscent of Bauhaus design, the large static set elements suggest—without representing—a cockpit, fuselage, propeller, and wings as part of a three-dimensional, highly geometrical collage. Again, we see a production whose representational gestures are highly attenuated in order to create a sense of distance or estrangement.

For a moment, I want to turn to the role of the radio, both as it was indicated on the Baden-Baden stage and as it figures in Brecht's dramaturgical theory more generally. Brecht used radio not just to broadcast performances of his work, but also to expound upon them. For instance, in March 1927, he delivered a brief introduction to Berlin Radio's broadcast of his play *Mann ist Mann* in which he commented on the relationship between mankind and advanced technologies.

> The great buildings of New York and the great discoveries of electricity are not of themselves enough to swell mankind's sense of triumph. What matters most is that *a new human type* should now be evolving, at this very moment, and that the entire interest of the world should be concentrated on his development. [...] It is my belief that [the new type] will not let himself be changed by machines but will himself change the machine[.][23]

Among the machines Brecht sought to change was the radio itself. In "The Radio as an Apparatus of Communication," published first as a program note to accompany the 1926 production of *Mann ist Mann* and then, in 1932, appearing as a stand-alone essay, Brecht argues for a reconception of the role the radio plays as a social apparatus.[24] Brecht contrasts his contemporary moment—Germany between the end of the First World War and the rise of Nazism—when "technology was advanced enough to produce the radio [but] society was not yet advanced enough to accept it"—with a foreseeable future when it would no longer be "one-sided":[25]

> So here is a positive suggestion: change this apparatus over from distribution to communication. The radio would be the finest possible communication apparatus in public life, a vast network of pipes.[26] That is to say, it would be if it knew how to receive as well as to transmit, how to let the listener speak as well as hear, how to bring him into a relationship instead of isolating him.[27]

Brecht hoped that such an advance in the radio's capacity would encourage an engaged, participatory, collaborative involvement with cultural production among users, noting that "[s]uch an attempt by the radio to put its instruction into an artistic form would link up with the efforts of modern artists to give art an instructive character."[28]

Brecht's hopes for the socially transformative potential of radio connects to his more general interest in the way a scientific and technical approach to the theatre might enable a more socially engaged and responsive art form by fostering "an audience for the scientific age."[29] In a 1936 letter to a number of theatre professionals in Europe and North America, Brecht proposed the foundation of the Diderot Society, an association devoted to deploying theatre as a means for rational social and cultural improvement. Although nothing seems to have come from the proposal, according to Mordecai Gorelik, who collaborated with Brecht on translating the proposal into English, the ideas Brecht propounds in the proposal offer further insight into Brecht's thinking about the relationship between theatre and innovations in science and technology.[30] According to Gorelik, the idea that

> art is "opposed" to science is a notion which did not exist for Brecht, who saw art and science as inseparable, complementary ways of looking at life. He believed, further, that in this scientific age, art has much to learn from the inventiveness, methodology, and impersonal discipline of science.[31]

The collaborative, experimental, and empirical methods of science, Brecht hoped, once applied to artistic endeavors, could mitigate art's hitherto "thoroughly individualistic character," especially in theatre where "the building and projection of this [objective, empirical] type of image [would be] a technical process beyond the limited capacity of individuals."[32] For Brecht rejected the idea of individual genius, located in the playwright, the director, or the star, seeing it as a retrograde, bourgeois, capitalist fantasy.

The collective character of the Diderot Society, then, would provide an alternative model for artistic innovation and creation, largely by means of reports by its members to be submitted for publication.[33] Brecht imagined an approach to theatrical creation and production that would take its cue from the great international scientific, medical, and research societies already well established in Europe and America. The hoped-for result would be a concept of theatre-as-praxis whose advances and innovations would no longer be tied to the personas of singular creative geniuses, *auteurs*, to borrow a term from film theory.

Brecht's de-individualizing impulse, aided by an objective, empirical approach to creation and production, extended to his concept of epic or "gestic" acting, expounded in part in his "Short Description of a New Technique of Acting which Produces and Alienation Effect," written a dozen years after the Baden-Baden premiere of *Lindbergh's Flight*.[34] In contrast to what would come to be known as "The Method," by means of which an actor attempts emotionally and physically inhabit or become a character, gestic acting—in other words, acting meant to demonstrate the socially embedded, culturally constructed nature of the characters, situations, and values on stage[35]—was to be manifestly artificial, performed as if the actor were, at the same time, observing and inwardly commenting on and judging their own performance. Gestic acting is thus a "showing" instead of a "transformation."[36] Its aims to emphasize the didactic, social purpose of the production and to encourage a similarly critical, observational spectatorial orientation. Thus, gestic acting forms part of a larger repertoire of alienating techniques meant to "purge" the stage and auditorium "of everything 'magical'" so that "no 'hypnotic tensions' be set up."[37] Gestic acting, then, is more like self-conscious imitation than portrayal in the usual sense of the word; it is "acting" very much in inverted commas. The distant, observational, rational, critical attitude Brecht advises the actor to take toward the role aligns with his techno-scientific aspirations for the Diderot Society. Much of Brecht's writing on acting, technology, and set design, including his *Short Organum for Theatre*, which attempts systematically to lay out his theories, was composed in the decades following the first performances of *Lindbergh's Flight*. Still, his notes on the Baden-Baden production and broadcast indicates how Brecht would continue to try to negotiate the paradox of a conception of theatre that both depends on and even celebrates technological advancements enabled by capitalist modes of production and social organization while also wishing to deploy and represent those technologies in works that attempt to trouble the unproblematic identification with, and validation of the individualistic subject of capitalism in order to promote a collectivist perspective. In his remarks, Brecht attempts to qualify his optimism in that regard. Even while he figures the radio as a means of dissemination and, like *The Spirit of St. Louis*, a synecdoche for the progressive possibilities of a collective technical and social apparatus, he also seems aware of the danger that the flier, his machine, and their success could evoke a kind of authoritarian, fascist fantasy-ideal of the a-historical hero type. For, according to Brecht, "the figure of a public hero in *Der Flug der Lindberghs* might be used to induce the listener at a *concert*"—that is, in a performance lacking the placards, staging, and gestic acting meant to alienate or distance the audience—"to identify himself with the hero and thus cut himself off from the masses." Thus, he advises that, to forestall this desiring identification with the heroic individual in a concert setting, "the Flier's part must be sung by a *chorus* if the sense of the entire work is not to be ruined. Only [a] concerted *I—singing* [...] can save something of the pedagogical effect."[38] The "I" of the Lindbergh/flier's position, Brecht suggest, must comprise a more broadly collective "we."

Brecht, then, appears to have imagined *Lindbergh's Flight* as having mounted a double defense against capitalist appropriation. First, the use of radio to broadcast the performance and to invite participatory engagement from listeners, and the conception of the listener/flier as a multiple position, suggest that cultural progress is always a question of group, rather than individual advancement. Second, the mechanical, gestic performance of the flier's part and the crude, approximate staging emphasize the status of this piece as interpretation, intervention, and experiment altogether, rather than as transparent representation or "magical" spectacle. In other words, performances of *Lindbergh's Flight* were to establish a critical, radically negative relation to the palliative commodity aesthetics of modern capital.

Despite Brecht's, and perhaps Weill's, critical intentions and the defenses Brecht tried to put in place against the absorption of the work by commodity culture, the Opéra National de Lyon's 2006 production, directed by French-Canadian filmmaker François Girard and featured at the Edinburgh International Festival in the fall of that year, demonstrates the susceptibility of Brecht and Weill's work to consumer-capitalist appropriation. Overall, the effect of that production, nearly 80 years after the work's premiere, can be described as stunning. The design and execution of Girard's spectacular vision lived up to elaborate Broadway or West End production aesthetics. Before an enormous silver screen, twenty-five chorus members, singing with bell-tone clarity and refinement, performed their roles, swaying enraptured to the music. Meanwhile, the flawless, crystalline tenor voice of Charles Workman, as the flier, emanated from a small, mechanical airplane arcing overhead from stage right to stage left. Behind the assembled singers, the fog, wind, and rain obscured and rippled the filmic surface of a projected sea, separating the black Mercator silhouettes of stage-right North America and stage-left Europe. Along the apron, at eye level, five radio microphones were suspended, an empty synecdoche of the Baden-Baden broadcast. Over the course of an hour, the flier made his way from New York to Paris, where waiting crowds feted his landing, dollar bills raining from the flies—a moment of explicitly capitalist triumph uninflected by any discernible irony or distance. On the whole, the considerable technical resources of the company and festival seem to have been deployed entirely in order to produce this cathartic triumph of human and machine over nature: a duo that stands in for the humans and machines responsible for producing what was billed as a theatrical triumph.

It is important to remember, here, that calling attention to the technical means of theatrical production is not necessarily a politically retrograde, unquestionably capitalist or fascistic gesture. Indeed, the technical reproducibility of the great treasures of Western art and the ability of photography and, most importantly, film to decontextualize, distribute, and recontextualize representation, for Marxist thinkers like Walter Benjamin, Brecht's friend and a champion of his work, held the potential to undermine the traditions upon which class capitalism reproduced itself. Namely, Benjamin saw in technologies of sound recording and still and moving photography the potential for diminishing an artwork's "aura"—the halo of reverence instilled by tradition and emanating from original works of art. Since, like Brecht—and later Marxist thinkers such as Louis Althusser—Benjamin located much of what was wrong with bourgeois ideology in its construction of liberal, individual subjects, recording and disseminating technologies could advance a Marxist social agenda by de-individualizing the creators and their creations alike.[39]

Benjamin's optimism has, quite obviously, not been repaid. The transformational potential he saw in photography, sound recording, and film has not, in the event, resulted in widespread political change. While the film (to take Benjamin's primary example as a case in point) *qua* object—or, as it were, the digital code, given the marked decrease in the use of actual film in cinemas over recent decades—and the moviegoing experience are, on the whole, relatively inexpensive and accessible, three factors militate against the dissipation of aura and its support of capitalist value systems. Together, these three factors demarcate something like a law of conservation of aura. First, filmmaking has become a mainstay of capitalist cultural production; consequently, film narratives, characterization, and production values, as well as the rituals of moviegoing, do the ideological work of advanced capitalism, with only infrequent exceptions. Second, while moviegoing and the film-object do not, in themselves, bear the aura of tradition and authenticity, that aura still remains: in the persons of movie stars and in the objects (set elements, props, and so forth) and real-life locations used to make the film. So it is that iconic memorabilia from famous film sets can fetch hundreds-of-thousands, or even millions of dollars at auction.

The third factor, however, concerns us most centrally here and connects to the earlier discussion of spectacle: As technological sophistication in film production increases with the use of special effects and high-fidelity visual and audio quality in cinemas, the spectacular or sensational value of the moviegoing experience becomes as compelling as plot and character—often more so. To repeat an earlier formulation, the spectacle of technical facility itself becomes an object of spectatorial fascination; and yet, since the apparatus responsible for producing these spectacles are often out of sight or even mysterious, in the case of computer-generated visual and sound effects, *aura*, as a visual metaphor, no longer suffices to name the quality in question. Rather, in the age of highly refined, technologically produced effects, Benjamin's *aura* has become something more like a *vibe*—a total feeling or sensation, a thrill, produced by the machinery of representation. And yet, in terms of the way it functions to extend the ideological power of the work, a movie's vibe has a quality very similar to Benjamin's notion of aura. Whereas Brecht, in collaboration with Neher, depended on a studied crudity in technical and visual design and implementation in his work as a means of forestalling a retrograde emotional investment in representational technology, mass-market filmmaking has depended upon the production of positive, ideologically affirmative vibes.

In contrast to Brecht's vision for *Lindbergh's Flight*, Girard's production for Opéra National de Lyon creates precisely these vibes. Far from making the flier's part choric or staging the performance in a way that would emphasize the collective spirit of his endeavor, the production cast the accomplished and well-known tenor Charles Workman as the flier and, throughout most of the performance, kept him elevated and isolated high above the stage. His imposing physical presence underscored the heroism of the individual flier, while the staging emphasized his highly personal relationship to his machine: the airplane. To highlight the individual, personal quality of this relationship, the flier even tenderly embraces the plane mid-flight.[40] This literal embrace, together with the sophisticated—and invisible— filmic and technical apparatus required for the production, points toward a figurative embrace, a celebration of the individual's triumphs enabled by the techno-scientific advances of late capitalism. As with any spectacle, the technology disappears behind its effects: Because of the way the stage is dominated by the film-scape of the sea and the elements, the guy wires hoisting the airplane, its propeller gratuitously whirling, became invisible before the projected backdrop, creating not just the representation of flight, but the illusion of it. Finally, once landed, the flier stood above the crowd, celebrated as a hero, statuesque in his cultish pose.

The webcast comments of Brian McMaster, the director of the Edinburgh International Festival in 2006, highlight how the Opéra National de Lyon's production deployed the slick, hyperproduced commodity aesthetic. Recalling that the premiere performance, a "fantastic triumph," was "greeted in the end [sic] by cheers," McMaster concludes that it is "a great show" that not only "speak[s] to anybody who enjoys a musical," but, indeed, will "excite and really thrill anybody."[41] Far from acknowledging the political, much less Marxist thrust of the piece, McMaster's comments sound more like advertising copy for the latest Broadway musical extravaganza—in other words, advertising for precisely the sort of theatre Brecht himself attempted to subvert. And, at $130 (in 2006) for first-balcony seats, its pricing alone suggests its aspirations to Broadway and West End appeal. Of course, it wouldn't in fact appeal on Broadway or the West End—the plot and music, after all, are very much at odds with more popular styles; that is, the piece has not entirely given up its resistance to easy commodification. But that resistance no longer finds its place in a production aesthetic whose aim is to "excite," "thrill," and "triumph"—to be a "great *show*."

Compared to the Baden-Baden broadcast or the Stadttheater Breslau production, this production demonstrates not only the increased sophistication of twenty-first-century technologies of theatrical production over that of the late 1920s, but also the sophistication of this particular production in relation to the more modest contemporary productions of literary theatrical works. The technical apparatus brought to bear in Girard's vision rivals the capabilities of the most magnificent and sensational musical productions of New York and London. Added to the marketing-and-advertising discourse McMaster's comments employ, the deployment of this technical capacity shows how completely the modalities of consumer capitalism are capable of appropriating Brechtian epic theatre and neutralizing it as spectacle. In doing so, it behaves just as Brecht described above: "processing" theatrical invention "to make fodder for [the] public entertainment machine, judging it by [the machine's] standards and guiding it into [the machine's] channels."[42]

The possibilities for a genuinely epic theatre, in the Brechtian sense, have become increasingly rare and difficult to sustain in the context of late capitalism's tendency to flatten out distinctions and to reduce political discourse to style. Moreover, as Squiers contends, "[w]hile once at the vanguard of dramaturgy, many of Brecht's estrangement effects have been so widely adopted not only in theatre but in cinema and television they are now [in 2014] rather commonplace."[43] Girard's use of a filmic seascape as the backdrop to the Opéra National de Lyon production of *Lindbergh's Flight*, and, indeed, the decision to commission Girard himself, known primarily for his cinematic direction, points toward one major factor in this difficulty: the dominance of a filmic sensibility in the late-twentieth and early-twentieth-century aesthetics of cultural production. The infiltration of motion-picture technology into every realm of expressive or artistic activity signals its naturalization as medium, even to the extent that motion picture and video no longer get recognized, generally, as mediums at all. The widespread availability of video recording and playback technologies, in the form of smartphones and web applications, has stripped video recording of its alienating potential. At the same time, the look and feel of professional video recording has become the standard by which representational excellence in theatre is often measured. The more filmic a live production is, employing lighting, music and sound, and digital and video technologies to produce apparently unmediated effects onstage, the more successful it is in terms of its spectacular quality. Even "the media" is imagined as an unalloyed abstraction disconnected, in the popular imagination, from the material conditions and constraints it any particular medium—newsprint, Web servers, digital code, and transmission and distribution infrastructures.[44] From this point of view, we might retrospectively theorize Brechtian epic drama, in terms of its formal concerns, as focused primarily on theatre as medium—its facticity and resistance to spectacular erasure—highlighting theatre's material conditions, including not only the physical materiality of the stage, lights, and sets, but also with its labor and economic practices.

Perhaps because its title character was, in history, so consumed by his public image and its dissemination in the news media, and because it continually quotes and alludes to the apparatus of video recording, communications technology, satellite transmission, and intercontinental and space travel, *Nixon in China* (1987), composed by John Adams, with libretto by Alice Goodman under the direction of Peter Sellars in its Houston Grand Opera premiere, more effectively foregrounds the mediated quality of historical events and their representation on stage. To the extent that it does so as a way of commenting on media, the construction of political identity, and the tension between two radically different worldviews—that of the United States, the global superpower, in contrast to the agrarian, isolationist People's Republic of China under Mao—*Nixon in China* succeeds as Brechtian epic, despite its not having been commonly recognized as such.

Nixon and China and *Lindbergh's Flight* share numerous similarities. Perhaps the most obvious, particularly in the 2006 production of the latter, is the landing of an aircraft onstage: Nixon's arrival in Peking (Beijing) aboard the *Spirit of 76* echoes Lindbergh's arrival in Paris in *The Spirit of Saint Louis*. Like *Lindbergh's Flight*, too, *Nixon in China* offers more a montage than narrative: scenes drawn from key moments during Pat and Richard Nixon's visit, including the Nixons' arrival; the president's visit with Mao Tse-Dong; the state dinner at which Chou En-Lai and Nixon exchange toasts; Mrs. Nixon's cultural tour of Peking; the Nixons' attendance at a performance of the Chinese National Opera directed by Mao's wife, Ch'iang Ching; and, finally, a tableau as the six principals spend the final evening of the Nixons' visit reflecting and imagining what may be to come. In its presentation of its subject, the opera is not heroic, tragic, or comic: rather, it remains muted in its judgments on Nixon and his mission and objective and neutral in its representation of world leaders from both sides of the Pacific. Sellars's staging is highly textualized, especially in the opening sequence, when large banners in Chinese hang in the middle distance, behind the presidential plane, and when Nixon and Kissinger meet Mao in his study, lined as it is with labeled boxes full of documents.

The epic approach to characterization in *Nixon in China* is evident both in the way the music and libretto, working sometimes together and some times at odds with one another, emphasize alienation and in the way the actors employ gesture, posture, and movement. While operatic "speech" and acting are always, to a degree, estranged by the fact of singing and the actors' and audiences' awareness of the music's overwhelming presence, in both the 1987 Houston Grand Opera Premier and in the 2010 Metropolitan Opera reprise of the original staging, the actors' blocking and gestural repertoire are so stylized, indicatory, and unnatural, particularly in ceremonial scenes, as to resist interpretations of them as naturalistically mimetic. Likewise, lines that may appear relatively natural in the printed libretto are set to Adams's post-minimalist music, their prosaic sense becoming both elevated, like poetry, and distorted, through repetition, rhythmic dissonance, and tonal painting. Finally, while the chorus sometimes stands in for crowds—laborers, diplomats, welcoming parties, spectators—in key moments, the use of the chorus, as complement and supplement to the text, recalls Brechtian alienation effects used in *Lindbergh's Flight* and elsewhere.

To take the role of the chorus first: In two scenes in particular—Nixon and Kissinger's meeting with Chairman Mao in the middle of the first act and the performance of Ch'iang Ching's *Women of the Red Brigade* in the middle of the second—the chorus augments, prompts, amplifies, and even substitutes for the soloists in ways that recall Brecht's commentary on the chorus in *Lindbergh's Flight*: namely, to forestall identifying the sentiments or views being uttered with the will or presence of mind of a particular individual. When the aged Mao, who speaks epigrammatically and cryptically throughout Act One, Scene Two, in what he himself describes as "riddle[s]," "paradox[es]," and "philosophy" discourses on revolution, three female secretaries follow his vocal line a beat or so behind, repeating and emphasizing his words.[45] The effect is uncanny in performance, the women's echo seeming both an amplification and an incantation at the same time.[46]

Chairman Mao's first sung line of the opera, in the second scene, is, appropriately, "I can't talk very well. My throat";[47] from the outset of that scene, then, we are informed of a disconnect among Mao-the-revolutionary, Mao-the-spokesman, and Mao's speech. The awareness of this disconnect is emphasized by the fact that the Mao's secretaries begin to sing his first words a quarter note before him, as if they were prompting, rather than echoing or emphasizing his words. This effect is repeated somewhat later in the scene. Mao, referring to the people of China, says, "The world to come has come, is theirs."[48] But, because he repeats the clause "The world to come has come" three more times, and within those repetitions, repeats "the world" two more times, before finishing his thought—"is theirs"—the secretaries finish articulating the complete sentence eight bars before he does, despite their coming in a full bar behind him.[49]

Elsewhere, the three secretaries seem to function as translators, articulating and repeating Mao's utterances for the benefit of his visitors and for the opera's audiences, although throughout much of the scene, Mao, Chou, Nixon, and Kissinger interact without the secretaries as intermediaries. At still other times, the secretaries seem to function as stenographers, recording the conversation and making note of particularly portentous pronouncements, as when, at the very end of the scene, Mao repeats a sentence he had uttered earlier in the scene under the stage direction *"dictating"*—"Founders come first—then profiteers"—and the secretaries mechanically repeat this formulation after him.[50] And, in at least one instance, at a climactic moment in the scene, when Mao has become frustrated with Nixon's apparent inability to follow his disjointed and cryptic lines of thought, the secretaries and Mao sing together, again in close harmony, as if their voices were one, the voice of a philosophy or historical inevitability rather than those of distinct individuals: "We no longer need Confucius! Let him rot."[51] Importantly, Mao, at this moment, is attempting to drive home to Nixon a point he has been repeatedly trying to make throughout their conversation: namely, the unimportance of historical figures relative to the grand sweep of history itself; thus, his sentiments match the effect of the voice-leading in erasing the individuality of the characters themselves.

This observation draws our attention to other moments in the scene when the relationships of speech to character, singing to singer, and speech to singing get emphasized, and, consequently, estranged in a way they are not in traditional opera. Returning again, then, to Mao's opening remark, "I can't talk very well," we are invited to note several complementary ironies operating at once. The first is that, while Mao refers to his ability to "talk," the audience is profoundly aware that they are receiving his speech as singing. Whatever difficulties Mao is experiencing with his "throat" do not manifest in the quality of the singing; rather, they are indicated in the syncopation of the sung rhythm, with the words, each equivalent to a quarter-note in time, separated by quarter rests. The result is a halting, slightly disoriented opening line. Second, emphasizing the disconnect of speech from singing and of Mao's vocal apparatus's from the singer's is what follows in Mao's vocal part: While the line "I can't talk very well" is sung in part of the male vocal range shared by basses, baritones, and tenors, as soon as Nixon has confessed to being "nearly speechless with delight," Mao is revealed as a heldentenor whose vocal line remains largely between

E_4 and B_4 (the tenor high-B).⁵² In short, while Mao may not "talk very well," the role is one that requires a singer who can sing a high, difficult part quite well indeed. In casting John Duykers in the role for the 1987 premiere, Adams and Sellars chose a singer of vast vocal power and depth combined with an apparent ease more typical of lyric tenors. The result is an ambiguous effect combining great effort and difficulty, on the one hand, with virtuosity and, at times, tenderness, on the other.⁵³

While repetition as a form of emphasis or estrangement or both operate in the libretto's setting in Scene Two, discussed above, its effects are most apparent in Nixon's opening aria, "News has a kind of mystery." Because of the centrality of technologies of mass media and intercontinental and space travel and of their perceived contrast to agrarian Chinese culture, this aria is worth prolonged and detailed analysis, particularly so because it takes up themes central to *Lindbergh's Flight*. It comes early in the opera and, as Timothy A. Johnson remarks, is "one of the most effective musical characterizations of the President in the opera."⁵⁴ The aria, delivered mostly as a long aside, reveals Nixon's thoughts, first as he greets numerous Chinese officials on the runway outside Peking, where his plane has just landed, and then extending to his first private moments in his quarters, before it finally morphs from waking thoughts into nightmare paranoia during a brief nap. Because so much of the aria is sung on the runway, the nose and front half of the fuselage of *The Spirit of 76* loom over the scene, reminding us, as we shall see, of the intersection of the theatrical *machina* and the technologies of twentieth-century air travel.

Once again, read straight through, absent the musical setting, the lyrics of Nixon's "News" aria present thoughts cogently expressed, even if they do at times seem tenuously linked to one another.

> News has a kind of mystery.
> When I shook hands with Chou En-Lai
> On this bare field outside Peking,
> Just now, the whole world was listening.
> [....] Though we spoke quietly,
> The eyes and ears of history

Caught every gesture [....]
And every word, transforming us
as we transfixed—
[...] Made history.
[....]
On our flight over from Shanghai
[....]—the countryside
Looked drab and grey. "Brueghel," Pat said.
"We came in peace for all man kind,"
I said, and I was put in mind
Of our Apollo astronauts,
Simply [....]
Achieving a great human dream.[55]

These straightforward opening verses, however, become estranged and alienating as set to Adams's music, requiring, as it does, repetitions of key words and recapitulations of phrases and sentences, so that, in performance, it takes nearly 130 bars for Nixon to complete his opening train of thought:

News news news news news news news
News news news news news news news
Has a has a has a has a kind of mystery
Has a has a has a kind of mystery.

When I shook hands
When I shook hands with Chou En-Lai
On this bare field outside Peking
Just now, the whole world was listening
The whole world was listening. Listening. Listening.
And though we spoke quietly, and though we spoke quietly,
And though we spoke quietly,
The eyes and ears of hisssstory, hissstory, hissstory
Caught every gesture, Caught every gesture
Caught every gesture and every word,
Transforming us as we transfixed,
Transforming us as we transfixed,
Transforming us as we transfixed,

Made hissstory, hissstory.
As we made hissstory.
The eyes and ears of hissstory,
As we made hissstory.

On our flight over from Shanghai, the countryside
Looked drab and grey. "Bruegel," Pat said.
"We came in peace for all man kind," I said.
I said, I said, I said, I said, "We came in peace for all mankind"
And I was put in mind of our Apollo astronauts,
Simply achieving a great human dream.[56]

The repetitions and elongations Adam's music imposes upon the linear lyrics of Goodman's libretto emphasize a recurring motif in Nixon's words throughout much of the opera: namely, his obsession with the way his image and reputation, as president, get captured and transmitted via the news media. Hence, the emphasis on the word "News," sung fourteen times in a row at the beginning of the aria, and later, on the way the "eyes and ears of history / Caught every gesture and every word,/ Transforming us as we transfixed." Even his repetition of "I said," following his pronouncement that they "came in peace for all mankind," dwells less on the content of his remark and more on ensuring that "the eyes and ears of history" know that Nixon was the one who made this historic pronouncement, even though this quotation, featured on the first lunar landing plaque, was crafted by Nixon's aides and speechwriters.

These repetitions are, from a purely formal point of view, partly the effect of setting words to music, an effect seen time and time again in opera: The musical phrasing and the overall structure of an aria in classical opera frequently call for the repetition of a sentiment or even, at times, the recapitulation of an entire verse. But both the fragmentary nature of the repeated bits and the extreme frequency of repetition as a formal device make Nixon's aria particularly alienating, even to the ear accustomed to classical opera. We must recall, however, that Brechtian alienation is not the result of a set of merely formal characteristics. Accordingly, I also want to point to the way the formally estranged repetitions call attention to a series of conceptual motifs that indicate socio-political orientation beyond the obviously political context of staging an international summit between the world leaders.

In emphasizing "news," as such, and the centrality of the presidential utterance ("I said"), and leading up to the lyrical expression of Nixon's passing thought about "our Apollo astronauts," the setting of this first part of the "News" aria prepares listeners for the recurrence of motifs concerning the degree to which Nixon's White House staged his visit for the media, for consumption by at-home viewers in America. As journalist Seymour Hersh reports,

> [f]or the White House the most important summit issue was television....By early 1972 Richard Nixon had all but given up on dealing with the nation's newspapers [...]. [T]he President's men had decided that while the three networks could have sixty-eight technicians on the 155-member press delegation that would accompany the President, it would include fewer than forty print journalists, including only twenty-one reporters to represent all the daily newspapers of America.[57]

Johnson amplifies Hersh's account by quoting Jerry Voorhis's claim that "a main purpose of the visit to China was to dominate the news for several weeks as an aid to Mr. Nixon's reelection."[58]

So, when Nixon returns to the "news" theme later in the aria, we have already been prepared for his obsessional relationship to television coverage of his presidency. As sung in the performance, now alone with Pat, Nixon, apparently now speaking aloud, gestures to his watch:

> News! News! News! News!
> News! News! News! News!
> It's prime time in the U.S.A.
> It's prime time in the U.S.A.
> It's yesterday night.
> It's yesterday night.
> They watch us, now;
> The three main networks colors' glow
> Livid through drapes, onto the lawn.[59]

So, the interrelationship among television news, intercontinental air travel, space exploration, and time dominates most of the opera's first scene, beginning with the arrival of *The Spirit of 76*, whose roaring engines find expression in the basses and tympani,[60] running through Chou En-Lai and Nixon's brief conversation upon his arrival, during which Nixon explains that they "stopped in Hawaii for a day / and Guam, to catch up on the time,/ it's easier that way"[61] and culminating in Nixon's anxious realization that it's "prime time in the U.S.A.," quoted above. Taken all together, this motific arc suggests time travel on Nixon's part, a fantasy of exaggerated power and control of a piece with Nixon's well-known and exaggerated sense of his own importance, even for a president.

These motifs return yet again in Act One, Scene Three, during Nixon's speech at the state dinner on the evening of his arrival, after his meeting with Chairman Mao. Having "mov[ed] / A vote of thanks to one and all / Whose efforts made this evening possible,"[62] Nixon begins to praise Chou En-Lai's "eloquent remarks," only to elaborate on the fact that "millions more hear what we say / Through satellite technology / Than ever heard a public speech / Before. No one is out of touch. / Telecommunication has / Broadcast your message into space."[63] Throughout Act One, the presence of news media and broadcast technology is indicated by the occasional appearance of cameras and microphones—as in Act One, Scene Two, when cameramen appear briefly to photograph Chou En-Lai, Mao, Nixon, and Kissinger together—or in Scene Three, when both the premier and the president speak into a bank of mics. Even when the technologies of video recording and broadcast are not visible, strobe lights suggest the flash of cameras, in particular throughout the raucous round of toasts that ends the state dinner. These technologies also find expression in the percussion line that accompanies both Nixon's "News" aria and his after-dinner remarks, which, as Johnson points out "lend a teletype-like flavor to [Nixon's] aria, suggesting the intense activity of the assembled journalists."[64]

Nixon's direct address to the audience during his "News" aria tells us that we have been made privy to his interior thoughts, and thus invites us to hear the music, at least in part, as comprised by those thoughts. We can thus understand the "teletype-like" rhythm as an indication that even when he is not thinking explicitly about the news media, he nevertheless remains faintly aware of its rhythms and cycles. So, when a similar rhythmic pacing, described in the notes to the score as "perc[ussion]—dry slap" in a galloping rhythm, runs through the first fifty bars of his speech at the state dinner, we know that Nixon's mind is divided between the present occasion and its representation in news media.[65]

Such a divided portrayal is central to Brechtian acting. In sketching out his theories for an alienated acting method, Brecht referred to "traditional Chinese acting,"[66] which achieves the alienation effect, "[a]bove all" by "never act[ing] as if there were a fourth wall."[67] Instead, the Chinese actor "expresses his awareness of being watched."[68] In addition to removing the audience's "illusion of being the unseen spectator at an event which is really taking place," as is customary in European opera and theatre, the Chinese style gives the impression that "the artist is observing himself"; "He will occasionally look at the audience as if to say: Isn't it just like that?"; "The performer's self-observation, an artful and artistic act of self-alienation, stop[s] the spectator from losing himself in the character completely, that is, to the point of giving up his own identity, and len[ds] a splendid remoteness to the events."[69]

Brecht's description here very much characterizes the way James Maddalena portrayed Nixon in both the 1987 premiere and in the 2011 Metropolitan Opera revival of the original staging.[70] While Maddalena's gestures are not so stylized as to suggest mime, they are certainly stylized, falling into two main modalities, the imitative—not mimetic—and the indicative, often somewhat mechanically or haltingly performed. In moments of imitative acting, Maddalena uses gesture to take on the rhythm and form of the technologies surrounding him, for instance, by marking the rhythm of the music or, in one case, framing his face with his hands as if he were appearing on television. The indicative mode emerges when Maddalena's Nixon points or gestures toward a technological context—either historical or theatrical—beyond the places and times we are to imagine the historical Nixon occupied during his visit. At the moment he realizes "[i]t's prime time in the U.S.A.," Maddalena's Nixon taps his wristwatch emphatically; "put in mind of our Apollo astronauts," he gazes upward, toward an imagined moon; aware of the cameras photographing his arrival, he waves grandly from the doorway of the plane and holds his handshake with Chou En-Lai for a long, still moment before a tiny bell signals the return to the normal flow of time. These gestures, and others like them, particularly noticeable during moments when Nixon is aware that he is being photographed or recorded, put quotation marks around the characterization.

Alienated action is more pronounced in the 2012 Théâtre du Chatelet production, directed by Chen Zhi-Zheng, which emphasized the opera's mechanical and technological motifs.[71] The arrival of the Nixons (Franco Pomponi and June Anderson) is effected by means of an undisguised steel elevator, lowering them gradually from the flies to the top of the waiting stairs. The state dinner of Act One, Scene Three, is visually dominated by Olivier Roset's hanging collage of light-emitting diode (LED) flat-screen televisions rendering composite, but fragmented, images of the historical Nixon drawn from archive news footage looking down upon an otherwise bare and dimly lit stage. The final act, bringing together the six principals, takes place beneath, before, and upon an enormous black-iron scaffold where soldiers of the revolution slowly erect a colossal statue of Chairman Mao. In keeping with the abstract and mechanized scenography, Pomponi's Nixon gestures and moves much more mechanically and haltingly than Maddalena's, almost robotically, as if propelled by crude gears and sudden surges of current. His denaturalized portrayal is all the more striking given the relative naturalism of Anderson's, Kyung Chun Kim's, and Alfred Kim's portrayals of Pat, Chou En-Lai, and Mao, respectively. Taken as a whole, Zhi-Zheng's production underscores the already alienating effects of Adams's opera by infusing the scenography and characterization with manifestly mechanical and technological effects.

Alienated portrayal as an effect of technology is the focus of the last half of Walter Benjamin's seminal essay "The Work of Art in the Age of its Technological Reproducibility."[72] In theorizing the effect of the camera and sound-recording apparatus of film on the actor, Benjamin argues that "the fact that the actor represents someone else before the audience matters much less than the fact that he represents himself before the apparatus."[73] Quoting Pirandello's remarks on film acting— "The film actor [...] feels as if exiled [...] not only from the stage but from his own person"[74]—Benjamin attributes this sense of exile or distance to the novel "situation" the film actor finds himself in: "For the first time—and this is the effect of film—the human being is placed in a position where he must operate with his whole living person, while forgoing its aura. For the aura is bound to his presence in the here and now. [... Whereas] *the stage actor identifies himself with a role*[, *t*]*he film actor is very often denied this opportunity.*"[75]

This form of estrangement is precisely Brechtian in spirit, even though the exact gestural repertoire Maddalena, Pomponi, and others employ in productions of *Nixon in China* are not identical to those used in Brecht's time. Indeed, on this point, Squiers's *Introduction to the Social and Political Philosophy of Bertolt Brecht* is particularly useful; for the foundational premise of Squiers's study is that the philosophical underpinnings of Brecht's drama are separable from their formal elements (gestic acting, a literalized stage, visible lights and guy wires, and so on), and that although the formal elements become naturalized relatively quickly, appropriated by hegemonic capitalist commodity production, the radical, resistant kernel of his social and political philosophy remain active and relevant. Specifically, with respect to estrangement and characterization, Squiers points out that "[t]he estrangement Brecht desired was an internal estrangement from one's current [...] worldview," and that gestic, distanced acting, for example, or split characters like Shen-Te/Shui-Ta in Brecht's *The Good Person of Szechuan* enacted the kind of internal estrangement Brecht hoped to encourage.

The same may be said of Nixon as portrayed both by Maddalena and Pomponi, whose shifts in attitude (from diplomatic to combative to idealistic to paranoiac in the space of a seven-minute aria), divisions of attention (as he both muses inwardly as he takes part in the welcoming ceremony on the tarmac), and denaturalization of gesture and posture, constantly put before us an idea of Nixon as a riven subject, divided (often against himself) by the imperatives of a very public, mediated presidency in opposition to his private contradictions and reservations. This self-estrangement, in *Nixon in China*, is enabled in large part by the presence—implicit and explicit—of broadcast and media technologies as well as by the technologies of staging that allow for the deployment of light, set, and orchestral cues to create quite sudden shifts in tone, place, and time.

Squiers is particularly interested in Brecht's denaturalization of time by means of an episodic dramatic structure, articulated scenes sutured or knotted together across time, as distinct from Aristotelian emplotment. Squiers quite rightly observes that such temporal estrangement sought to undermine "the myth of the organic nature of temporal order."[76] Subjects of twentieth-century industrial societies would have perceived temporal linearity and unity as natural and given. As Charles Tung has shown, however, linear temporality, and the conceptions of subjectivity, agency, and causality that depend on it, had been constructed not just culturally in the West by the early twentieth century—that is, an effect in the superstructure—but were economically and technologically constructed, imposed by the needs of industrial labor, empire, and transportation. Tung reads much of modern literature and art as troubling this linearity; however, while Tung's reading focuses on the literary and visual arts' troubling of temporal order primarily—although not exclusively—as having formal and aesthetic consequences, Squiers emphasizes that Brecht's dramaturgy troubles the coherence of time and space as a means of critiquing a "totalizing" bourgeois worldview.[77] "Brecht was [...] attempting to dispel the myth of other social conventions which are understood as commonsense matters and taken-for-granted truisms of bourgeois society."[78]

With respect to temporal dehiscence in *Nixon in China*, Johnson's analysis proves useful again. While Johnson does not take up the question of temporality at length and does not suggest a link between *Nixon in China*'s temporal manipulations and political or social estrangement, he nevertheless draws attention to the time effects of Adam's music and Goodman's libretto. For instance, he notes Adams's frequent use of "metrical dissonance," perhaps the most immediately noticeable and disorienting manipulation of time in the opera, which "occurs when interpretive layers of an underlying pulse stream are not in alignment."[79] "Time," in Adams's score, is literally "out of joint," to quote Hamlet, causing listeners continually to lose their place in the music; as a consequence singers' entrances and phrasing, transformations in chord structure, and the transition from one attitude or tone to another defy a listener's attempts to anticipate them or synthesize them in a unified whole and thus to conceptualize the structure of the music in its entirety. Even a fairly music-literate person listening to the opera repeatedly will find it difficult to follow these shifts, their sense of timing divided between or among "dissonant" or "misaligned" rhythmic structures.[80] Johnson, relying in part on the work of Stephan M. Prock, also points out the way the dramatic effect of Nixon's aria "warps the sense of the passage of time,"[81] thus complementing the music's emphasis on temporality throughout the opera through abrupt shifts in tempo,[82] moments of musical and rhythmic stasis,[83] and a sense of temporal persistence,[84] among other effects. Together with the opera's episodic structure, the music heightens the sense that time in *Nixon in China* is malleable and subject to manipulation by real-world news media and theatrical techne alike. It thus troubles media representations of world-historical events as coherent, governed by Aristotelian notions of causality and plausibility, and shaped by self-conscious, free-willed subjects.

Ironically, the PBS broadcast of the Houston Grand Opera's production of *Nixon in China* in 1987 used scene breaks and intermissions as the occasion for Walter Cronkite to provide historicizing commentary on the events of February 1972, at which he was present as a member of the television news media, showing photographs of the Nixons during their visit. In doing so, the broadcast filled in the gaps, reimposing narrative and historical coherence onto an opera that attempts to subvert it. And so, while the disjointed temporalities and episodic structure, in Brechtian drama, invites audiences into a "new way of seeing" that resists the ideological imposition of narrative coherence, in suturing the events represented (and often simply imagined or misrepresented) in *Nixon in China* to historical so-called realities, the PBS broadcast threatens to undo the ideological critique the opera otherwise deploys.

The formal, thematic, and political alienations—of audience from performance, of actor from role, and of subject from ideological worldview—suggested by the formal and thematic features of both Brecht and Weill's *Lindbergh's Flight* and Adams and Goodman's *Nixon in China* find much more explicit, even exaggerated enactment in Don DeLillo's 1999 play *Valparaiso*.[85] Unlike both *Lindbergh's Flight* and *Nixon in China*, *Valparaiso* is a straight play. But, while this generic difference certainly stands out as a notable formal distinction, beyond that, the similarities of *Valparaiso* to these two works are quite striking: all three rely on an episodic structure and self-alienated conceptions of character, are shaped by the mass-media environment of their times, and critique a manifestly bourgeois ideology of cultural and spatiotemporal coherence. A careful consideration of *Valparaiso*, however, also demonstrates that the play goes somewhat beyond the ideology critique enabled by *Lindbergh's Flight* and *Nixon in China* to suggest that the human subject is not simply shaped or affected by the increasing dominance of broadcast and other media technologies, but is, in fact, created by it: The human, in *Valparaiso*, is a product of the machines; moreover, the mode of production DeLillo's machineries of communication and recording employ is a manifestly theatrical one.

The plot's backstory, which emerges in repeated retellings throughout the play, is implausible in a post-9/11 world in which airline travel is tightly controlled, the flow of passengers regulated by ubiquitous surveillance and security checkpoints, online registration systems, and numerous confirmations of identity. Michael Majeski, the play's main character, has become an overnight celebrity thanks to a series of missteps and errors in judgment that turned a routine business trip into a transcontinental wild goose chase. On his way to a meeting he believed was to take place in Valparaiso, Indiana, he suddenly began to fear that his intended destination was, in fact, Valparaiso, Florida. Having changed his itinerary en route, he boarded a flight that would have allowed him to connect to the Florida destination, only to once again doubt himself. So, following the advice of a ticket agent, he rebooked for Valparaiso, Chile; but, during that flight, it dawned on him how grossly he had erred in allowing himself to get swept so off course by the inexorable flow of airline travel, and so attempted to commit suicide—perhaps out of a sense of shame and embarrassment, perhaps as a result of deeper, underlying issues—by suffocating himself in the plane's lavatory with the plastic liner the airline's travel blankets are packaged in. His attempt failed, however, in part because of the oxygen-saturated cabin air and in part because, during a moment of turbulence, he reflexively obeyed the call for passengers to return to their seats. By that time, the plane's surveillance camera had already recorded his idiotic and futile attempt at suicide.

By the beginning of the play, Michael is world-famous; for the story of his misadventure has found its way onto news wires, twenty-four-hour news television, and talk radio. The opening scene features the in-flight video recording projected on the upstage wall of the Majeski home, where Livia, Michael's wife, pedals intensely on her stationary bike, which, we will learn, has become almost an obsession for her. The fact that the bike is stationary suggests the abstraction of the machinic into pure form: the repetitive pedaling is manifestly unproductive labor and articulates to the mechanization of leisure Stuart Ewen discusses in his book *All-Consuming Images*. In it Ewen analyzes the way bodily perfection is sought among urban, body-conscious American men of the 1980s, noting the degree to which the body is refined through highly mechanical repetitions on exercise machines designed to isolate and work particular muscle groups.[86] So, while Livia's repetitions are unproductive in the industrial capital sense of the term, they do literally produce her—her physical body as well as the mental discipline and stamina required by the exercise routine. The literal machinery of the bicycle and the presence of Livia's machined body, counterpoint the diffuse, virtual machineries of satellite and internet communications technology through which her husband's identity will be constructed, revised, and disseminated. This second technological register—that of the news media—will dominate the remainder of the play: Reporters, talk-show hosts, radio producers, cameramen, and other agents of mass media seek Michael out for sound bites and accounts of his journey, to the point that Michael must leave his job in order to attend to the constant requests for interviews and media appearances, at which point his whole self-conception inheres in media representations of him, increasingly formulaic and vapid. Only death extracts him from his obsession with his relationship to mass media when, on the set of a television talk show, the host, Delfina Treadwell, suffocates him by forcing her handheld microphone down his throat.

In what follows, I wish to argue for a post-human reading of *Valparaiso*, one that counters the reading proposed by Rebecca Rey in her study *Staging Don DeLillo* (2016).[87] Explicitly drawing on DeLillo's notes and on his remarks in correspondence and interviews to authorize her claims, Rey observes that, despite the hyper-mediated environment in which the characters live, "meaningful relationships do indeed still exist" in *Valparaiso*, as in DeLillo's other works.[88] While I would not dispute this claim, it does not follow that "[c]ommunication technologies" in *Valparaiso*, "presented as personified and driven towards self-replication, dissemination, and control" are only "metaphorical" in their expression of a technological "will."[89] Rey explains that

> DeLillo purposely gives technology an animate presence for the purpose of better representing the process of mediation. The impulsion that is given to technology is a non-literal personification "tool" to help us realise how the *will* is manifest within *ourselves* as users of technology. Consequently, DeLillo's repetitive inclusion of screens and data is not motivated by his interest in the screens and data themselves, but in their human users.[90]

Reading the play, then, according to what she perceives were DeLillo's "purpose[s]" and intentions, Rey elaborates: "[T]he *will* of technology is not entirely within devices, independent of human users"[91]—the inclusion of the word "entirely" making this claim an incontrovertible one. However, even though the will of the machine is not *entirely* within devices, it is not necessarily the case that it "is in fact actually the *will* of its users" that controls it.[92] To make this interpretive leap, from not entirely in the machine to, therefore, entirely in the users, Rey must silently assume a clear and impermeable boundary between the machine and the human to begin with—a distinction we have already seen imagined in the works of Sophie Treadwell, Elmer Rice, and Arthur Miller in Chapter 2. However, Livia's self-fashioning by means of a stationary bicycle already indicates that human interactions even with quite simple technologies blur the organic/machinic distinction in *Valparaiso*. Outside the frame of the play itself, the field of cybernetics, with its attempts to reduce human consciousness to, and translate it into digital information, had already undone the easy assumption of a human/technological divide. By 1999, cyborg theory and posthuman studies were well established fields, not just in the rarefied world of academic research, but in the mainstream: the emergence of Web 2.0 and filmic depictions of artificial intelligence and human/machine hybridity invited everyday people to imagine the human as intermingled with the technological. Certainly, by 2016, the publication date of Rey's book, any claim about the independence of human will from sophisticated, programmable technologies and the massive global systems that support them would have been unsupportable, as we shall see in greater depth in Chapter 5.

And so, when Rey claims, for instance, that the play has primarily to do with Michael's "desire to better understand himself and construct an identity through his interaction with his technological surroundings," she maintains an imaginary distinction between the human "himself"— his "desires" and his "identity"—and the "technological surroundings," a distinction that had already been a nostalgic fantasy for fifty years in the West by the time of *Valparaiso*.[93] And it may be true that DeLillo himself, and even *Valparaiso*, do long for that fantasy. However, even if *Valparaiso* can be read as an articulation of a nostalgic longing for an unconstructed human subject *à la* the European enlightenment, it also repeatedly undermines that imaginary, independent, will-endowed model of subjectivity.

One of the most obvious means by which *Valparaiso* represents how technology and techno-rationalist ideology shapes human will takes place during the commercial breaks interpolated into the play's second act. Three times during the extended scene of a live taping of a morning talk show where Michael and Livia appear as guests, advanced aviation technology finds itself formalized into a kind of choric ritual. A three-person "Chorus" of flight attendants, with exaggerated costumes and makeup, recite, in clipped, formulaic, and mechanical style—reminiscent of Cocteau's phonographs discussed in Chapter 1—a pastiche of words, phrases, and questions drawn from preflight and pre-landing safety announcements and pop-psychology, while the lead member delivers lines more decidedly drawn from commercial marketing to create a kind of collage jargon and ad-speak, promising comfort, convenience, and even airborne sexual encounters.

These brief interpolations address an anonymous, generalized "you"—a consumer-"you" entirely devoid of individualizing qualities. Accompanying these recitations are the chorus's gestures, which the stage directions stipulate are to imitate the mechanical, rote gestures accompanying preflight safety checks. While the chorus of ancient Greek theatre was employed to act as secondary characters, such as crowds and bystanders, to interrogate the principal characters, or to articulate the broader truths and questions raised by a play, this chorus speaks for the apparatus and through the apparatus, its message both highly stylized and, finally, nonsensical. They thus share with both *Nixon in China* and *Lindbergh's Flight* an essential function: They decontextualize their own utterances through fragmentation and repetition, and thus they enact a disconnect between the speaking subject and the spoken utterance.

While the aesthetics and logic of communication technologies characterize the formal elements of *Valparaiso*, the play also emphasizes the presence and identity-formation function of quite literal machines as well. Along with the exercise bicycle and screen that appear at the beginning of the play, numerous apparatus of communications and mass media appear onstage: microphones, mixing boards, telephones, radio sets, televisions, and so on, which are meant to "glow" at key moments. When talk-show host Delfina Treadwell caresses Michael's crotch with her microphone, the instrument glows. Likewise, early in the play, as Michael is being interviewed in his home, when he and the interviewer speak, the interviewer's tape recorder also glows.[94] Preparing for an interview, Livia sports a DayGlo lapel mic, just as, later, an interviewer will write with DayGlo pen.[95] These and other instances of glowing "instruments"—the term recalls the Spanish Inquisition—suggest a lineage of technology, from pen-and-paper, through sound recording and telephony, all the way to television taping and broadcast. Moreover, in glowing, these technologies have acquired an auratic quality, bathed in haloes and giving off what Ewen calls "the aura of technical perfection"[96]—what I have called "vibe" earlier in this chapter—and reminding us of the limits of Benjamin's optimistic view of media technology's revolutionary potential. The apparatus has become an angelic, mysterious herald of the post-human world.

If the episodic structure of *Valparaiso*'s first act, the ritual incantations of the flight crew/chorus in the second, and the high-visibility mechanisms throughout the play—bicycle, cameras, and microphones—both remind us of Brechtian alienation devices and point explicitly toward mass media as the mechanism responsible for the alienation of everyday life at the end of the twentieth century, the dialogue concerning Michael's experiences indicts media saturation as both symptom and enabler of capitalist ideology. Frequently exhorted to reveal more and more about his experience and his life, and to do so more and more quickly, Michael increasingly identifies with the version of himself promulgated by mass media. He even reveals to one interviewer his decision to quit his job to focus on giving interviews.

Just as Michael's celebrity persona begins to occupy his ordinary, everyday life, so too do the boundaries between the interviewers and Michael, as interview subject, begin to blur. Often, interviewers begin to speak in Michael's voice, from Michael's point of view, as if not only to echo and prompt him but, vicariously for their audiences' sake, to become him momentarily. And, in a complementary switch during one interview, Michael himself takes on the discourse of the interviewer, asking her about her own personal life and relationships. By the end of their interaction, late in the first act, Michael's and the interviewer's positions have become indistinguishable, their voices merging into the seamless, impersonal discourse of the interview.[97]

In addition to the melding of the two voices—an effect that carries on intermittently throughout their whole conversation—a jarring blend of the mundane and the erotic, the shift from question-and-answer to a more conversational interaction, and the frequent moments of hyper-reflexivity, when the fact of the interview becomes itself a topic of the interview, enact the highly articulated, fragmented, and directionless form modern media discourse takes.[98] We can hear in the shifts of this conversation not just the patchwork snippets of changing channels but also echoes of the operatic Nixon's tangential and disconnected thought processes and speech. When, at last, Delfina brings Michael to the inevitable realization of the emptiness of his own life—an emptiness that preceded his disordered flight—the characters and audience have come to see the insight of an apparently throwaway observation one interviewer makes early in *Valparaiso*: "Everything is on the record. Everything is the interview."[99] In short, by the play's end, there is no Michael separate from the media apparatus; his desires, hopes, aspirations, sense of self and of purpose, have all been shaped by, processed through, and finally, produced by mediating technologies.

In closing these reflections on *Valparaiso*, I'd like to spend a few moments considering its two central deaths: Michael's failed suicide that serves as its inciting incident and the microphonic homicide that serves as its denouement. Both are mediated by advanced recording and broadcast technologies, but the contrast between the two moments is particularly telling in what it shows us about agency and subjectivity in the technological age—concerns central to *Lindbergh's Flight* and Brecht's political theory, if somewhat more implicit in *Nixon in China*. The suicide attempt, which occurs before the beginning of the play, is the result of an intentional, if sudden and misguided decision taken by the play's protagonist. As a gesture of self-annihilation, this act may be read as the ultimate assertion of a particularly human subjectivity, suicide being as it is a uniquely human act. But this desperate grasp for autonomy—motivated, we learn in the final act of *Valparaiso*, not just because Michael is embarrassed at having found himself aboard a plane to Chile, but also because he is haunted by the drunk-driving accident that seriously injured his young son and irreparably damaged his marriage—is thwarted by the very apparatus Michael finds himself unwittingly enmeshed within. For the richly oxygenated air of the airplane's cabin, the surveillance camera installed in the lavatory (which he sees immediately before aborting his attempted suicide), and the lighted sign warning him to return to his seat, all prevent him from succeeding in killing himself.

While the space-age technologies of airline travel prevent Michael from exercising his autonomy in service of his own demise, and while radio and television media act as a kind of life support system through most of the play, Delfina's microphone is finally the instrument that not only suffocates him but ironically (given its intended function) silences him in the process. With regard to the staged technologies of *Valparaiso*, what remains constant is the progressive diminution of the human agent's ability to act, to speak, and even authentically to experience and judge the world he inhabits, both outer and inner. Michael's inability to speak authentically—that is, intentionally to express himself in accordance with a desire of which he is aware—becomes increasingly apparent each time he recites, ever more robotically, the account of his misadventure. His at first deliberate, thoughtful, reflective narrative has become rote and self-propelled by the time he has retold it on numerous occasions. It has become so shopworn and predictable that, by the end of the first act, the interviewers to whom he speaks are able to prompt him and recite his responses along with him, not unlike the chorus parts in *Lindbergh's Flight* and the three secretaries in scene two of *Nixon in China*'s first act.

These examples of what I called *dislocutions* in Chapter 1 are not simply representations. Because of the technical sophistication of the theatrical apparatus required for *Valparaiso*, *Nixon in China* and, in its Opéra National de Lyon production, *Lindbergh's Flight*, dislocution is manifestly theatrical: That is, in splitting or dislocating voices, not only do these plays comment on the relationship among agency, utterance, and technology in the real world, they also call our attention to the way conventions of dramatic theatrical production always constrain speech and split identities, by virtue of the very practices of memorization and recitation, performance and its repetitions, and technological doubling, distortion, and illusion. To understand these pieces' nostalgia for a unified, will-endowed human agent is to read against the medium of theatre itself, a medium to which these pieces repeatedly call spectatorial attention. At the same time, these dislocutions, both represented and enacted, offer proximate versions of the more widespread and distant forms of dislocation effected by the real-world broadcast media to which the recording and transmitting devices featured in all three of the plays central to this chapter are connected. Michael, like Nixon and Brecht's flier, in submitting to the apparatus of techno-celebrity, increasingly lose their subjective coherence as individuals. As all three pieces conclude, the mechanisms of mass media have colonized their principal characters' subjectivities, eliding the kind of self-reflection and authenticity usually signaled by arias in opera[100] and the confessional modes of media programming with which Michael engages. But, while *Lindbergh's Flight* meant, at least in Brecht's view, for the evacuation of individuality to be the occasion for the development of a more generalized class consciousness, and *Nixon in China* focuses its attention on powerful actors on the world stage and thereby suggests that this elision of authenticity is, in a way, a political reality, *Valparaiso* anatomizes the plight of the subject formed by and entangled in the everyday technological apparatus of late capitalism.

The later production of *Lindbergh's Flight*, along with *Valparaiso* and *Nixon in China*, may give the impression that in the North American and European contexts, Brechtian critique of techno-rationalist ideologies and their dominating tendencies have begun to require a high degree of technological sophistication in the theatre itself. However, forty-five years after the stage premiere of *Lindbergh's Flight*, we still find in white South African playwright Athol Fugard's *The Island*, devised in collaboration with actors John Kani and Winston Ntshona, testament to the persistent power of the kind of studied crudity Neher's designs championed.

Like many of the works examined in this book, *The Island* is self-consciously theatrical.[101] It focuses on John and Winston, named for the actors who created the roles, who within the play are inmates on Robben Island, a prison island housing political protesters in apartheid South Africa, including most famously Nelson Mandela, who spent much of his twenty-seven years' imprisonment there (1964–1982). The action follows John and Winston as they labor in pointless penal servitude, share memories of life before their imprisonment, fantasize about reconnecting with friends and family they have left behind, and, principally, preparing to perform a condensed two-man rendition of Euripides' *Antigone* for an upcoming prison exhibition.

Before we learn of their preparations, however, we witness a lengthy enactment of John and Winston's labor, under the watch of *hodoshe*—the gadfly—the prisoners' nickname for the prison guard. The guard, however, is not an embodied character; or, more precisely, he is not portrayed by a live actor. Rather, his presence is signaled by John and Winston's reactions to his abuses and is indexed by the whistle, which, we are given to understand, he uses to issue commands. While segregation laws under apartheid would have forbidden a white man to play the role of prison guard on the same stage where the black actors John and Winston portray prisoners, we cannot account for the nonmimetic, indexical representation of the guard as a consequence of apartheid alone. After all, even after apartheid, under Fugard's direction, the play has been produced again and again without featuring a live actor in the role of the guard. Moreover, the guard is not the only nonmimetically represented aspect of the play; when John and Winston are shackled together as they move from worksite to prison yard to cell, they mime being bound at the ankles, much as they use mime to signal other features of their environment: digging and filling holes, banging on a cell door, and urinating. For the set consists only of "a raised area representing a cell on Robben Island. Blankets and sleeping-mats—the prisoners sleep on the floor—are neatly folded. In one corner are a bucket of water and two tin mugs."[102] Lighting changes, sound cues, and the characters' physical business suggest all other details, with the exception of a few personal props, including the outside environment and the passage of time.

The relatively sparse mise-en-scène, however, does not impoverish theatrical effect. Rather, the sound and lighting apparatus, minimal as they are, stand in both for the more sophisticated design and tech elements typical of Western drama of the type we have been examining to this point and also point to the apparatus of domination and enforcement deployed by the white government of South Africa against the nonwhite majority underclass. Fugard's centering of Antigone as political allegory, which requires Winston to play the role of Antigone before his fellow prisoners, wearing a wig, false breasts, and a necklace made of old nails, emphasizes the theatricality already established by the mime and the silent, unseen guard, as does a lengthy episode in which the two pass the time by pretending to talk to their old friends by phone. In other words, we are not, as in realist theatre, being invited to suspend our disbelief; rather, the disbelief, or the difficulty in sustaining the theatrical illusion, implicitly reveals the state of South African society as, itself, an illusion that can be sustained only by means of an invisible state apparatus. And so, while the technology of Fugard's staging is quite simple, particularly by comparison to the highly developed theatrical and social technologies of its European and American counterparts, we can nevertheless perceive a dynamic whereby the little theatre technology that does interpose nevertheless implicates and critiques a much more advanced—and menacing—apparatus of power and domination by revealing its moral impoverishment and ideological fragility.

Although manifestly Brechtian—and, perhaps more specifically, Neheresque—in its production values, *The Island* conveniently points also to the themes that will occupy my attention in the next chapter: namely, a simultaneous re-centering and decentering of the stage as a site of technological domination, on the one hand, and an exploration of live theatre as an apparatus of physical and psychological constraint, on the other, in high absurdism. The mid-century plays of Harold Pinter and Samuel Beckett represent their characters as entangled in futile attempts to bring themselves into being as fully realized human subjects; however, in those plays, the subject emerges, in part, as a theatrical construct, both enabled in speech and action and constrained less by the technologies of the extra-theatrical world than by those of the theatre itself. Theatre's materiality and the technologies of its medium, in these plays, will become objects of representation and analysis in and of themselves.

4

Machineries of Constraint: Samuel Beckett, Harold Pinter, and Badal Sircar

The preceding chapters have focused attention on highly dynamic plays in which avant-garde flights-of-fancy with their fast-paced, often episodic narratives and highly active flow of bodies, machines, and energy offer enactive critiques of and resistance to the machine logic of modernism and late capitalism. Technologies of travel—trains, planes, bicycles, steam engines, automobiles, and elevators—and of communication—television, radio, voice recorder, and the internet—literalize these plays' complex spatiotemporalities. They offer characters and circumstances shaped by transatlantic, transpacific, and trans-American flight; the flow of commuters and telegrams alike beneath, through, and even above cities; and the surreal fragmentation and transformation of the human into the inhuman. These earlier chapters introduce technological advancements as both literal and metaphorical, the Taylorist logic of the factory floor and the rhizomatics of transportation and transformation informing plot, characterization, and staging. By contrast, the three playwrights' works examination in this chapter—Samuel Beckett's *Krapp's Last Tape* (1958), *Play* (1964), and *What Where* (1983); Harold Pinter's *The Dumb Waiter* (1960); and Badal Sircar's *and Indrajit* (1962)—emphasize stasis and constraint: Whereas the technologies manifest in works discussed so far broadened the conceptual and geographic scope of the stage and the world it represents, those of Pinter, Beckett, and Sircar, as we shall see, circumscribe it, imagining the theatre's human–technology interface as a bounded site of constraint and delimitation.

Beckett's works for the stage, particularly those of the 1960s and 1970s, call attention to the technical apparatus of the theatre on which they rely. The visual isolation of the human mouth in *Not I* (1972) and the interplay of prerecorded voices and breath in *That Time* (1976), for instance, attest to Beckettian drama's demands upon theatre's technologies, and these technologies' demands upon actors and characters alike. Even in some later plays, when the technological apparatus is less in evidence, more attenuated on stage, the actors' bodies often take its place, performing repetitive, precisely timed gesture and choreographed, angular, seemingly machinic movement. The strictly lockstep ambulation of the four figures in *Quad* (1982), the counterpoint of motion and stasis in *Rockaby* (1981), and switching on and off of speech in *Ohio Impromptu* (1981) enact the internalization of the stage machineries by the characters and actors.[1] They become embodied machines, recalling Vsevolod Meyerhold's biomechanics.[2] Two of Beckett's plays under discussion here, *Play* and *What Where*, both represent and enact the machineries of the stage, interconnecting the actor's body, the character's body, the staged technologies, the theatre apparatus, and the techno-rational context of everyday life. In doing so, they condense and abstract elements evident in Beckett's early stage play *Krapp's Last Tape*, reducing the concrete and the human elements and emphasizing the abstract and machinic ones.

While Harold Pinter's drama does not, for the most part, enact the formal logic of the machine to the degree to which Beckett's plays do, his work nevertheless articulates to a techno-rationalist ideology in ways that resonate with Beckett's works. In *The Room* (1960), the grumpy and, eventually, violent Bert takes pleasure only in forcing his delivery van to his will;[3] the criminal enterprise within which Goldberg and McCann operate in *The Birthday Party* resembles the metaphorical machines of power, extortion, and enforced loyalty;[4] and the machineries of warfare and totalitarian state power lurk behind the scenes of *Party Time* (1993), *One for the Road* (1985), and *Mountain Language* (1988).[5] Still, in contrast to Beckett's stage works, which evolved toward abstraction, constraint, and formal precision, Pinter's moved somewhat in the opposite direction, increasingly opening onto large historical and deeply human ethical questions alive in the contemporary world beyond the stage of his late works. As a consequence, we find the clearest expression of a machine–human interface in his early play *The Dumb Waiter*, itself a riff on Beckett's *Waiting for Godot*. Together with Beckett's *Krapp's Last Tape*, *Play*, and *What Where*, Pinter's *The Dumb Waiter* crystallizes the way mid-century absurdism in English investigated the relationship between techno-rationalist ideology and conceptions of individual agency, authority, and power, and they do so by suggesting analogies to that relationship in the interplay of theatre technology and the actor. In examining the way the works of Pinter and Beckett disport with the machine, then, we must inevitably ask how doing so presents notions of character and subjectivity different from the humanistic conceptions central to the actor's method, realism, and the structures of meaning they inhabit.

In *Krapp's Last Tape* (1958), Beckett's only play to stage what would have been considered in its time advanced technology, the personal tape recorder, the various machine effects emerge with greater complexity and clarity than they will in later works, thanks in part to the centrality of a machine to the mise en scène.[6] After examining the mechanics of staging Krapp's machine and of Krapp-as-machine, which presage later manifestations of machineries and machine logic in Pinter and Beckett's works, I will turn to Pinter's nearly contemporary *The Dumb Waiter*, before returning to a full examination of Beckett's two later plays *What Where* and *Play*.

Krapp's Last Tape anticipates the mid-twentieth-century emergence of an ideology of "purposive-rational action" in economically developed societies, which social philosopher Jürgen Habermas would describe in his 1968 essay "Technology and Science as Ideology."[7] According to Habermas, who relies heavily on the insights of Max Weber and Herbert Marcuse,

[r]ationalization means, first of all, the extension of areas of society subject to the criteria of rational decision. Second, social labor is

industrialized, with the result that criteria of instrumental action also penetrate into other areas of life (urbanization of the mode of life, technification of transport and communication). Both trends exemplify the type of purposive-rational action, which refers to either the organization of means or choice between alternatives.[8]

Connected to the "progressive 'rationalization' of society" is the "institutionalization of scientific and technical development," which "transform[s]" social institutions of all kinds, undermining "old legitimations," including mythology, faith, tradition, morality, and aesthetics.[9] This "institutionalization" of a techno-rational worldview takes the "form of [an] unacknowledged political domination" that "removes the total social framework […] from the scope of reflection" and decision-making and thus "requires a type of action that implies domination, whether of nature or of society."[10] At the same time, techno-rationalist thought becomes invisible, an irreducible given, and thus ideological, cloaking overt modes of "domination" in the discourse of "progress."[11] In a society where such a techno-rational ideology operates, we would expect to see its values and assumptions reified in the habits of everyday life, even those that do not pursue rational or productive ends, such as leisure, aesthetics, and play.

Krapp's Last Tape anatomizes these ideological effects by demanding that the actor subject himself to the role of Krapp and to the technical apparatus of the theatre in the same way that the subject of liberal capitalist society is expected to relate to the techno-rationalist apparatus of social order: the metaphorical and literal mechanics of everyday life, including the machineries that increasingly surround and enable the liberal bourgeois subject. Indeed, we have already seen, in Chapter 3's discussion of DeLillo's *Valparaiso*, an exaggerated view of subject formation in a technologically sophisticated media context, and in Chapter 2, we saw the same ideology at work in Miller's *Death of a Salesman*, albeit in a expressionist and ideologically ambiguous way. The analysis *Krapp's Last Tape* performs, however, becomes possible only when the production commits itself fully to the rigors of Beckett's text; to do so, actor and director alike must abandon notions of interiority and "the method" which, as Amy Strahler Holzapfel and Shawn Kairshner have separately demonstrated, itself emerged in the late nineteenth century from medical technologies of microscopy, vivisection, X-ray, and other means of literal bodily insight.[12] It is not so much that a Krapp built out of the raw materials of an actor's inner life, experience, sense-memory, and so forth—the stuff of theatrical realism—is a less compelling, less interesting, or less pleasing Krapp. Rather, to humanize Krapp by making him a realist subject in conformity to an ideologically dominant notion of the independent human agent of liberal capitalism (as Rebecca Rey attempts to do to DeLillo's Michael Majeski, discussed in Chapter 3) neutralizes, if it does not entirely erase, the play's crucial analysis of high-capitalist subject formation.

By contrast, instead of inviting an approach to production and characterization like those demanded by realist drama, *Krapp's Last Tape* asks for what I will call, following Habermas, an "instrumentalist" approach to performance. It understands the performance as a function of the textual and theatrical apparatus, and it calls upon the actor, director, and technical designer to foreground the instrumentality of staged representation. Likewise, Krapp himself behaves in ways that suggest his integration into a instrumentalist, purposive-rational universe: His obsessive recording, redacting, replaying, cataloguing, and organizing of his audio diaries; his carefully timed shots of whisky; his repetitive and nearly ritualized consumption of bananas; and his investment in strict binaries of light and dark, love and labor, and present and past testify to his subjection to rationalist criteria, even as he pursues activities that are, from an industrial-capitalist point of view, unproductive. Indeed, his lifelong struggle with constipation and his eventual inability to speak literalize his lack of productivity. Nevertheless, a few hours spent at the pub on his thirty-ninth birthday become the occasion for "jott[ing] down a few notes on the back of an envelope";[13] these notes, in turn, will serve as the basis of one of his "old P.M.s"—post mortems—which he will record, label, catalogue, and file.[14]

Thirty years later, Krapp's failure to record his last tape, commemorating his sixty-ninth birthday, and the irreducible sense of loss and regret that haunts his moments of silence and stillness presage the silences that will characterize Beckett's later plays and lay bare the gaps and fissures of purposive-rational criteria themselves. These moments suggest an outside to ideology by representing radically negative spaces, devoid of form and content to which one might assign a rational telos, in the midst of so highly formalized a pastime as Krapp's. But, along with the promise of something other than what is ideologically given, *Krapp's Last Tape* offers a view of social and personal value measured against purpose and utility. For both the play and the ideological forces it reveals circumscribe, if they do not completely foreclose, liberal humanist notions of rational agency, casting Krapp and the actor who plays him as instruments of the machinery that, while it is apparently within their control, is actually beyond it.

On the stage, the larger social and ideological apparatus at work is represented, both synecdochally and metonymically, by the unambiguously real, hulking, humming presence of the reel-to-reel tape recorder on Krapp's desk. And, because almost all the staged speech emanates from this machine, or at least is meant to appear to do so, the machine literally dictates the timing of most of the performance, not unlike the role of the phonographs in Cocteau's *Eiffel Tower Wedding Party* examined in Chapter 1. But unlike Cocteau's piece, in which the phonographs often followed the lead of the actors and dancers moving onstage, in Beckett's play, the actor and Krapp, both of whom once dictated to the machine, are now subject to its demands. The actor must master the awkward and, today, seemingly crude controls atop the machine. He is responsible for starting and stopping the tape at the right moment and—if the sound is actually produced by the onstage machine, and not in the sound booth—for rewinding and fast-forwarding the tape to the correct cues.[15] Because, in this case, the cues would have been prerecorded on the tape, the actor must follow the machine's lead. He must, like Chaplin's tramp in *Modern Times*, discipline his body to the rhythms of the mechanism. For, unlike in most plays, the actor controls very little of his own gesture and pacing once the playback has begun. This lack of control extends to preperformance preparations as well. The actor no longer needs to build his character according to the elaborate method established by Stanislavsky and developed (and debated) in the United States by The Group Theatre's Lee Strasberg and Stella Adler. Backstory and exposition are entirely a matter for the prerecorded voice. On the first two occasions when the actor speaks— that is, when the voice heard by the audience is produced live by the actor on stage—it is when Krapp is reading, either out of a ledger or from a dictionary.[16] Even during his abortive attempt to record his latest installment in his audio diary, Krapp is working from notes. And when he crumples the notes and attempts extemporaneous reflection, he is left with "[n]othing to say. Not a squeak."[17] Staged speech in *Krapp's Last Tape* is to be understood not as the immediate, unmediated, extemporaneous expression of the liberal human subject that the actor's method sustains, but rather as highly mediated, pre-scripted, rehearsed, and recited. It does not, in other words, emanate from some locus of essential, a priori personhood.

The constraints of such rigid scriptedness—indeed, of scriptedness within a script—make the actor as much an instrument of the stage apparatus as Krapp is of the social apparatus that imposes purposive-rational models of behavior. Indeed, the stage directions introducing the action read as much like choreography as they do a page from a script:

> Krapp remains a moment motionless, heaves a great sigh, looks at his watch, fumbles in his pockets, takes out an envelope, puts it back, fumbles, takes out a small bunch of keys, raises it to his eyes, chooses a key, gets up and moves to the front of the table. He stoops, unlocks the first door, peers into it, feels about inside it, takes out a reel of tape, peers at it, puts it back, locks drawer, unlocks second drawer, peers into it, feels about inside it, takes out a large banana, peers at it, locks drawer, puts keys back in pocket.[18]

And so on, for several more pages and at least ten minutes of performance time. The speechless, patterned, and extensively scripted action before the first words are spoken suggests the need for characterization dependent much more on disciplined physical routine rather than on deep-seated interior emotional or mental states. Moreover, the actions that may be taken as expressive of Krapp's Krappness—he "sighs," "fumbles," "stoops," and "peers"—generally suggest bodily exhaustion and failure without reliably signifying an interiority. The audience—perhaps even more than the reader of the play—is invited to see Krapp first as a set of quasi-automatic functions; and, I suggest, we are invited to see the actor in the same way.

This last observation raises a larger question: Put this way, aren't *all* actors carrying out quasi-automatic functions, as I argued was also the case with *Valparaiso* in Chapter 3? Hasn't the repetition of rehearsal and memorization, the taking of direction and the dominance of the script and director over the production, already usurped a good deal of whatever agency the stage actor might have exercised otherwise? Isn't this precisely the relationship of every actor to every scripted performance—leaving aside improvisation, environmental theatre, and the like? To the extent that actors are given words to say and, either by the script or by a director, gestures, intonations, expressions, and blocking to which they must conform, they are indeed quasi-automatic, instrumental functionaries, at least partly preprogrammed. Further, those who act in plays in order to earn a living—buy things, pay rent, settle debts, and so on—are embedded in a more general instrumentality: They ply their trade as a means for remaining functional social and economic machineries, literal and figurative, of all kinds.

But the difference between the way *Krapp's Last Tape* subjects the actor to the production apparatus' constraints and the way expressionist drama, as we saw in Chapter 2, does so, is that in realist staging, the apparatus demanding the actor's conformity disappears into the performance. Watching Andrew Undershaft in Bernard Shaw's *Major Barbara* (1905), a character intimately familiar with the machinery of armament manufacturing and whose very name suggests mechanization, the audience is *not* encouraged also to see, in the person of the actor playing him a laborer at the mercy of the machinery on stage.[19] The air of mastery Undershaft projects can only convince if the work of acting as such is put entirely under erasure.[20] In realist productions, playwrights, directors, actors, and crews suppress the theatricality and the theatre mechanics of the performance, eliding the fact of the representational apparatus as much as possible.

By contrast, the actor playing Krapp becomes a spectacle of the actor playing Krapp, in much the same way the machinery enabling the Opéra National de Lyon's 2006 production of Brecht and Weill's *Lindbergh's Flight* discussed in Chapter 3 projects the spectacle of theatrical machinery. That is to say, the physical work of acting never quite disappears from sight; the spectacular, excessive actorly body remains as a trace, unlike the actor who allows himself or herself to be wholly subsumed by the character. Indeed, the analogy I proposed in this regard may be reversed. Instead of saying the actor is as much an instrument of the stage apparatus as Krapp is of the social apparatus, I might just as well say that Krapp is precisely as much an instrument of the social apparatus as the actor is of the stage apparatus.

I should clarify that the actor in question here is the actor who adheres to Beckett's stage directions. For, while it is sometimes the case that actors and directors of conventional plays—particularly historically distant ones—treat the stage directions as optional, to be obeyed or ignored at the discretion of the director, such is not the case with Beckett's work. Often, Beckett himself would direct the premiere productions of his own plays, especially later in his career; famously, to achieve just the effect he wanted for the character "Mouth" in *Not I* (1977), Beckett insisted on immobilizing Billie Whitelaw for the 1972 London premiere. James Knowlson reports that the chair she would occupy during performances, designed to keep her body—and, most importantly, her mouth—from moving out of the tiny spot of light that would isolate it

> looked disquietingly like an electric chair; in late rehearsals, it seemed as if Whitelaw were being prepared for some medieval torture. [...H]er body was strapped into the chair with a belt around her waist; her head

was clamped firmly between two pieces of sponger rubber, so that her mouth could not move.²¹

Jonathan Bignell explains that Beckett's attention to the most minute of details was more than just an occasional fixation. Citing his "rigid views about how his work should be realized," Bignell notes that Beckett

> had a reputation (as does his estate after his death) for being a controlling and precise director of his own work and a highly prescriptive author, in whose writing stage-direction, set design, lighting cues and costumes are all very carefully described. This authorial control exercised via the scripts and subsequently the published texts of the plays is supplemented in Beckett's case by his own involvement in productions or even his direction of them.²²

Actors and directors who, unlike Whitelaw, "d[o] not accept these rigorous constraints" can easily alter the tone and impact of Beckett's plays.

John Hurt's portrayal of Krapp under Atom Egoyan's direction in the *Beckett on Film* project (2001) provides a case in point, demonstrating the degree to which humanizing Krapp according to a realist character-building paradigm neutralizes the play's potential for ideological analysis.²³ Importantly, this neutralization results partly from interpretive choices made in the production and partly from elisions of particular stage directives altogether. Without question, Hurt's Krapp is manifestly human; he emerges, in this production, as Lear-like, a character whose pain and regret in old age is at once profoundly particular and hauntingly generalizable. His are not the exaggerated, even clownish features called for the text: "White face. Purple nose."²⁴ We may, of course, read these descriptions as themselves exaggerated, as if they meant merely *wan* face and *roseolate* nose, although to do so would be to ignore Beckett's reputation for precision in his writing and directing. Even so, however, Hurt and Egoyan's Krapp is strikingly everyday in his appearance: the makeup is naturalistic, the hair only somewhat "disordered," and a closely cropped mustache replaces the "[u]nshaven" face stipulated in the text.²⁵ Nothing, in other words, marks this face as *theatrically* aged: It is simply an old face.

The text also calls for a "[s]urprising pair of dirty white boots, size ten at least, very narrow and pointed,"[26] emphasizing Krapp's clownish qualities. On this point, we have no basis for comparison to Hurt's Krapp because the camera never reveals any part of the mise en scène below waist level. The locking and unlocking of, and fumbling about in desk drawers, so distinctly spelled out in the text, are invisible to the film's spectator. Accordingly, we are not presented with a vision of Krapp slipping on the banana peel, and are thus deprived of the expectation of his fall that our familiarity with the banana-peel gag would engender in watching the play staged live. When Hurt's Krapp does fall, he falls out of the frame and remains for some time below the camera's view, groaning in deep pain, before slowly regaining his feet. How different this performance is from its description in the stage directions: "He treads on [banana] skin, nearly falls, recovers himself, stoops and peers at skin and finally pushes it, still stooping, with his foot over the edge of the stage into the pit."[27] The comedy of this moment, which would necessarily disrupt realist identification, comes not only from the familiar banana routine, but also from Krapp's recognition of the edge of the stage, over which he is careful to throw the peel of the next banana he eats. There is no pit in the film, and the floor of Krapp's room is out of view. And so, the whole business with the banana peel is substituted, in Egoyan's version, with the groans of an everyday old man in pain: truly Hurt.

As a result, the familiar, indeed cliché vaudeville clowning gets erased and the play gets re-encoded as sentimental drama. To amplify the sentimentality, Hurt's Krapp drinks less often and less ritualistically and weeps one viscous tear from his rheumy eyes, in close-up, at the end of the play. To be sure, the tape recorder remains central, but because Hurt's Krapp is characterized as a deeply sentimental person, longing for the past he is unable to reclaim, the machine undergoes an analogous sentimentalization: Hurt caresses and fondles it; he gestures toward it in impatience and frustration; and he speaks not just *into* it, but *to* it. In making Krapp a figure encouraging sentimental identification, Egoyan's direction and Hurt's portrayal relocate the play's concern with an analysis of the human–machine interface to an exploration of a very particular individual's relationship to himself and his own past, enabled—it just so happens—by a machine. Whereas Beckett's *Krapp's Last Tape* verges on post-humanist theatre, Egoyan's is a profoundly and nostalgically human rendition.

The post-human dynamic emergent in *Krapp's Last Tape* is the focus of much of N. Katherine Hayle's essay "Voices out of Bodies, Bodies out of Voices."[28] In it, Hayles draws particular attention to the way the displacement of Krapp's voice—what Chapter 1 called "dislocution" in reference to Cocteau's phonographs—complicates humanist assumptions about the relationship of the voice to the body and of both to subjectivity. "Can the tape recorder be understood as a surrogate body?" she asks. If so, "does the body become a tape recorder?":

> Is the interior monologue a recording played on the body-as-tape-recorder? What happens if this interior monologue is externalized and made into a tape played on another recorder, mechanical or organic? What happens to the stories we and others tell if the production of these stories is no longer situated in the body's subvocalizations but in the machine?[29]

By raising these questions, Hayles argues, *Krapp's Last Tape* and other modernist experiments with voice recording introduce "instabilities" on the Cartesian model of subjectivity. For it troubles presence of all kinds, not least self-presence, by allowing the reception of speech to be deferred over time, for speech to be precisely repeated, and for speech to go on without a body, and for speech to be directed toward listeners not imagined at the moment of speech. The listening Krapp becomes, then, both speaker and addressee; but, as a listener, he too is a different Krapp from the Krapp who recorded the tapes, as evidenced by his repeated inability to recall, the meanings of a word he once used ("viduity"[30]) or the significance of a sensation he had predicted, thirty years ago, he would "feel [...] until [his] dying day."[31] The disconnect Krapp in the present experiences in listening to the recorded voice of a much younger version of himself emphasizes the way "the body-as-tape-recorder [can] also undergo time-delay mutation" as a result of the body's "metonymic […] participat[ion] in the transformation the voice underwent" in the "new medium" of tape recording.³² To the extent, then, that the voice has for thousands of years been privileged over writing as a mode of establishing and sustaining subjective presence and self-presence, the dislocutions enacted by Krapp's tape recorder—which include not just trans-embodiment, but temporal and spatial dilation, as well—trouble attempts to situate agency within the subject and to situate both in a stable relationship to the body. In anatomizing these complexities, which become apparent only in the context of advanced voice-recording technologies, *Krapp's Last Tape* raises questions very similar to those discussed vis-à-vis DeLillo's *Valparaiso* and Adams's setting of Goodman's libretto for *Nixon in China* in Chapter 3.

Hayles uses Jean Martin's experience in 1970 of playing Krapp, mentioned above, as an example of how dislocution affects the actor's interface with the tape recorder and, to a certain extent, with theatre's representational apparatus more generally, quoting his account of deciding how to voice the two versions of Krapp that predominate in the play:

> [Y]ou must choose either to change the voice of the actor playing the old Krapp or change the voice of the recording made by the younger Krapp…I chose as a solution to keep my normal voice for the Krapp of thirty years ago. And when acting I made the voice of the later Krapp a little older, a little heavier, and a little slower.³³

Within the frame of this chapter's focus on the constraining effect of advanced technologies in absurdist plays, I am especially interested in Martin's formulation: "you must choose either […] or." As Martin is about to speak about the constraints he perceives on the actor's ability to make his own choices, the "you" distances Martin-as-actor from Martin-the-commentator. It is not "I" who had to choose; rather, it is Martin-as-"you" who must do so. The distancing/disavowal enacted in this testimony replicates one of the dynamics created by Krapp's interactions with the machine that both receives his speech and gives it back to him as both familiar and alien, as a disembodied, uncanny revenant. Moreover, the "you" does not just distance Martin-the-rememberer from Martin-the-remembered; it also generalizes what he has to say, the idea being that the same constraint will confront *any actor* playing Krapp.

Second, the imperative "must choose" demands some interrogation. What authority issues this imperative? One might imagine it is Beckett himself, who, as we have seen, took an active role in the staging of his works. But the fact that the "must" of Martin's formulation, the marker of constraint, is followed by a sign of liberty, "choose," suggests that there is something about the role itself, rather than this or that particular, individual, human authority, that forces the actor to "choose." Martin, here, again replicates the logic according to which Krapp engages with the recorder: The machine—in terms of both its material, mechanical properties and the content of the playback—enacts an authority over Krapp, constraining his choices, but also constraining him *to choices.* Abdication, stark refusal, seems out of the question as much for Krapp as for the generalized actor Martin imagines playing Krapp. The annual routine of diary keeping, figured both metaphorically and synecdochally in the tape recorder, imposes itself as a requirement.

It is true, of course, that an actor, finally, *must* make certain choices. The whole history of scripted, rehearsed drama demands it. Postdramatic theatre and liminal ritual practices aside, an actor must not, according to the formal limits of the genre, go about onstage willy-nilly, making no choices at all. Indeed, the choice is really either to make choices as an actor or to leave acting altogether. Still, easy as it is for us to accept the validity of these conditions, these constraints upon what it means to be act onstage, they are nevertheless not self-evidently given. It is not simply natural that a thing called acting or playmaking should have come to be in the world, that they should have developed as they have done over the past three thousand years, and that we contemporary critics, playwrights, and theatregoers should continue to adhere to them. We enter, more or less voluntarily, with more or less perspicacity, into a kind of contract with, and constraint by the traditions of Western dramatic theatre. Sometimes, as with productions of Beckett's plays, this contract is quite literal, detailed, and binding, bearing the imperative to perform plays according to the letter and the intention of the text.

The traditions of dramatic theatre as a practice and a genre and the contractual obligations accepted by companies engaged in productions of Beckett's work all conspire to recreate, as the a priori conditions of performance, the very forces under analysis in *Krapp's Last Tape*. As with an actor playing Krapp, it is thinkable that any member of any theatre company producing any play *could choose* literally to part company; that any company chafing under the constraints imposed by this or that grant of rights could decline, after all, to perform the work in question. But, having already accepted the basic material conditions of doing the work they have decided upon, having in short committed themselves to performing this play, the actors and the company as a whole "must choose" how to proceed with the production within the constraints they have accepted. In this reading, Krapp's machine becomes a synecdoche for the whole apparatus of live theatre, and, indeed, of the whole jurisprudential and economic system that subtends the very idea of intellectual property, performance rights, and contractual relationships in the first place.

Moreover, considering theatre's conventions—whether matters of convention or of legally binding contract—allows us to elaborate on Hayles's analysis of the instability of the voice/body/subjectivity relationship that undoes long-standing assumptions about agency and presence: Even without a voice recorder, voices already multiply on stage, dislocate themselves from the actorly body to the body of the character, bear the trace of authenticities constructed, built, or enacted provisionally only for the sake of performance. Thus, *Krapp's Last Tape* reveals not only that the body of Krapp is a machine for producing a voice and subjectivity effects, and that the machine is a machine for reproducing a body, but also that theatre is a machine for doing the same things. What Hayles allows us to see, although Hayles herself does not articulate this point, is that Beckett's play makes this dynamic, always in play, explicit.

The fact of theatre as machine is more starkly visible in Pinter's *The Dumb Waiter*. Midway through it, the eponymous mechanism makes its first appearance, after which it remains central to the dialogue and action.

> There is a loud clatter and racket in the bulge of wall between the beds, as of something descending. [Ben and Gus] grab their revolvers, jump up and face the wall. The noise comes to a stop. Silence. [...] Gus approaches the wall slowly. He bangs it with his revolver. It is hollow. Ben moves to the head of the bed, his revolver cocked. Gus puts his revolver on his bed and pats along the bottom of the centre panel. He finds a rim. He lifts the panel. Disclosed is a serving hatch, a "dumb waiter."[34]

The appearance of the dumb waiter derails the narrative of what appeared to be a fairly conventional, if somewhat dilated and comic, *noir* opening: Two hit men, small parts of a large crime syndicate, hiding in the basement of an apparently abandoned former restaurant, await further instructions about a murder they are to carry out; as they do so, the dynamic of their relationship begins to emerge and, in short order, deteriorate. Gus, the junior partner, begins to voice doubts, anxieties, and questions about their job and their roles in the organization. As Gus expresses his reservations increasingly openly, through probing and suggestive questions, Ben becomes increasingly defensive, retreating behind his newspaper and his bravado to avoid answering Gus's questions (if he knows the answers) or appearing unsure of himself (if he doesn't know them); instead, he puts Gus's questions off with nonanswers and evasions.

The dumb waiter's arrival, however, introduces a sense of urgency into their waiting and, at the same time, reorients their sense of purpose. In Aristotelian terms, it introduces an implausible and unnecessary element into the established situation: Apparently, a restaurant upstairs has lurched to life, and from it emanate increasingly complex food orders, ranging from tea and sago pudding to macaroni pastitsio, ormitha macarounada, and scampi. That a restaurant should somehow begin operation, calling upon the resources of its defunct kitchen converted into lower-level sleeping quarters defies credulity—ours and the characters'. In a manifestly human world—with its implied narrative of revenge and criminal coercion as well as the all-too-human doubts and reservations Gus himself expresses—the dumb waiter introduces machine desire, and with it the possibility that social systems sustained and controlled by people—in this case, a criminal, metaphorical "machine"—are liable to usurpation or elimination by even the simplest of technologies. Furthermore, while the machines of this play are indeed simple—pulleys, valves, a speaking tube, plumbing—a proto-digitality begins to emerge as well; for the analogue techne fails as a more articulated, discontinuous, and dissociated structures (narrative and logistic) gain the ascendant.

Faced with the arrival of meal orders, Ben and Gus find themselves at a loss to fill them, sending up their meager store of snack foods to appease their ersatz patrons. After all, they cannot even light the gas stove in the adjoining kitchen to make tea, much less "char siu."[35] But the stove and the dumb waiter are not the only technologies out of order in *The Dumb Waiter*: Ben and Gus discover that the toilet, also offstage, won't flush properly because, Ben surmises, of a "deficient ballcock."[36] Indeed, *The Dumb Waiter*'s offstage spaces repeatedly emerge as sites of unregulated, unmanageable, unpredictable, diverted, or clogged flows—of water, gas, urine, food, information, and, finally, bodies. That this dysfluidity effects Gus's uncanny return as the target, and not a perpetrator, of the hit at the end, as he somehow enters the scene through a door different from the one he had just moments ago left through, makes explicit how significant the management of flows is to the way mechanized space configures itself in *The Dumb Waiter*.[37]

As I have already suggested, those machinic configurations operate in the service of engendering, managing, foreclosing, or—although rarely in Pinter—satisfying desire. In doing so, they serve an ideological as well as a psychological function. In other words, the food orders come not just as demands for dishes, but as demands that Gus and Ben conceive of themselves as part of a particular social formation despite their apparent subterranean isolation. Indeed, the slips of paper that arrive via the dumb waiter are only intelligible as demands of any kind because they index an entire social context. As a consequence of their willingness immediately to respond to the sudden change in the nature of their job, Ben and Gus also find themselves mechanized, instrumentalized to suit the commands of their immediate superiors. As several commentators have noted, Ben and Gus, in awaiting orders—for food or for murder—become "dumb waiters," mechanized by the very apparatus from which they take their orders.

This mechanization of the human in *The Dumb Waiter* is highlighted by a concomitant reversal: the humanization of the machine. For, when Gus and Ben first notice that food orders have arrived, they are at a loss as to how to communicate with those placing the orders upstairs. After yelling up the chute in vain, they discover the communicating mechanism:

Gus What's this?
Ben What?
Gus This.
Ben (*examining it*): That? It's a speaking-tube.
Gus How long has that been there?
Ben Just the job. We should have used it before, instead of shouting up there.
Gus Funny I never noticed it before.[38]

The term "speaking-tube" enacts a double entendre: On the one hand, it is a tube through which to speak; on the other hand, a literal understanding of the term would mean that the tube itself speaks. Thus, when Ben addresses his concerns about providing adequate meals, he does so, as the stage directions indicate, "*with great deference*": "Good evening. I'm sorry to—bother you, but we just thought we'd better let you know we haven't got anything left. We sent up all we had. There's no more food down here."[39] Ben has begun an interpersonal relationship with the disembodied voice emanating from a machine that demands a degree of respect he has not yet shown to Gus, the actual human with whom he more frequently interacts.

Because Ben does not know who might be at the top of the machine, his choice to defer to, rather than resist, the orders he receives suggests that his deference is inspired not in spite of the mechanized, distanced, disembodied nature of the orders, but precisely because of it, as if he were taking part in a bizarre version of the Turing test. Ben, in short, has been conditioned by the social and organizational apparatus, manifested here by the dumb waiter and its adjunct speaking tube, to show deference to the machine as an index of social power. In this world, the machines have taken over the role of humans, demanding respect and intimacy and literally consuming Ben and Gus's food. Indeed, given the dumb waiter's demands for very particular foods, indeed, it appears endowed with both appetites and tastes. Meanwhile, the play's humans—Ben and Gus, to be sure, but also those mentioned without appearing, like Wilson, the unnamed female victim of a recent hit, and the imagined next victim—have become machine functions.

Another way of reading the dumb waiter, by no means incommensurate with the view that it inspires automatic deference outlined above, presents itself as well: a reading more explicitly theatrical. Positioned in the center of the upstage wall, with its hatch that will rise and fall, and outfitted with cables and a rudimentary sound system, the dumb waiter appears as a stage within the stage. In this way, it is similar to Krapp's desk, which serves as a stage for the replaying of Krapp's past, complete with sound system and lighting. Desk and serving hatch alike thus effect a mise en scène en abyme not unlike the play-within-a-play that structures *Hamlet* or the recursive dynamic we will see at work in Heiner Müller's *Hamletmachine* in Chapter 5. In other words, the dumb waiter stages a performance within Gus and Ben's performance of "getting ready," itself a performance within a performance of a play called *The Dumb Waiter*, just as Krapp's recorded diaries emerge as the site of a performance before an audience of one within *Krapp's Last Tape*. The dumb-waiter-as-microcosmic-stage offers a performance of desires that circumscribe Ben and Gus's exercise of agency, already limited by their place within the vague criminal organization's machinery. Its imposition of constraint on Ben and Gus through a performance of desire recapitulates ideological constraints upon its subjects and, importantly, theatre's constraints upon its audience. For, like the dumb waiter, considered here as a stage-within-a-stage, staged drama, and particularly plays within the absurdist tradition, perform desires without end in such a way as to thwart spectatorial desire for closure, clarity, and narrative fulfillment. This deep meta-theatricality thus reproduces machine ideology at three levels simultaneously.

Ben and Gus's "rehearsal" of the upcoming hit, near the end of the play, makes clear the degree to which they have been instrumentalized as components of the machine—the dumb waiter, the criminal organization, and the theatre. Ben catechizes Gus on the mechanics of the hit, requiring Gus to repeat each instruction, down to the fact that he must take out his gun before he fires it. This rehearsal shows, again, how deeply Ben and Gus's behavior has been conditioned by their self-conception as cogs in the machine. This rehearsal of the hit paraphrases the impending job precisely as Sanford Meisner's acting technique—a post-Stanislavskian approach to character-building "the method" that emphasizes behavior over interiority—structures performance rehearsals. In doing so, it creates a moment of meta-theatre, foregrounding the performance-based aspects of everyday life. In momentarily performing performance, this rehearsal-within-a-play restates the analogy we have already seen at work in Beckett's *Krapp's Last Tape*, above: namely, that the character's relation to the social apparatus and the actor's relation to the theatre apparatus are analogs of each other, each mirroring, enlarging, and analyzing the other. The very techniques of an actor's preparation—rehearsal, paraphrase, and muscle memory—inform Ben and Gus's behavior and highlight their role-playing within parameters defined by a mechanism seemingly beyond their control.

However, the subject/system dichotomy is somewhat more complex still in *The Dumb Waiter*. As Lance Norman argues, "the protagonists of [...] *The Dumb Waiter* initiate the outside power that keeps them toiling and replicating familiar patterns," demonstrating that "the powers that induce the protagonists to perform"—a term Norman uses advisedly to suggest the meta-theatricality of the Gus and Ben's interactions—"exist because the protagonists establish such powers in their dialogue and actions."[40] In other words, while there is little doubt that Ben and Gus are, in fact, operatives of a large and dominating criminal system, that system gets manifested in their interaction not only by intruding directly into it and exercising authoritative control, but also because Ben and Gus themselves repeatedly invoke it and enact it. They have internalized the system to such a degree that they have become its proxy mechanisms, its instruments, repeatedly reproducing it for themselves over and over again, just as Krapp engages in somewhat more literal reproductions of the techno-rationalism he has internalized.

One way in which this invocation of the machine works both in *Krapp's Last Tape* and in *The Dumb Waiter* is through the characters' interactions with texts. Krapp's engagement with his previously recorded diary, some thirty years before the night of his last tape, is preceded by consultations of his rigorously organized and cross-referenced ledger and is interrupted when he consults his dictionary to remind himself of the meaning of a word he had used in recording the tape he is listening to. Ben and Gus's fraught interaction with Ben's newspaper is more salient with respect to the way it analyzes technology's imposition of constraint. If we understand the newspaper as an index of the whole system of communication, printing, and distribution necessary for its existence, then we can begin to see that the newspaper, as an ideological apparatus, effects what McLuhan describes as "the extension of power in an ever more homogeneous and uniform space."[41] Twice during *The Dumb Waiter*, Ben reads aloud from his newspaper, inviting Gus to comment on the accounts he shares. In both cases, Gus and Ben react strongly to what the newspaper reports, questioning the accuracy of the account or analyzing the actions and events reported on. However, the third such reading makes starkly apparent the uniformity imposed by the machineries of media communication:

Ben *turns back to his paper.*
Silence.

Ben *throws his paper down.*
Ben Kaw!
    He picks up the paper and looks at it.
    Listen to this!
    Pause.
    What about that, eh?
    Pause.
    Kaw!
    Pause
    Have you ever heard such a thing?
Gus (*dully*) Go on.
Ben It's true.
Gus Get away.
Ben It's down here in black and white.
Gus (*very low*) Is that a fact?
Ben Can you imagine it.
Gus It's unbelievable.
Ben It's enough to make you want to puke, isn't it?
Gus (*almost inaudible*) Incredible.[42]

This exchange, near the very end of the play, demonstrates the degree to which Ben and Gus's interactions have become routinized and automated. Whereas in earlier conversations about the newspaper, they reacted to the reported facts, in this instance, the actual content of the newspaper article remains unspoken. Nevertheless, Ben and Gus act as if Gus had articulated what the newspaper reports. It appears that, having endured the demands of the dumb waiter and having been conditioned by the criminal machine of which they are a part, Ben and Gus have become highly formalized, automated functions, engaging in a nearly pure abstraction of conversation. This scene once more reinforces the analogy among machine power and desire, on the one hand, and performance, on the other.

These relational analogies in *Krapp's Last Tape* and *The Dumb Waiter* are precisely ideological, anatomizing what Louis Althusser, in his seminal essay "Ideology and Ideological State Apparatuses," calls "interpellation," the production of subjectivity by specifically capitalist ideology.[43] For Athusser, whose insights will also inform my understanding of Heiner Müller's *Hamletmachine* in Chapter 5, the work of ideology subtends the continuation of capitalist systems of production, power, and domination, forever reproducing the means by which capitalism produces itself and the apparatus of industrial and commodity labor and consumption. This reproduction of the means of production requires widespread material practices, adopted by individuals who believe they have chosen freely, that support and expand capitalism's necessary social relationships at the same time that they appear, to the seemingly self-conscious subject, to be expressions of one's own unique personhood. Ideology thus produces representations of the imaginary relationship of individuals to their real conditions of existence, such that the imagined relationship obscures the reality of domination, exploitation, and subjugation. At the same time, it produces in its subjects the desire, perceived as authentic, to engage as if voluntarily in capitalist production and consumption. Martin's "must choose" discussed above precisely captures this ideological compulsion-of-choice.

In Europe and America, theatre has typically, although of course not always, occupied the social margins. The London's liberties, beyond the city walls, were the site of the first English permanent theatres in the sixteenth and seventeenth centuries, for instance, and the existence, until 1968, of the Lord Chamberlain's censor in England attests to the suspicious regard in which "official" culture held theatre. Even to this day in Europe, England, and the United States, theatre practitioners do not fit easily into categories of capitalist consumption and production: their "labor" does not produce value in the usual sense of productivity, and their employment conditions lie precariously between wage labor and gig labor, despite unionization, even while theatregoing remains a respectable and cogent demonstration of refinement and class. So, it should come as no surprise that theatre is often the site of ambiguous social analysis: As we shall see in more depth in Chapter 5, literary theatrical production, as distinct from the Broadway or West End smash hit, takes part in capitalist economies without being quite *of* the capitalist economy. Likewise, as with *Krapp's Last Tape* and *The Dumb Waiter*, in analyzing the machinic aspects of ideological interpellation, theatre reserves the right to critique and analyze machine logic and its instrumentalization of human subjectivity even as theatre's very conventions of rehearsal, characterization, representation, and production enact that logic and instrumentalizing impulse.

Beckett's later plays, including *Play* and *What Where*, make these ambiguities even more stark, given their minimalism and formal abstraction and their progressive movement away from mimetic representation and toward a more enactive, formal anatomy of theatre-as-machine-system. *What Where*, Beckett's last play, and among his briefest, ends with three enigmatic lines, in the voice of Bam, emitted from a megaphone positioned above the stage, well away from the small playing area where the main action takes place:

That is all.
Make sense who may.
I switch off.[44]

Preceding this "switching off" has been an almost ritualized series of preludes to a series of three offstage inquisitions meant to coerce each of three characters, Bem, Bim, and Bom, into revealing "it," which, we are given to understand, will answer the questions "what?" and "where?" More about the elusive object of these inquiries we do not learn. These preludes and the offstage interrogations last, in stage time, for less than ten minutes; but the megaphone, styled in the stage directions as *V* for "voice," reports the passage of an entire year, with each interrogation taking something like three months to unfold before the subject "pass[es] out" unable to be "revived."[45] Overseeing and orchestrating these interrogations is Bam, who occupies his place on stage as an embodied character played by an actor, but whose voice emerges from the megaphone, too, to narrate the passage of time, to direct the action, and to judge the merits of the performance itself.[46]

And so, at the end of the play when V pronounces "That is all," the "all" in question is very little indeed. Moreover, the very little that it is is in question; for, when each of the interrogators returns to report that each of the subjects has passed out without confessing "it," "what," or "where," Bam accuses him of lying, thus instigating another round of interrogations. Not only do we not know what *it, what,* and *where* refer to—what, in other words, the complete questions compressed into these pronouns are—we are also invited to doubt the veracity of the reports Bam (and we) receive about what has happened offstage during the action's foreshortened three-month hiatus. Thus, the claim that "that is all" comes less as summing up and more as an emptying out, as if it were meant to say, "That'll have to do," or, "Don't expect any more."

This suggestion that the "all" that "that is" is not enough is underscored in those closing lines by the imperative, "Make sense who may." Importantly, the line is not, "Make sense who *can*." Contrasted to "make sense who can," "make sense who may" sounds more like a dare to the foolhardy rather than an invitation to some fuller understanding, some "sense" plausibly to be revealed by analysis and interpretation. If we take this imperative as a dare, the final line, "I switch off," is both a statement of fact—for the whole production apparatus shuts down, leaving only a darkened, silent stage—and also an abdication of any further responsibility. Whoever may wish to take up the dare to "make sense" is on their own.

In what follows, then, I will not attempt to "make sense" of the play in the conventional sense of interpretation or explication. Rather, I want to read *What Where* as an enactment of anti-critical, meta-theatrical bringing-to-awareness of the machineries of theatrical representation as such. The play's title, *What Where*, names the two main objects of inquiry that drive the action, such as it is. The first of these interrogative adjectives points to the questions a literary critic or spectator might ask: *What* does this mean? *What* is Beckett trying to say? *What* is really going on here? The second, following closely, begins to pose the questions a production team might ask—questions about staging, blocking, and mise en scène. The two words of the title, in short, both index *and fail to index* questions motivating theatrical interpretation and production.

Taken in this way, the title resists the highly political turn of British drama in the 1980s including Pinter's torture plays *One for the Road*, *Mountain Language*, *The New World Order*, and *Party Time*, along with new works by Caryl Churchill, Tom Stoppard, and David Hare, among others. In these plays, the *what* and *where* extended beyond the sequestered confines of the stage to comment on the resurgence of conservatism in British and American politics, the plight of the poor and disenfranchised in Western democracies, the atrocities of far-right dictatorships in developing nations, and the struggle of pro-democracy activists in Eastern Europe and the Near East. Reviews of and academic articles about these playwrights and their politically charged drama, for a time, focused almost exclusively on explicating the political theses these plays offered.

By contrast, *What Where* seems to offer only the irreducible facticity of theatrical performance as such. Instead of inviting investigation into the socio-political realities that obtain beyond the theatre, this play warrants an investigation into the nature of theatrical representation and it does so explicitly. The piece opens with V, an obvious effect of an obvious stage technology, switching on, a move signaled quite manifestly by V's first speech:

> We are the last five.
> In the present as were we still.
> It is spring.
> Time passes.
> First without words.
> I switch on.[47]

This "switching on" entails light coming up on the "playing area," designated as such in the stage directions, a three-meter by two-meter rectangle upstage and left of the position of the megaphone from which V's voice emerges;[48] although the voice is Bam's, who appears on stage as an embodied character, the "I" comprises the whole theatrical apparatus: the lights, the stage, the characters, the blocking, and, of course, the megaphone itself. That "I" asks us to imagine a point of view that subsumes both the object of spectation—the whole production—and a vantage point outside that production which can see, hear, and pass judgment on it. For, immediately, when it is revealed that both Bam and Bom occupy the playing area at the first lights-up, V declares "Not good. I switch off."[49] The stage returns to darkness before the voice once more "switch[es] on" to reveal a different tableau, Bam alone on stage, which V pronounces "Good."[50] Several more times throughout the play, V will judge the enactment of the interactions between Bam and each of the remaining three characters—Bem, Bim, and Bom—that precede and follow each of the offstage interrogations (which, being offstage, may or may not have taken place anyway) as either "good" or "not good." In the latter case, V will insist that all or part of the scene be replayed. Late in the play, when the enactment repeats itself for the third time, V interrupts with "So on," thus skipping a section of dialogue we have already heard twice before.[51] Increasingly, V, with its judgments and interruptions, its directions and prolepses, begins to resemble a stage manager commenting on, cueing, refining, and calling a performance during rehearsal.

Thus, a kind of laying bare of the usually overlooked or hidden dynamics of theatrical production takes place, where the blocking—executed in a dry run, without dialogue, as a dumb show first—along with performance notes, rehearsal-style repetitions of bits and beats, and a kind of Meisnerian paraphrase become manifest in the produced performance itself. And this laying bare also entails a rehearsal, whereby the action we would be most interested in, the discovery of *what* and *where*, and the meaning of these two truncated interrogatives, remains offstage, unseen and unheard. So, whereas *What Where* employs the form of a play within a play, it produces the effect of a play adjacent to a play—or rather, a rehearsal of a play adjacent to a play—where the outer play, the one we see, fails to quite frame the principal drama, but instead elides it.

The misaligned framing here becomes especially notable Damien O'Donnell's version of *What Where*, which he directed for the *Beckett on Film* project.[52] The camera is quite active, employing extreme close-up to capture the actors' facial expressions and reverse shots to give the impression that two characters, both played by Gary Lewis, occupy the space at the same time. Rarely does the camera allow us to see the whole playing space at once and then only from an extreme overhead point of view. One consequence is that O'Donnell's rendering creates a sense of disorientation, making it difficult to locate entrances and exits and Bem, Bim, and Bom's positions in relation to the central position occupied by Bam. Consequently, the obvious, even intrusive, camera work heightens the play's sense of urgency in the search for what and where, because as spectators we find ourselves dislocated with respect to the action. The stable orientation of audience is replaced by the camera's movement, which usurps control over the spectating gaze. In this way, the technology of film gets layered atop that of the stage, dissolving the fourth wall and bringing the audience under the seemingly omnipotent control of the camera. At the same time, O'Donnell's mise en scène emphasizes a technological representational aesthetic, recreating a mid-1960s version of an imagined future reminiscent of the original Star Trek series. While the action seems to take place in a vast library, with impossibly tall shelves of leather-bound volumes surrounding an open space, this library is presented as an archive of a past from the vantage point of a distant future where electronics and hydraulics are in control of the environment. Banks of lights running along the vertical ends of each shelf and the eerie indirect lighting that illuminates the shelves recall the high-tech archives of today's most modern libraries. As lights go out or come on and as automatic doors open and close, the soundscape signals the presence of a massive, unseen technological apparatus with the sound of heavy, hydraulically controlled switches being thrown and the buzz of current, giving the impression that the whole space is controlled by a distant, electronic, voice-activated machine.

By drawing attention to the theatre apparatus as such—the sound and light cues, the mechanics of blocking and rehearsal—and presenting it as liable to fail, interrupt itself, or need tuning, *What Where* hints at the salience of a question articulated manifestly in Beckett's slightly earlier *Play*: "When will all this have been…just play?"[53] And, as we will see,

What Where offers us a similar, and similarly implicit answer: never. Rather, *What Where* presents the work of theatre as an ongoing labor, a deployment of bodily and theatrical instrumentality always held in abeyance, always requiring tweaking and adjusting, its timing always just out of joint, never quite ready for an infinitely deferred opening night.

Like *What Where*, *Play* contends directly with theatre practice and the theatre technologies that enable it. *Play* presents two women and a man each trapped in a large urn, with only their heads visible, facing forward, seemingly forced to repeatedly—perhaps eternally—recount the history of their love triangle. Apparently confined to a kind of purgatory of retelling, the characters recount their history in fragments, each interleaved with the fragments of the others, cued to speak by a beam of light that shines first on one face, then another. To emphasize the sense that this retelling will go on forever, the stage directions stipulate a repeat of the entire play, with perhaps only slight variations, such as a dimmer beam of light and lowered voices. They also suggest that the lines be delivered with an increasingly "breathless quality" in the repeat.[54]

Of primary interest here is the light's function, about which Beckett's stage directions are characteristically detailed:

> The source of light is single and must not be situated outside the ideal space (stage) occupied by its victims.
> The optimum position for the spot is at the centre of the footlights, the faces being thus lit at close quarters and from below.
> [....]
> [A] single mobile spot should be used, swiveling at maximum speed from one face to another as required.
> The method consisting in assigning to each face a separate fixed spot is unsatisfactory in that it is less expressive of a unique inquisitor than the single mobile spot.[55]

Tellingly, the spotlight is figured as "expressive of a unique inquisitor," and that it is "not [...] situated outside the ideal space (stage) occupied by its victims." This inquisitor–victim relationship is mediated by the light. That is, the light "express[es]" an "inquisitor," but is not necessarily to be understood as the inquisitor itself.[56] Its position within the same space as its "victims," however, lets us know that the light is meant to express the presence of an inquisitor not just to the spectators, but to the characters as well. In other words, it is an expression of an inquisitorial presence within the frame of the action. That the light is perceived as an inquisitor, demanding that the characters speak aloud their memory of past events, is evidenced by their occasional reactions to it: "Get off me! Get off me!" cries Woman One midway through the play. A few lines later, Woman Two remarks to the light "You might get very angry and blaze me clean out of my wits."[57] Man wonders aloud "Have I lost… the thing you want? Why go out?" and Woman Two asks "What do you do when you go out," this latter question employing a double entendre, "going out" being something both a light and a philandering husband will do.[58] These interactions with the light make it clear that the lighting effects take place within the play, and are not, as is typically the case with lighting sourced off-stage, a means for making the action visible to the audience, but a means otherwise unnoticed by the characters. The consequence of employing a spot light in this way, as both a lighting effect and as a stage light, creates a palimpsest by which the inquisitor-light/character relationship is overlaid onto stage-light/actor relationship; they are precisely coterminous, yet distinctly legible. In other words, we do not, in *Play*, witness the complete collapse of the theatre apparatus into the frame of representation; the layers are still perceptible. However, what we see is both theatrical apparatus and represented apparatus at the same time, their contours and boundaries precisely congruent.

This palimpsestic doubling of the stage technology does not quite take effect in the *Beckett on Film* version of *Play*, directed by Anthony Minghella, to the extent it does so in versions staged according to the text's directions.[59] Minghella deploys camera work in place of the intrusive, inquisitorial light of the staged original, drawing our continual attention to it by abrupt cuts, changes in focus and angle, and interpolated blank frames and test patterns. The sound of the camera's autofocus and of the film moving through a projector or camera, along with the hiss and static on the soundtrack, keep the filmic medium *as such* in view throughout. But, because as spectators we watch the piece *through* the camera, our position and that of the inquisitor are now the same, whereas in a staged version, with what Graley Herren, in his comprehensive study *Samuel Beckett's Plays on Film and Television*, describes as its "stance of direct, fixed confrontation,"[60] the audience occupies a third position, one that invites disinterested objectivity rather than identification with the inquisitorial point of view. Moreover, because the filming is self-consciously virtuosic, as opposed to the rather more low-tech spotlight of Beckett's stage directions, Minghella's film risks fetishizing the production technologies themselves, eliciting an aura of technical facility, what I have called "vibe" in Chapter 3. Still, Minghella's version of *Play*, like O'Donnell's *What Where*, makes especially salient the technological dynamics of the filmic medium and allows us to read the stage play with its mediation more fully in mind.

Beckett's late pieces for theatre, in their brevity and abstraction, in addition to their individual narrative and formal dynamics, each can be seen to have isolated one or a few elements of theatrical representation and to have worked them up into a deliberate and careful analysis. *Breath* (1969), for instance, isolates the relationship of the voice and breath to the formal ground of the mise en scène; *That Time* (1976) enacts the multiplication of voices I earlier argued was an effect of all theatrical production; *Come and Go* (1966) engages with the breakdown of narrative into French scenes, marked by entrances and exits; *Catastrophe* (1982), with its prerecorded applause, analyzes spectation as a fact always implied already even in moments of nonperformance; *What Where* contends with the relationship of rehearsal to performance and of onstage to offstage space; and *Play* confronts the irreducibility of performance as such and the constrained temporality of its representational dynamics. The salience of the theatre's technical apparatus in *What Where* and *Play*, however, makes them especially germane to this study, recalling as they do Beckett's and Pinter's more traditionally dramatic machine plays: *Krapp's Last Tape* and *The Dumb Waiter*, respectively.

In grouping Pinter and Beckett among the absurdists, Martin Esslin situated them in a lineage of dramatists concerned with the persistent reduction of existential questions to absurdity: "Theatre of the Absurd," Esslin famously explains, "strives to express its sense of the senselessness of the human condition and the inadequacy of the rational approach by the open abandonment of rational devices and discursive thought," arguing that the absurd is more "adequate as an expression of [existentialist] philosophy" than the philosophical and theatrical writings of such existentialists as Sartre and Camus themselves.[61] The ideas Esslin strove to clarify in this theatrical mode, however, remained rooted in a manifestly European and American tradition of dramatic writing: in the works of Beckett and Pinter, to be sure, but also of Ionesco, Jean Genet, Edward Albee, Günther Grass, and others.

Little known in the West, the work of Bengali playwright Badal Sircar allows us to see that the themes and theatricality discussed so far in this chapter pertain not particularly to Western thought alone, but to any context in which rapid modernization and the concomitant urbanization and professionalization of everyday life foment individual and social disorientations. Sircar's *and Indrajit* (Bengali: *Evam Indrajit*; 1962), shares with Fugard's *The Island*, discussed in the previous chapter, and with Pinter and Beckett's works a manifest theatricality, one reminiscent of Luigi Pirandello's *Six Characters in Search of an Author* (1921) as well, because it concerns, in part, the struggle of an author—called "The Writer"—to reconcile his own desire to compose a drama with the title character's resistance to conducting his life in a linear, predictable way.[62] Against Aristotelian narrative's demand for plausibility, necessity, and unity of character and of action, Indrajit lives a somewhat aimless life, never quite settling down to one thing, constantly aware of the cosmic insignificance of the individual's existence and the futility of human desires. Indeed, the mythoheroic name Indrajit is imposed upon him by The Writer when, having met him at the beginning of the play, he finds his given name—Nirmal—too conventional. (Indeed, the Sanskrit origins of *Nirmal* suggest purity or cleanliness, not far from bourgeois values of the "normal," creating a fortuitous play on words in the English translation of Sircar's original Bengali.) The play's meta-theatrical quality serves to highlight the systematicity of cultural norms and expectations *as such* and permits the piece to connect this abstract sense of systematicity to the technologies of everyday middle-class life in Calcutta: technologies of transportation, communication, and financial transaction. The play itself and theatrical production more broadly, as a set of routinized, standardized, and literally productive practices, come to stand in for both the abstract socioeconomic systems Indrajit/Nirmal resists and the technologies and techno-rationalist ideologies that sustain those systems.

The Writer is compelled and constrained by his own need to write—literally, to produce—a play, even though he himself does not have a clear idea about what its themes should be. We are thus given to understand that *and Indrajit* is, itself, both a dramatization of his attempt to write a play *and also* the play he is writing. Throughout, The Writer exhorts his principal characters—Amal, Vimal, Kamal, and Indrajit (the play takes its title from Indrajit's last place in this list)—whom he has chosen seemingly at random from among the audience, to make something of their lives, something upon which he might base his play. Because The Writer and, by extension, bourgeois dramatic theatre, align themselves with capitalist ideological norms of subjectivity and the actions appropriate to it, Indrajit's resistance to The Writer's exhortations both constitutes the dramatic conflict and signals a more general ideological resistance.

Despite Indrajit's inability or unwillingness to acquiesce to bourgeois values, his three fellow principals submit to them wholeheartedly, and it is primarily through their experience that the play links bourgeois norms to technology and techno-rationalism. For instance, having taken professional positions, they complain to The Writer, who doubles from time to time as their office lackey, of late trains, broken down trams, and crowded buses, just like The Young Woman of Treadwell's *Machinal*, discussed in Chapter 2. Likewise, scenes of their professional life are marked by disjointed words and phrases drawn from bourgeois professional discourse but conveying no clear, unified sense, again reminiscent of *Machinal*'s pointless business jargon. Only Indrajit and The Writer begin to realize that this way of life seems part of a larger, even more cosmically pointless machine, endlessly "going round and round" like a "giant ferris wheel."[63] This image of pointless revolution at one point is punctuated by "loud music" that "drowns out Indrajit's voice" during final oral examinations, much as Zero and the Boss's dialogue are disrupted by theatrical sound effects in *The Adding Machine*.[64] I wish to suggest that these momentary references to extra-theatrical technologies take on special significance in the context of Sircar's theatre aesthetic, standing out as indices of the kind of sophistication *and Indrajit*'s production values eschew. Even so, like Beckett's shorter works and Pinter's *Dumb Waiter, and Indrajit* does, finally, succeed in both *being a play* and *refusing to be a play*, anatomizing and critiquing the constraints of theatrical form upon the subjective desires of its characters. Sircar's inclusion of The Writer as a central figure in the play thus creates a kind of mise en abyme not unlike that of Beckett's lighting and sound apparatus and Pinter's dumb-waiter-cum-stage-within-a-stage.

In doing so, *and Indrajit*, along with *The Dumb Waiter, Krapp's Last Tape, What Where,* and *Play*, remind us of how the persistence of theatrical and ideological mechanisms of constraint, control, and representation gesture to the social machineries and systems of all kinds that, in the everyday world, enable constraints and modes of domination whose consequences are far greater than those to be seen on any stage. In the next chapter, this self-reflexive, sometimes recursive dynamic, centering attention on the technologies and conventions of staged representation, intensifies in works that critically disrupt the boundaries of the stage, expanding the site of performance beyond the delineated playing spaces we have encountered so far. As we shall see,

Heiner Müller's *Hamletmachine*, Julia Taymor, Bono, and the Edge's *Spider-Man: Turn Off the Dark*, and Tod Machover and Robert Pinsky's *Death and the Powers* gesture to a digital, as opposed to analogue, conception of experience and representation and sketch what may be thought of as a post-human dramatic aesthetic.

5

Post-Human Recursivity: Heiner Müller, Julie Taymor, and Tod Machover & Robert Pinsky

In Chapter 2, we saw how three plays of the American Modernist canon deployed humanist nostalgia to express the sense of loss, helplessness, and constraint imposed upon the everyday person—the clerk, the wife, the salesman—by the technologies of capitalism in the late industrial period. In works by Elmer Rice, Sophie Treadwell, and Arthur Miller, the machineries and techno-rationalist ideologies born of machine logic in the first half of the twentieth century contrast with the bucolic, agrarian, and frontier fantasies of liberty, self-discovery, and agency. Each of these works holds out the possibility, however remote, of an authentic, organic human experience as an alternative to the malaise of modernity and as an aspirational model of human subjectivity in its own right. Hearkening back to a Jeffersonian notion of the American dream—opportunity, hard work, and liberty—and reinforcing the Hooverian ideal of rugged individualism as the bedrock of American identity, these plays indict technology, and particularly the techno-rationalism of business, as an obstacle to self-fulfillment, where the "self" is imagined as an unproblematic given prior to culture or ideology. They did not, in other words, go so far as to indict that ideal itself. In the middle chapters, however, that notion of that machine has become increasingly attenuated: abstract, metaphorical, and characteristic of a systematicity and logic that exceeds technology's material substrate, and along with it, that notion of a unified self.

The theatre works I will examine in this chapter, continue that arc, raising questions about that antediluvian ideal of the human subject as a coherent, self-willed, individual agent. Different as they are, they enact post-human conceptions of consciousness and agency and the organic boundedness of the body, conceptions that both rely on and are consequences of technological innovation. Heiner Müller's *Hamletmachine* (1979), Tod Machover and Robert Pinsky's "Robot's Opera" *Death and the Powers* (2010), and Julia Taymor's production, in collaboration with Glen Berger, Roberto Aguirre-Sacasa, Philip William McKinley, George Tsypin, and U2 band members Bono and The Edge, of *Spider-Man: Turn Off the Dark* (2011) deploy advanced technologies to stage menacing encounters between technologically enhanced heroes and villains in a technologically dominated world. But these works do so in ways that are quite distinct from the plays discussed in the previous chapters. First, while technologies saturate these work—as objects of representation, as means of production, and even as onstage agents—and are, for some of the characters (and perhaps for the audiences, too) a source of menace, the works themselves mostly reserve judgment, at least explicitly. Technology in these post-human works is presented as a fact of the world; and, while each of these works makes much of the power and potential of advanced technology, they do so in ways that suggest a neutral posture that takes technological advancement for granted.

Second, they use advanced technology to complicate the very idea of character as it evolved over the twentieth century. In all three works, the notion of character inherited from the Enlightenment through Stanislavsky no longer suffices. This insufficiency emerges, in part, from genre conventions in two of these works. *Spider-Man*, as a lavish Broadway musical based on a Marvel comic, and *Death and the Powers*, as an opera, both partake in their respective performance traditions' reliance on voice, music, costume, choreography and sets over characterization and mimetic portrayal to convey character, presented in these traditions more as stock types than as fully developed, interiorized human subjects. Nevertheless, in all three works, the rejection of mimetic portrayal is heightened by the usurpation of character representation by nonhuman agents or human/nonhuman hybrids: machines, monsters, and digital code.[1]

And, finally, they present the human as out of proportion to their world. In all three works, the very large and the very small have gained ascendancy, the one confronting the human with its insignificance and the other with its penetrability and lack of adaptive agility. These menaces of scale, moreover, manifest themselves both explicitly and implicitly and characterize the relationship of the actor to the production as much as they do that of the character to their worlds; indeed, in the case of *Spider-Man: Turn Off the Dark*, the sheer scale of the production seems to have overwhelmed almost every member of the crew and creative team. In all three cases, the disproportionality of the human to the world takes on a scientific and technological dimension, inviting us to imagine the end of the Anthropocene era—what Pinsky and Machover's robots will call the "Organic Age"[2]—and the beginning of an age where the very small (DNA, bytes, and bits) and the very large (the accrual of history, the metropolis, global systems of commerce and power, and the technosphere) will leave increasingly little space for the human to exercise agency and power, if any of either remain to it.

During the three-and-a-half decades separating Taymor's and Machover's pieces from Müller's, technological innovation in theatre and other performance modes, including dance, performance art, installation art, and music, became widespread, to such a degree that, in his remarks on New York's 1984 New Wave Festival, critic and scholar Johannes Birringer could find little to distinguish between the "fashionability" of pop culture and mainstream "technolog[ies] of cultural promotion" and "advanced art":

> The question of avant-garde fashionability [...] has become a serious problem, since it is no longer possible to review aesthetic practices and their meanings separate from the institutional (publicity, promotion, funding, production) and technological environment in which they are sold to the public as "new."[3]

Here, Birringer's inverted commas around "new" underscore his skepticism about what he sees as a collusion between avant-garde performance and the affirmative ideologies of late capitalism. He particularly takes to task Robert Wilson's five-hour production of Philip Glass's *Einstein on the Beach*, which he finds both relentless and vapid, "an overstimulating ensemble of pseudo-performances that no longer follow a perceivable logic of 'theatre,'" with its "posing of familiar images of technology" resulting in the "complete effacement of [modernism's] thematic content," which it quotes for stylistic effect alone.[4] Somewhat more enabling, from Birringer's point of view, Meredith Monk and Ping Chong's *The Games*, with Chong's "elliptical computer graphics" complicated by Monk's music, along with

> her own performance of the sexually unidentifiable role of "Gamemaster" [...] addresses the crucial question, not only of the representability of the human body within such visual-aural collages, but also the spectator's or auditor's relationship to the competing audiovisual languages [...] that take place before me but not for me.[5]

Nevertheless, Birringer's overall response to the experimental pieces on display is blasé, seeing them as little more than showpieces for technological spectacle.

Whereas Birringer's skepticism responds to the large-scale effects of avant-garde performance's technologization generally, in this chapter, I wish both to broaden the scope of discussion to include manifestly popular performance, represented here by the Broadway extravaganza *Spider-Man: Turn Off the Dark*, and to narrow it to focus on works where technology is not just a means of producing effects, but is in fact an object of representation. By doing so, I hope to uncover a fraught relationship between the staging of technology and the staged technologies that leaves open the possibility of critical engagement, analysis, and interpretation.

Of the three pieces under discussion here, the earliest is also the one in which the machineries of late capitalism are represented in the most attenuated, least explicit way: Heiner Müller's *Hamletmachine* (1977, trans. 1979). However, if we take the "machine" Müller's title as a sign of the technology's centrality to the play, several questions arise: What does this machine do? What are its components and processes? What are its inputs, its raw materials? What are its products or effects? Given its late-1970s origin, how does it situate itself with respect to the digital revolution, digital computing, and other emergent concerns in science and mathematics? And what do possible answers to these questions tell us about theatre and drama in the late twentieth and early twenty-first century and about the relationship between theatre practices and rapidly changing conceptions of the human during the rise of post-structuralist philosophy, postmodern culture, and the emergent field of cyborg studies? In other words, if the machine of *Hamletmachine* is more than just a stylistic gewgaw, a nod toward "fashionability," how can we begin to understand the play's machinic qualities and themes?

Admittedly, that's a big *if*. The play, a kind of hyper-collage of mainly twentieth-century literary, dramatic, and popular texts, often echoing authors who themselves produced highly fragmented and cutup works, seems only loosely tethered to the *Hamlet* of its title. *Hamletmachine* may be accused of using Shakespeare's most famous plays and characters more as an occasion for experimenting in form than as a thematic or formal center, expanding to include political and economic theory and questions of gender, power, bodily integrity, and subjectivity that drive *Hamletmachine* well beyond the limits of its purported ground text. Moreover, just as the play contains much that is not *Hamlet*, it also contains much that is not machine: Images of the body, particularly the dismembered, tortured, and desiring body, abound; quite human appetites and longings—for sex, food, love, recognition, and revenge—appear to give the play a persistently organic, somatic, and psychological quality. Images of bleeding, dismemberment, murder, suicide, and gluttony and references to a range of human emotions and experiences create a highly visceral experience reminiscent of Artaud's "theatre of cruelty" and presaging later decades' "New Brutalism" and what Aleks Sierz has dubbed "In-Yer-Face Theatre."[6] Consequently, *Hamletmachine*'s overt themes and tonalities would seem to share little in common with the machineries and works we have examined in the preceding chapters. The fracturing and sheer excess of *Hamletmachine*, which defies even the minimal linearity and causality necessary for plot or stability of discourse and self-presentation required for character suggests a machine of a kind very different from what we conventionally call mechanical, technological, or even virtual.

To be sure, the piece names technologies in its speech and sometimes embeds machineries—three televisions and a refrigerator, for instance—into its scenography.[7] The speaker sometimes called Hamlet evokes a smoking stove[8] and voices the longing to "be a machine. Arms for grabbing. Legs to walk on, no pain, no thoughts,"[9] claiming, at one point, to be "the typewriter" and, at another, to "feed [his] own data into the computers," thereby becoming "the databank."[10] Another speaker, as Ophelia, claims to "wrench the clock that was [her] heart out of [her] breast," using imagery that perhaps recalls the dismembering dynamic of *The Gas Heart* and the obsessive temporality of *Machinal* and of Taylorist notions of efficiency.[11]

While these moments merit discussion—the density of the play's text does not admit to throwaway lines—these mechanistic registers are overwhelmed by images of the failing or suffering body, emotional longing and despair, psychological conflictedness and self-doubt. The Hamlet-speaker complains of "LUGGING [HIS] OVERWEIGHT BRAIN LIKE A HUNCHBACK" and suggests that "[w]e could butcher each other [...] if life gets too long for us or our throats too tight for our screams";[12] he anatomizes his mother's "breasts [as] a rosebud, her womb a snakepit"; [13] and he recounts how "SOMETIMES IN WINTER THEY CAME INTO THE VILLAGE / AND TORE APART A PEASANT."[14] Likewise, the Ophelia-speaker evokes the suffering, death, and perhaps uncanny resurrection of the female body in her soliloquy that composes the entirety of Act Two:

> I am Ophelia. The one the river didn't keep. The woman dangling from the rope. The woman with her arteries cut open. The woman with the overdose. SNOW ON HER LIPS. The woman with her head in the gas-stove. Yesterday I stopped killing myself. I'm alone with my breasts my thighs my womb. [....] With my bleeding hands I tear the photos of the men I loved and who used me on the bed on the table on the chair on the ground. [....] I walk into the street clothed in my blood. [15]

Occasionally, as when the Hamlet-speaker evokes the "daily nausea" of the "television," perhaps a play on "the daily news," a binary opposition between machine and body seems to coalesce but only momentarily.[16] The machine moments and the far more common organic, visceral ones resist the consistent structuring effect of binarity, instead entering into apparently fluid, polymorphic, and polysemous arrangements.

And so, upon first encountering *Hamletmachine*, one cannot see immediately or clearly what, precisely, the titular *machine* is or to what degree it is really central to any understanding of the play. The play stands, in many ways, as a challenge to speak about the machine as such, so clogged is it with its own literally and figuratively "raw" materials. The challenge of doing so is evinced in a range of scholarly responses to the piece, particularly those that came after Robert Wilson's 1986 production at New York University. Elizabeth Klaver, for instance, focuses her attention on the television screens called for in the play, which index "a boundless megatext, a three-dimensional architecture in which textual free play occurs,"[17] thus intensifying the play's "intertextuality" and the "self-irony generated when one text is perforated by an inappropriate one," as *Hamletmachine* certainly is.[18] This focus on the television's perforation of the scene allows Klaver to see the viewer as a "textual assembler" whose spectation must work against the fact that "cohesive structure disappears altogether."[19] Similarly concerned with media effects, Nicholas Zurbrugg is interested in the way Wilson's production of *Hamletmachine* heightens its "multimedia sensibility," which accounts for variations in rhythm and pace as well as image and sound juxtapositions seemingly unmotivated by the text.[20] Unlike Klaver, however, Zurbrugg takes a dismissive tone toward Müller's play and Wilson's staging alike, seeing both as idiosyncratic and stale. By contrast to both Klaver and Zurbrugg, instead of focusing on a particular machine represented within the text and productions of *Hamletmachine*, Kirk Williams says that Müller's "machine remains stalled in a moment of melancholic incorporation."[21] For Williams, memory, the body, and the ghost are primary in *Hamletmachine*, the machine a metaphor for or overlay upon these more urgent and central thematic concerns. While Joseph M. Dudley notes the play's machine effects, such as "doubling," "reassembl[ing], and fracture[ing]," he is more concerned with questions of ontology and epistemology as they relate to the real and imagined spaces in and around performances of *Hamletmachine*.[22] In all four cases, by no means exhausting the critical literature on *Hamletmachine*, but certainly representative of it, scholars either narrow their focus on a particular machinic aspect of Müller's play or, while acknowledging them, address questions only obliquely related to the piece as mechanism.

These encounters with *Hamletmachine* are effective in opening up the piece as a site of critical engagement precisely because they come at the machine obliquely or in piecemeal fashion. That is, they use the machine as a way into a range of questions that expand beyond the limits of a focused examination on the play's mechanisms and its mechanistic themes. In keeping with the focus of this book, however, and as I implied in raising my earlier questions, I do propose to speak of *Hamletmachine* as a whole machine, recognizing that, in doing so, my analysis will necessarily downplay the piece's disport with the organic body, with literary and philosophical traditions, and with global political conflict.

In brief, I see *Hamletmachine* as a machine for reproducing *Hamletmachines*; it is not the first machine to do so: Arguably *Hamlet* itself may have been, or perhaps Aeschylus' *Oresteia* or Euripides' Theban cycle, whose material Shakespeare's *Hamlet* updates, condenses, and recycles. Indeed, one of the effects of Hamlet machines of all kinds is to disrupt chronology. Between Shakespeare and Müller, many other Hamlet machines have engaged in those reproductions: from Henry Irving's severely edited productions of Shakespeare at the Lyceum Theatre meant to serve popular commercial ends in late-nineteenth-century London theatre[23] to "the Ophelia phenomenon" in eighteenth- and nineteenth-century visual art[24] to the ironically jazzy "Shakespeherian rag" of Eliot's *The Waste Land* (1921)[25] to Stoppard's *Rosencranz and Guildenstern Are Dead* (1967), to name only a few. And so, in one sense, the production and reproduction of Hamlet machines by *Hamletmachine* works retroactively, retooling Shakespeare and Euripides, but also Eliot, Weiss, Brecht, Marx, Mao, Hemingway, Mussolini, Conrad, Sartre, Miller, Beckett, and many others from the long tradition of Western thought, theatre, and writing, retrofitting them as themselves *Hamletmachine* machines. If capitalist ideology, as Althusser posits, makes imperative "the reproduction of the conditions of [capitalist] production," *Hamletmachine* imposes upon the texts that precede it *the reproduction of the conditions for reproductions* of *Hamletmachine(s)*.[26] It retroactively reconfigures its forebears as always reproducing themselves as Hamlet machines already; likewise, it extends the reproduction of those conditions for reproduction into the future, not only making theatres, companies, and directors who stage future versions of *Hamletmachine*—and the critics and scholars who subject the text and its productions to analysis and interpretation—into Hamlet machines, but also proactively transforming all future theatrical productions of all kinds into *Hamlet* machines. *Hamletmachine* dramatizes its own position vis-à-vis theatre as already the product of the machines that have preceded it; but instead of imagining itself as the telos of tradition, it becomes a processor-conduit, the means by which what comes after gets produced as a Hamlet machine, thus recalling Deleuze and Guattari's rhizomic assemblage discussed in Chapter 1.

By this reading, it is not the *machine* of the title that is incidental or attenuated; rather, it is the Hamlet. *Hamlet*, the auratic Shakespearean text, gives way to the *machine*, the process of consuming raw material, recycling it, and using it to continue to produce the machine itself, in varying degrees of complexity at various scales and levels of detail. For instance, a 2000 New World Performance Lab production at the Cleveland Public Theater, taking its cue from Jerzy Grotowsky's poor theatre, rendered a "very 'non-high-tech' version of Müller's landscape—a triangular empty space filled only with three actors, three lights, a telescope, and four small boxes of personal memorabilia."[27] Linda Eisenstein of *The Plain Dealer* called that production "a springboard for a series of inventive surrealist images and transformations."[28] That same year, University of California, Los Angeles, Bauhaus University

(Germany), and the University of South Wales (Australia) collaborated on a digital installation that used visitors' shadows cast onto light-density sensors to trigger and determine the volume of the playback of one or several or all of fifteen audio fragments of different lengths into which an audio recording of Müller's text had been cut, resulting in a text that "is both sheltered and shattered by the perfect preservation and repetition possible with digital technology, while its complementary capacity for dynamic manipulation of media allowed each experience to be a different collage of sound and meaning."[29] Müller's text, more than almost any other in contemporary drama, has invited a degree of intervention, rearrangement, and rescripting at times so radical as to include resituating within media, modalities, and spaces unimaginable in the text alone: light-sensitive audio collage, guerilla performance art, an interpolation into *Hamlet*, textual performance, and even a rewriting of the play titled *Opheliamachine*.[30]

Read in this way, *Hamletmachine* resonates more with Beckett's later plays than it would first appear to do, reminding us of their concern with representing theatrical representation as such, as I discussed in the preceding chapter. But, whereas Beckett's plays present themselves as finished pieces, final products, the creative scope and free play for future productions of which are constrained and codified in licenses and stage directions, *Hamletmachine* presents itself as a process, radically open and unfinished, always in motion already. Its failure to coalesce as a scrutable, even momentarily stable object of interpretation emerges not so much from the way it plays with the tropes of the European modernist avant-garde, with which it has at times been unfavorably compared,[31] as from its status as a recursive process: decomposition, churn, torque, compression, attenuation, and production. In this way, *Hamletmachine* and its mutated progeny enact the very logic of theatrical production and reproduction, emphasizing what I have elsewhere characterized as the "transience, interpretive fecundity, and multiplicity" that "constitutes [theatre] as a practice."[32]

In engendering these semi-self-similar reproductions, adaptations, and variations, Müller's text operates in ways that echo 1970s experiments with recursive coding and digitality: for example, chaos theory, fractal mathematics, and recombinant DNA. While I have used the terms *complexity, levels of detail, scale, semi-self-similar,* and *recursivity* above because they adequately characterize the way *Hamletmachine*'s various outputs distinguish themselves from one another without losing their quality of being outputs of the same machine, I also wish to foreground the way the productive dynamic of *Hamletmachine* articulates to fractal, rather than linear formal dynamics. If the line is the geometry of Aristotelian action, the fractal—and particularly, chaotic fractal dynamics as they were conceived by Benoit B. Mandelbrot—is the mathematical function of *Hamletmachine*'s operations. Coined in 1975, Mandelbrot's term "fractal" compresses the term "fractional dimension," the dimensional quality of a figure—a curve or a line, say—whose one-dimensionality increases without even becoming two-dimensionality by the infinite expansion-by-recursion of any discrete segment or arc. Or, more simply, it is a function repeatedly iterated to create increasingly small and increasingly complex versions of itself: "a rough or fragmented geometric shape that can be split into parts, each of which is (at least approximately) a reduced-size copy of the whole."[33] Mandlebrot's innovation in fractal mathematics lies primarily in having theorized the study of what we now know as fractals as a coherent branch of geometry. The set named for him, the Mandelbrot set, demonstrates complexity that, when visually rendered, results not to the exact reproduction of a form at every level of detail (which a strictly self-similar fractal would, such as the Cantor set, the Koch curve, and the Sierpinsky triangle), but rather, in variations, sometimes similar and sometimes radically different, depending on how many recursion cycles the function has gone through. Thus, in looking at a visual rendering of the Mandelbrot set—which became possible only once digital computing became fast enough to render many hundreds of thousands of these iterations—one sees apparent repetitions of scaled-down first-recursion forms as outgrowths or emergent properties of later recursions; at the same time, one also sees forms that seem to bear no similarity to early-recursion forms. The important thing is that repetition, recognizable similarity, and apparently radical dissimilarity in the visual rendering or mapping of nonlinear fractal functions are, all alike, the result of the recursion of *the identical function*. Variation is the consequence of the repetition of the same function.

What all fractals share in common is that they are "dimensionally discordant."[34] That is to say that they enact, in their recursions, a dimensionality that is no longer representable by a whole number. Whereas we are accustomed to thinking of geometric figures as one-, two-, and three-dimensional, fractals, because they are infinitely scalable to increasingly smaller and smaller orders of detail, have effective dimensions that exceed their apparent, intuitive whole-number dimensionality. A one-dimensional line, subjected to recursive fragmentation, elongates infinitely without ever becoming entirely two-dimensional. Known as Hausdorff–Besicovitch dimensions, the discordant dimensions of the fractal, put simply, mean that its fractal dimension exceeds its topology, the space it occupies.[35]

Fractal mathematics, and specifically Mandelbrot's clarifications of it as a field in the late 1970s and early 1980s, thus provide a conceptual model for understanding *Hamletmachine*'s function *as a machine* and help to situate it within the context of technological and mathematical innovations at the time of its creation and early stagings. Like fractal mathematics, *Hamletmachine* emerges as one cultural product of the early years of the digital revolution, along with chaos theory and cyborg theory, that relies on recursive processes to reproduce both similarity and difference. While it would be pressing a point too far to suggest an exact correlation between Müller's aesthetics and a formal, mathematical rendering of fractal formation, putting Müller's work in conversation with Mandelbrot's reveals the salience of recursivity, scale, and complexity to the way *Hamletmachine* confronts theatre and human as it is traditionally conceived.

Particularly striking, in my view, is the idea of the fractal form as exceeding its own topography. While the "spatial turn" in drama studies would not come into its own for another twenty years, aided largely by Chaudhuri's *Staging Place* (1995), theatre has always been exquisitely aware of its own topographies and has always, in one way or another, sought to exceed them. But Robert Wilson's 1986 production of *Hamletmachine* represents a novel approach to fulfilling that impulse. Because Wilson claims to have worked out the spatial elements of the play—including movement and gesture—before beginning to work with Müller's text, his production represented the scope of the history and traditions the piece invokes in ways not accounted for in the text itself.[36] Birringer in particular emphasizes the disconnect of production design from text:

> It is now fashionable to watch a Wilson show without bothering to ask questions about its contents, as if the viewing merely confirmed our absence from a concrete historical scene. In his staging of *Hamletmachine*, Wilson relinquishes any attempt to interpret or even illustrate Müller's scenography of the "frozen storm" that presses the feminine discourse of the "anarchic-natural" into the wheelchair of passive cultural nihilism. Completely separating the acoustic score of Müller's text (live amplified and taped voices) from the single visual stage tableau that is choreographically constructed and repeated five times in five different angles, Wilson here lets the text create its own plasticity, an "other" space that is not seen but heard.[37]

While Birringer would clearly have preferred a rendering of Müller's text that was more faithful to it, I wish to suggest that if we take the *machine* of *Hamletmachine*'s title seriously and consider it in light of Mandelbrot's work on fractals, we should not be surprised when it occasionally produces something other than fidelity to its text (rigorous self-similarity) or when it seems to exceed the text's strict parameters (its dimensionality exceeds its topology).

In arguing that "*Hamletmachine* is set against the space of a theatre—a single place where many spaces are represented," and thus "occup[ies] doubled spaces" and "fracture[s], reassemble[s], and fracture[s] once again" the audience's "gaze," Joseph M. Dudley gestures toward the way Müller's text seems to call for a fractal-like expansion of theatre's spatial coordinates.[38] After all, the play is itself a rendering and fragmentation of numerous and disparate source texts; but it is also an enlargement of, and upon, those fragmented texts. Like the result of a recursive mathematical function or computer code, Wilson's production, as described by Birringer, subjects *Hamletmachine* to its own processes, figured as the disfigurement of its source texts; those processes result in a reproduction not of *Hamletmachine* as some fixed, originary, text-bound concept, but rather as a dynamic system, which itself always *processes* itself as its own raw material. This reprocessing and reproduction of its own systematicity *as such* produces a version of itself that disrupts the conventional dimensions of stage space—both literal and conceptual. This disruption allows Birringer to claim that the "acoustic score" is "completely separate[ed]" from the "visual tableau," itself iterated—"repeated five times in five different angles"—even while these elements are not, in fact, separated: they occupy the same stage space and stage time. This effect of simultaneous difference and sameness is a fractal effect, one that emerges from a play conceptualized as a machine process rather than a machine-object.

If Wilson's production of *Hamletmachine* reenacts the computational and recombinatory processes according to which the play reproduces itself in its future productions, Müller's decision to embed the piece between Acts Four and Five of his staging of Shakespeare's *Hamlet* in East Berlin in 1990 demonstrates the way *Hamletmachine* was always the product of prior versions of the Hamlet machine already. Describing this production as a "monumental [...] epitaph"[39] on Shakespeare, East Germany, and even history, Andreas Höfele's account notes that the seven-and-a-half-hour-long production begins with *Hamlet*'s final line and interpolates into it lines from *Hamletmachine* even outside of Müller's entr'acte interlude. The production's soundscape employs a "muted loudspeaker murmur[ing] the original Russian radio obituary for Stalin,"[40] and "Erich Wonder's stage [...] depicted this rotting nightmare world as a vast decaying bunker," which would be replaced in Act Three "by a pastiche of Tintoretto's magnificent 'Translation of the Body of St. Mark' [...] while the downstage area changes into a huge subway tunnel."[41] The diction was "deliberately de-psychologized" throughout and the "slow, stylized movement" of the actors and the "muted [...] immobili[ty]" of the Danish court, "like switched-off robots" at the beginning of the production emphasize Müller's mechanical, dehumanized vision of *Hamlet*.

While Höfele scoffs at the production's excesses—"What next? A twelve-hour *Lear* perhaps?"—this production makes clear that *Hamletmachine* imagines itself as part of a long series of machine processes; retroactively inserted into the texture of Shakespeare's *Hamlet*, it infects it, takes over the original play's processes, fragmenting it and slowing it down like the computer viruses that would become digital threats in the decades to follow. *Hamletmachine*, Müller's *Hamlet* production suggests, was already embedded in *Hamlet* from the beginning, already programmed into its processes, both as an input and as an output. This interpolation-as-immanence retroactively reconfigures the whole tradition of Western thought, including literary and theatrical production, not as a linear teleology toward progress or completion, but as a recursive process of breakdown and reconstruction at different orders of magnitude. Importantly, this process is not the cycle of eternal return, whose metaphysical and mythical overtones Müller's texts reject, but a cold and inexorable machine process whose logic rigorously reproduces itself in the materiality of text and practice.

Together, Müller's *Hamletmachine*, Wilson's bifurcated production of it, and, finally Müller's reconfiguration of Shakespeare's *Hamlet* as always containing within it *Hamletmachine* as code and virus, considered in the context of fractal logic whose reemergence as a primary concern and popularized by fractal art and concerted efforts to mainstream at least simplified understandings of fractal theory in the 1970s and 1980s, highlight themes with which this chapter is principally concerned. First, the problem of scale: post-human theatre confronts the human, whether audience member, actor, or character, with both the overwhelmingly large (seven-hour productions, the suffocating weight of history) and the imperceptibly small (virus, gene, code), both registers threatening the coherence of the human and the legibility of the human world.

Second, the usurpation of organic processes by machine processes, and particularly processes related to digital computing and cybernetic theory. Resonating with Katherine Hayles's conception of the posthuman, these works and productions participate in a theatrical mode that

> privileges informational pattern over material instantiation, so that embodiment in a biological substrate is seen as an accident of history rather an inevitability[;] considers consciousness, regarded as the seat of human identity in the Western tradition [...], as an epiphenomenon[;] thinks of the body as the original prosthesis [...], so that extending or replacing the body with other prostheses becomes a continuation of a process that began before we were born[; and] configures the human being so that it can be seamlessly articulated with intelligent machines.[42]

And, third, the enactment of recursivity: Meta-theatricality increasingly gestures toward stage representation as an iterable, recursive process that reproduces variations on those processes *as such*, regardless of the content or object of representation. Theatre's constitutive recursivity becomes primary over the actions, events, and characters it represents. While this enumeration allows for a moment of conceptual clarity, we have seen and shall continue to notice considerable overlap among these themes. Recursivity, for instance, often suggests a scalar dynamic, and post-human theory already implies an emphasis on abstract processes.

Hamletmachine's response to the emergence of the post-human is neither to resist nor embrace it, but to escape it or to fall apart in the face of it. Reading its thematic development yields exceedingly pessimistic interpretations, its hue and cry finally resolving into something like resignation or surrender. Twenty years after *Hamletmachine*'s recapitulation in Müller's production of *Hamlet*, however, dramatic theatre has continued to explore ways of becoming post-human, sometimes only symbolically or representationally, and at other times quite literally. Tod Machover and Robert Pinsky's *Death and the Powers* and Bono, The Edge, and Taymor's *Spider-Man: Turn Off the Dark* offer somewhat more enabling ways of using and interpreting the role of the highly technologically sophisticated theatre apparatus as more than an enabler of stylistic effect. They do so because, like many of the works discussed in this book, they take as at least a significant proportion of their subject matter—their "content"—the problem of scientific and technological innovation. The stage and the characters alike both rise to the challenge posed by Fredric Jameson's *Postmodernity* (1989), in which he suggests that "postmodern hyperspace"[43] requires that its denizens "grow new organs" and "expand our sensorium and our body to some new, yet unimaginable, perhaps ultimately impossible dimensions"[44] that might make it possible for us to "map the great global multinational and decentered communicational network in which we find ourselves caught as individual subjects."[45] Constructed from 1974 to 1976—precisely contemporary with Mandelbrot's fractal innovations and Müller's *Hamletmachine*—the Westin Bonaventure Hotel, whose atrium gives rise to Jameson's reflections, also suggests the self-referential recursivity and counterintuitive dimensionalities of fractal geometry. At the same time, its use of automated movement to intensify the effects of volume and verticality in its lobby echoes Peter Brook's earlier innovations in staging in his work with the Royal Shakespeare Company's 1970 production of *Midsummer Night's Dream*. It would seem that Western theatre production, by the 1970s, had already begun developing the very organs and sensoria that Jameson's everyday postmodern subject still lacked in 1991.

These new organs and advanced sensoria take center stage in Machover and Pinsky's "Robot's Opera," *Death and the Powers* (2010), which imagines an age in which robots have replaced organic systems of all kinds, but nevertheless recapitulate human practices of theatrical storytelling, compelled to do so by commands encoded by their human creators. The opera presents itself as a frame narrative: The outer frame features several robots that, while clearly made of metal and plastic, roughly resemble human bodies, with axial and appendicular elements and white triangular headpieces. Although Pinsky's stage directions have these robots transforming themselves into simulacra of humans a few minutes into the opera, in the premiere production set to Machover's music, with set elements designed and programmed through The Massachusetts Institute of Technology's (MIT) Media Lab, the robots remain manifestly robots, elegant, modern, vaguely human-shaped modules whose sleek elegance and the design of their glowing, triangular white headpieces manifestly echo the look and feel of Apple computers and accessories.[46] In this form, itself perhaps merely a three-dimensional rendering of digital code, the robots prepare for a ritual performance that reenacts a key moment in now distant history—the moment Simon Powers went digital. At this point, the robots engage in a brief—and, from a purely robotic point of view, seemingly pointless—exchange about manifestly human question of existence and intention: What is death? Why did their human programmers mandate this performance? Obviously, these robots are unacquainted with Beckett's *What Where*, whose mechanized framing and reframing, whose second guessings, and whose ultimate disavowal of sense-making they unwittingly recapitulate. Despite their inability to fully comprehend death, being an organic process, except by positing possible digital analogs (if I may), such as deleted or misplaced data—much less human suffering—they proceed with their performance, each of the four robots who transform temporarily into human forms to receive "One Thousand Human Rights Status Credits," whatever those may be.[47]

Thus begins the framed narrative, the story of Simon Powers, an immensely wealthy inventor whose business holdings have expanded into every sphere of global economic exchange, warfare, and government. Faced with the decline of his health after a stroke, he bids farewell to his daughter Miranda (whose name evokes Shakespeare's *The Tempest* and casts Simon as a latter-day Prospero), his second wife and Miranda's stepmother Evvy, and his assistant Nicholas, a computer-engineering doctoral student whom Simon adopted and fitted out with cyborg prosthetics to compensate for crippling birth defects. During this long farewell, Simon explains that he and Nicholas have invented a means for his consciousness to be reduced to purely digital information and uploaded into the computer systems that control his domestic environment and connect to his business and financial holdings. In the moments leading up to this transformation, Simon repeatedly refers to poetry, including W. B. Yeats's "Sailing to Byzantium" and May Swenson's "Question," both to situate his vision of digital immortality against that of literary fame and to push against poetic notions of death and hybridity. So, like the Hamlet-speaker of Müller's *Hamletmachine*, Simon resists the weight of human history and tradition and imagines himself as a "databank."[48] And yet, in "feed[ing his] own data into the computers,"[49] Simon does not wish to escape the human altogether, as the Hamlet-speaker does, but to preserve what is essentially human in the machine. For the love between his daughter and her stepmother proves to Simon that what it means to be human is separable from the biological bodies and bloodlines of maternity and, by extension, of the whole human organism. Simon takes this love between biologically unrelated humans as proof that love, that most human of emotion, does not depend on the particularities of embodiment, which is only an accidental and unnecessary substrate for the human. As they listen to his twisted logic, soon enough Evvy and Miranda, along with Nicholas, join in with him to express their agreement, at least on the point of human love's transcendent nature.

Importantly, even as he advocates for the liberating possibilities offered by pure digitality, Simon deploys metaphors—"vibrations" and "places"—literary allusion, and wordplay, rhyme, homophony, and double entendre to make his point, invoking sign systems whose considerable ambiguities and plays of meaning could not be rendered into a stable code. Even so, when the translation of Simon's consciousness into code occurs, it seems mostly to succeed, and he remains himself, the disappearance of his body from the scene seeming to have had no immediate effect on his experience of himself. Decorporation and encodedness appear to have preserved his essential subjectivity, which now speaks through the machine. At least for the moment, Simon's fantasy of pure encodedness comes true as the opera, somewhat too easily, answers the question Jean-François Lyotard raised, in 1988, in *The Posthuman*: "Can thought go on without a body?"[50]

Simon is not the first to have articulated this desire. Indeed, from its very inception, in the Macy Conferences on Cybernetics from 1943 to 1954, cybernetics has attempted to articulate a "theory of communication and control" that would "appl[y] equally to animals, humans, and machines." As Hayles goes on to explain early in her book *How We Became Posthuman* (1999), "to succeed," cybernetic theorists

> needed a theory of information [...], a model of neural functioning that showed how neurons worked as information-processing systems [...], computers that processed binary code and that could conceivably reproduce themselves, thus reinforcing the analogy with binary systems [...], and a visionary who could articulate the larger implications of the cybernetic paradigm and make clear its cosmic significance [...]. The result of this breathtaking enterprise was [...] a new way of looking at human beings. Henceforth, humans were to be seen primarily as information-processing entities who are *essentially* similar to intelligent machines.[51]

This reduction of human thought and consciousness—of experience and of itself—would eventually make it possible for Hans Moravec, in 1988, to theorize the possibility of completely translating human consciousness into binary code and uploading (or downloading, depending on one's perspective) that code into computer systems, thus achieving a machinic immortality.

Hayles recalls her own skeptical response upon first encountering Moravec's work, a skepticism that echoes Evvy and Miranda's hesitation in the face of Simon's will-to-digitality. Thus Hayles:

> [Moravec] invents a fantasy scenario in which a robot surgeon [...] read[s] the information in each molecular layer [of the brain] as it is stripped away and transferring the information into a computer. At the end of the operation, the cranial cavity is empty, and the patient, now inhabiting the metallic body of the computer, wakes to find his consciousness exactly the same as before.
>
> How, I asked myself, was it possible for someone of Moravec's obvious intelligence to believe that mind could be separated from

body? Even assuming such a separation was possible, how could anyone think that consciousness in an entirely different medium would remain unchanged, as if it had no connection to embodiment?[52]

As Hayles notes later, Moravec's view of human consciousness as information relies on a definition of information that made it "calcula[ble] as the same value regardless of the contexts in which it was embedded," a definition, which "divorced it from meaning" for the sake of mathematical expressibility.[53] "*Taken out of context*," Hayles explains, "the definition allowed information to be conceptualized as if it were an entity that can flow unchanged between different material substrates, as when Moravec envisions the information contained in a brain being downloaded into a computer":

> Ironically, this reification of information is enacted through the same kind of decontextualizing moves that the theory uses to define information as such. The theory decontextualizes information; Moravec decontextualizes the theory. Thus, a simplification necessitated by engineering considerations becomes an ideology in which a reified concept of information is treated as if it were fully commensurate with the complexities of human thought.[54]

McCluhan obviously saw in 1964 what Moravec did not in 1988: That the abstraction of information from medium is only thinkable as a metaphor. And it is also something the Hamlet-speaker of *Hamletmachine* recognizes when he sees that by transferring his "data" into a digital system and becoming "machine," he might escape, *not preserve*, his humanity and the "part" he "won't play [...] anymore."[55]

In both the framed and framing narratives of their opera, Machover and Pinsky also raise questions about the possibility of the machine, however sophisticated, becoming able to understand human experience. The inability of the robots who open and close the opera to grasp death or the motivations that led their human programmers to require them to continually reproduce their performance of Simon, Evvy, Miranda, and Nicholas's last moments together suggests that both mortality and theatrical representation lie beyond their virtual grasp. Moreover, in taking machine communication out of the realm of silent code silently exchanged via radio waves or fiber-optic cable, and instantiating it in human speech, Pinsky's libretto reintroduces the ambiguity and play of language, the very sign system whose human limitations cybernetics has been trying to overcome all along. Their speech thus emerges as a concession to the human practice of staged performance.

Within the framed narrative, in a long scene in which Evvy begs for the now digital Simon's touch, longing for the physical intimacy she can no longer share with her uploaded husband, she at times seems close to reexperiencing his physical presence, manifested as a huge, harp-like metal apparatus that descends over her, under which she lies supine and undulating in ecstasy as she sings. However, following a final request for his touch, as she engages in what on stage suggests masturbation, and not interpersonal intimacy, she verbalizes her awareness that her just-concluded moment of sexual ecstasy took place at a distance from Simon, who has not taken part in it: her aria turns away from touch and toward memory, giving the final word on the limits of the human–machine interface. Intimacy is absent, a memory, relegated to a past in which Evvy can only recall Simon's embodiment, even as Simon, now silent, seems to have disengaged.

While Evvy's longing leads her finally to accept Simon's invitation to join him in his digital world, Miranda remains in the fallen, increasingly chaotic, violent world of embodied humans, right up the ambiguous end of the framed narrative, when in a flash of light, the robot's reenactment ends before we learn whether Miranda has accepted death and suffering as conditions of authentic humanity by remaining in her embodied form or has given into the call of digital immortality. Again, the opera wavers on the question of the degree to which the burdens and perils of embodiment along with its emotions and sensations are truly essential to being fully human. It thus pushes back against the reductive certainties of cybernetics Hayles describes.

Indeed, Machover, himself a member of MIT's Media Lab, in choosing to compose an opera on these themes, situated Pinsky's words and his own expressive music in a genre whose conventions emphasize embodiment. Diane Paulus's stage direction and Karole Armitage's choreography for the 2010 Monte Carlo production, reproduced for the 2014 Dallas Opera's broadcast production, emphasize the movements and limitations of the performing body, requiring the four singers to maintain their vocal and breath control while variously climbing the set elements, lying on the stage floor, being carried by other performers, or crawling and writhing. As theories of embodied performance remind us again and again, the experience of the singers' vocal mastery is irreducible, untranslatable into linguistic sign systems, let alone binary digital code, as is suggested by the distortion James Maddalena's voice, in the original production, and Robert Orth's, in the 2014 restaging, undergo once Simon has entered the machine.

And so, even as *Death and the Powers* imagines a future in which Moravec's conception of a post-human, disembodied consciousness—and, by extension, the entire fantasy project of cybernetics—is technically possible, it continuously reminds us of the limits of that vision by emphasizing embodiment and voice in its performance; evincing skepticism, regret, and confusion in the framed and framing dialogue; and invoking poetry and wordplay as part of a sign system against which digital code cannot prevail. Even the robots acquiesce to the conventions of embodied performance, offering a mechanized approximation of a bow during the final curtain call.

Despite the overt and subtle ways in which *Death and the Powers* suggests the limits of, and the possibilities of resistance against a purely digital conception of the post-human, media coverage, interviews, and reviews also invite a fascinated admiration for the technologies its production deploys and represents. Philip Kennicott reports in *Opera News* that the opera's "small orchestra" is "complemented by computers, a complex array of speakers and sophisticated electronics" to produce the soundscape of a work whose "technological ambition is high: Machover and Pinsky want the theater itself to be suffused with the personality and life force of the absent Simon Powers, as if he were psychically inhabiting the theatrical space."[56] Writing for the *Sunday Times of London*, Robbie Hudson quotes Machover's remarks on the advanced technology designed to "transmit [...] human gesture through time and space."[57] It does so, according to Machover, writing for the *New York Times* Opinionator blog, by deploying a set designed to

> translate and amplify Simon Powers's human presence, challenging current limits of our ability to measure and interpret all the subtleties of great performance. The techniques currently being developed are already yielding surprising results, turning elegantly refined gestures, barely perceptible touch, and the gentlest breath into sounds, shapes and movements that convey personality and feeling without looking or seeming exactly like a human being. It is a new kind of instrument, and we are learning how to play it.[58]

Machover calls the resulting human–computer interface "Disembodied Performance," explaining that "[w]hen the actor playing Simon is backstage singing," after Powers has disappeared bodily into the system,

> he is monitored by computer vision, vocal analysis and a host of sensors that measure everything from posture to muscle tension to breathing patterns. Together they capture his emotional state, which is infused into the stage through lighting, images, sound and robotics. The set emotes.[59]

If this description sounds a little far-fetched, it is. Simply viewing and listening to the opera, one is not aware of this offstage interface, the inputs and outputs of monitors and sensors. The movement of the set elements, the sound effects, and the lighting appear just as one would imagine they would if they were controlled in more conventional ways, by technicians or preprogrammed computers. The only way to *experience* this level of technological sophistication is to know about it, through publicity, news media, or other framing texts—which is to say, not to experience it as such, except as an intellectual awareness that technology's effects are, indeed, technological.

As if aware of the impossibility of a machine phenomenology, Machover, the MIT Media Lab, and The Dallas Opera presented a live-stream matinee production on February 16, 2014, which allowed remote viewers to using the Powers Live smartphone application to "receive […] additional audio, video, and multimedia," according to the sidebar text of Pio Barone Lumaga's "Dialogue" with Machover.

The added content allowed audience members to virtually experience the main character's thoughts and bring the sights and sounds of the live performance in Dallas "within reach." Using the mobile app, remote audiences could affect *The Moody Foundation Chandelier's* illumination and motion in real time during significant moments in the opera. The audience seated in the Dallas Opera, Winspear Opera House felt the presence of others watching the opera around the world as they witnessed the chandelier's dramatic changes.[60]

This Milgram-esque experiment with interactivity surely did not result in the felt "presence" in the auditorium of the remote viewers; the claim that it did can only be read as an excess of phenomenological wishful thinking. But it also lays bare the anxieties that arise when an opera is rendered robotic, if only marginally so, and when the human is seen to have diminished in its ability to have an effect on its world through the exercise of its agency by means of its organic presence in space and time.

Paratextual fascination with the machineries of stage production also shaped reception of *Spider-Man: Turn Off the Dark*. By the time this extravagant musical opened at Broadway's Foxwood's Theatre on March 15, 2011, it had already become one of the most talked and written about productions in Broadway history. Paul David Hewson, lead singer and lyricist for the Irish rock band U2, under his stage name Bono, and his bandmate David Howell Evans, known as The Edge, had been commissioned to compose the show's angular, booming, electric score. The show's creator and first director, Julie Taymor, awarded a MacArthur "Genius" Grant for her work on plays, musicals, operas, and film, had already achieved Broadway fame with her 1996 staging of Disney's *The Lion King* using puppets wielded by dancers and puppeteers. During *Spider-Man*'s many months of rehearsal, reports of acrobats' career-threatening injuries, enormous overbudget spending, fundraising woes, and strife among the creative team and producers created buzz on scale more in line with a smash hit than a faltering production yet to see the lights of opening night. When news that Taymor had been relieved of her directorial duties (she also cowrote the book and designed the masks) appeared, speculation swirled that the production would be canceled before it opened. When the show did finally open, Taymor was billed as having provided "Original Direction," with her replacement, Philip William McKinley, brought in to stanch Taymor's excesses and complete the production, listed as the show's director, registering only a trace of the acrimonious transfer of power that had been covered so fully in entertainment and mainstream media alike.

Patrick Healy, working sometimes with Kevin Flynn, covered the "drama behind the [...] musical" that "seem[ed] like theatre of the absurd" for the *New York Times* in 2010 and 2011.[61] Below a headline declaring the show "A Broadway Superlative for All the Wrong Reasons," Healy and Flynn reported, in March 2011, that the show's budget, estimated at $31 million in February 2009, had grown to "$70 million and counting" in just over two years, as "budgets were busted and spending soared."[62] Besides the financial bloat, four members of the cast had been hurt, three principals had left the show, and scenery regularly malfunctioned in the record-breakingly long preview period.[63] The drama had begun quite early in the production and rehearsal process: the *New York Post*'s Michael Riedel reported, in May 2010, that the production had nearly been canceled when five months after the show had been cast and rehearsals begun, the producer "had no money to pay" the cast. *Spider-Man*, Riedel went on to report, "was $25 million in the hole." As a result, "[a]ll work on 'Spider-Man'—construction, casting, marketing, ticket sales—was suspended." According to Riedel, the creative team was "furious," "embarrassed," and "shocked."[64]

The controversy over the show's financial mismanagement and the fall of Julie Taymor, characterized by Healy as "the theatre world's star auteur," was fueled by—and in turn added fuel to—interest in the creative aspects of the production itself. When George Tsypin joined the production as the show's set designer, Robert Hughes offered a profile of the artist in the *New York Observer*.[65] Noting that the musical had been the "subject of endless theatrical speculation," particularly over whether the creative team would be able to pull off the kind of "spectacle that [would] play to crowds long enough to recoup its considerable investment," Hughes reports that Tsypin would attempt to offer audiences an "immersive, environmental" experience of New York City's skyline that allowed them to see the city as if they themselves were swinging from rooftop to rooftop.[66] Describing the planned design as "pop-up," Tsypin said that, on Broadway, "you have to have a big effect every two or three minutes" and that he set out to "creat[e] a machine" that would provide these effects to secure the show's longevity.[67]

Tsypin's invocation of "a machine" is important because it highlights the degree to which the technical apparatus of Broadway theatre is essential to a show's financial viability. Those aspects of a production often thought of as secondary, peripheral, marginal, or invisible, such as the design choices, creative deliberations, financial arrangements, and rehearsals that precede opening night, are central to Hughes's piece, which itself helped to sustain curiosity and raise speculation about the musical. Notably, Hughes's profile of Tsypin appeared more than eight months before the show's repeatedly delayed opening, and so it was, itself, part of the peripheral apparatus of media and marketing shaping audience's expectations and, by extension, their experiences.

Glen Berger, the original scriptwriter, in his tell-all retrospective account of *Spider-Man*'s complex, acrimonious, and halting journey from concept to production also repeatedly invokes the machinic aspects of the work. For instance, he describes the difficulties in programming the computers controlling the cables supporting the aerial acrobatics throughout the show and in deploying the automated set elements that frequently failed to operate as expected.[68] Indeed, the theatre's technological capabilities became the primary factor in the eventual gutting and reconceiving of the whole production, giving the lie to Rebecca Rey's humanist optimism, in the context of

DeLillo's *Valparaiso*, about the degree to which people are in control of technology, discussed in Chapter 3.

Striking is the way Berger imagines *Spider-Man* not just as a literal machine for producing stage effects, but also as a cosmic machine in a moment of epiphany after a particularly grueling production meeting:

> What IS this place? I have arrhythmia. My arms are prickling. I thought I was so smart. I was going to save the show. But there IS no show! Spider-Man the Musical *was never* Spider-Man the Musical. *I see that now. It's always been nothing more than a diabolical machine built by the gods to teach humility. And I'm trapped in the dead center of its workings.*[69]

Recalling Cocteau, we hear the echo of his preamble to *The Infernal Machine*, discussed in Chapter 1. Unlike Cocteau's machine, however, *Spider-Man*'s "diabolical machine" is not the staged story, but the backstage drama, the machinations, betrayals, and dysfunctions that precede, surround, and threaten to derail the production altogether. Berger's diabolical machine is an offstage machine, part of the (dys)function of the theatre apparatus at a nearly (but not quite) metaphorical level.

Likewise, the complications and controversies that preceded the show's opening—again, ancillary to the actual quality and success of the production—drew attention away from what we might call, for the sake of convenience, the content of the piece: the music, lyrics, script, acting (such as it was), plot, acrobatics, and so on. Instead, the public were invited from the outset to fixate on the periphery, or what Genette would have termed the "paratexts" of the production.[70] As the Introduction explains, Genette's term refers in its original 1987 context to the various texts, often presumed secondary, that frame a central text: prefaces, forewords, epilogues, dedications, acknowledgments, tables of context, cover copy, author biographies, indices, epigraphs, and all the other elements of a text conventionally considered part of the exergue. These outworks are traditionally overlooked as objects of interpretation and analysis, and yet they are essential for making possible and, often, for stabilizing the main, central text—a novel, say, or a memoir—and making it legible not just as a text, but as *the* text. The preproduction publicity and buzz function as paratexts as extensions of the stage machineries that include guy wires, light boards, windlasses, pulleys, grooves, sound systems, and the architecture of the theatre itself that we pretend not to see when absorbed into a show, when we "suspend our disbelief."[71] The term *paratext* also highlights the salience of the news, gossip, and reportage that preceded the production, as well as reviews, interviews, profiles, and playbills that frame the production and, far from truly revealing the behind-the-scenes workings of the production, help to heighten "a kind of mystery," to quote Alice Goodman's Nixon's fixation on news media from *Nixon in China*, discussed at length in Chapter 3.

As it turns out, the way the preproduction buzz surrounding *Spider-Man* focused public attention on the show's paratexts and peripheries trained audiences-to-be in how to watch the performance itself. For, in fact, the real show is not the worn, hackneyed, contradictory, and entirely circumstantial, accidental, and situational series of events that comprise what one can call *plot* only in an access of post-Aristotelian generosity; rather, the real show in the Foxwoods Theatre was everything else. For instance, not only was no attempt made to hide the computer-guided aerial rigging and harnesses that suspended the numerous acrobats playing Spider-Man above the stage and the audience, but the stagehands responsible for catching and launching our hero from platforms just inside the torms were fully in view as well. Ushers in plain sight opened and closed doors to allow one stunt-double (or triple or quadruple) Spider-Man to exit the auditorium just as another would appear leaping from the catwalk or scaling the pop-up skyline. So central to the total effect of the show were the acrobatics of no fewer than nine Spider-Men, by my count, that the prime seating area, traditionally referred to as the Dress Circle in most theatres, was temporarily renamed the "Jump Circle" at the Foxwoods, because it comprised the seats from which one could get the best view of *Spider-Man*'s aerial choreography.

The acrobats' rigging and their attendants in the wings were not the only starkly visible peripherals during the show. In an early scene depicting Peter Parker's metamorphosis from gangly nerd into his new agile and powerful persona, the walls of his bedroom, made of lightweight carbon fiber, were held up by stagehands who manipulated them to accommodate his literal wall climbing. The room quakes and trembles, seeming on the verge of coming apart, as wonder-boy Peter bounces from one wall to the next and clings to the ceiling.[72] Soon after the bedroom scene, when Peter enters a prize-fight against a local heavyweight, his opponent is represented by a giant-sized, inflatable dummy, held up and animated by an unapologetically apparent stagehand.

The obvious apparatus literally behind these effects joins with other effects whose sources are less apparent: Projections of scenery, crowd scenes, and abstract colors and lights on towering obelisk-like LED screens are reminiscent of Adolphe Appia's monumental stage designs and Gordon Craig's patented screen system a century earlier,[73] while a treadmill embedded in the stage floor allows Peter and Mary Jane to walk from urban Manhattan to the modest residential suburb where they both live without traversing stage space. Although they are less apparent, as compared to the overt and sometimes cartoonish effects mentioned above, these are not invisible mechanisms producing visible effects. Even if they had been intended to achieve invisibility, the fact that the preproduction press and more visible aspects of the technical apparatus had already trained us to look for, and then to *look at* these kinds of sleight of hand made it difficult not to notice even the most subtle of the stage technologies. This shift in focus and its effect on training audiences to keep an eye on the apparatus recapitulates the fascinated admiration for stage technologies discussed above with respect to *Death and the Powers*, and it reinforces the machinic spectacle discussed in Chapter 3: the sense of "vibe" that one gets from the spectacle of technical facility.

One particular example, I hope, will suffice to demonstrate this point. In conventional musicals, the orchestra responsible for producing the music is situated in a pit, the recessed and sunken area beneath and somewhat in front of the stage apron. Even in blackout scenes, the faint lights of the music stands glow in the auditorium's darkness, and the conductor's back and baton are often quite visible from the front rows and balconies. Apart from acoustic concerns, the pit is positioned between audience and stage so that the singers on stage can follow the conductor while still singing and acting outward, toward the audience. Even Richard Wagner, who in designing his Bayreuth Festspielhaus, which opened in 1876, maintained the practice of placing the pit before the stage, even though he wanted to mask its appearance as much as possible to deemphasize the representational quality of his productions.

During *Spider-Man*, as it was staged at the Foxwoods in October 2011, the orchestra did not occupy an open pit. Rather, closed-circuit television monitors mounted to the front of the balconies and facing the stage carried a live broadcast of the conductor, so that actors could follow her lead without her being visible to the audience. For my own part, however, once I noticed the television screens, it was difficult for me not to watch them; even when I focused on the performance, I remained aware of her televisual presence in my peripheral vision. The presence I would have ignored had it been situated directly before me became a kind of uncanny return of the repressed haunting the auditorium. Only at the very end of the show, during the curtain call, was the conductor acknowledged: An image of her in action, accepting the audience's applause, was projected onto the onstage screens.

This moment of recursivity—the image of that which is usually visible, now invisible, suddenly become hyper-visible, but mediated—points to another register of recursivity shared between *Death and the Powers* and *Spider-Man*: Namely, that both plays are both *about* and *enabled by* code, binary information transferred in tiny packets, like the fragments that *Hamletmachine* condenses. And yet, a strange kind of dissonance exists between *Spider-Man*'s celebratory spectacle of the theatre's apparatus, on the one hand, and the apparent ambiguity of its storyline toward scientific inquiry and its technological applications, on the other. For Peter Parker's transformation in *Spider-Man* comes about when, visiting the lab of bioengineer Norman Osborn with his high-school science class, he is bitten by a genetically engineered spider. Osborn, an echo of Pinsky and Machover's Simon Powers, and his associates, including his wife, Emily, have been experimenting with various means, including radiation and genetic modification, to encourage spiders to evolve—to increase in strength, speed, and sensory perception.

These experiments, Osborn explains to Parker and his class in a song titled "D.I.Y World," are meant to yield information that will help humans survive in a world beset by natural disasters, climate change, and pervasive violence—a world not unlike the one in which Machover and Pinsky's Miranda remains after her father's digital disintegration. Invoking what Judith Roof calls the "poetics of DNA," Osborn argues that left to natural selection alone, evolution takes too long;[74] if you want to evolve, you have to "do it yourself." Despite the warnings of Emily and others that he may be moving too fast, and regardless of the fact that increasingly nervous investors are withholding much-needed capital to pay for further refinements to his method (a moment of accidental meta-theatre, given the show's financial troubles), Osborn presses forward. Instead of accepting buyout offers from Viper Corporation, a government contractor developing biological weapons for the US military, Osborn submits to the experimental process himself. The trial goes badly wrong, resulting in an explosion that kills Emily, and transforming Osborn into the Green Goblin, a glowing, winged, lizard-like humanoid bent on unleashing pandemonium throughout New York City.

Osborn is presented, throughout the first act, as a mostly sympathetic character, beset by the original fatal flaw: hubris. His motives are entirely humanitarian, as he searches for a technological intervention into what he sees as humanity's otherwise disastrous and unavoidable self-destruction. And, in resisting Viper's offers and continuing his research despite the departure of his top scientists, Osborn appears selfless and altruistic, if somewhat precipitate in his actions and obsessively driven by his foregone conclusions. Within and outside the superhero genre, Osborn's character is a common type, and the narrative of a scientific experiment gone wrong frequently serves as the backstory for the creation of heroes and villains alike. But, in *Spider-Man: Turn Off the Dark*, even as we are invited to lament Osborn's transformation and Emily's death, we are also given to understand that scientific inquiry and discovery hold the key to humanity's survival. Osborn's vision of a future cataclysm hastened by a political and cultural resistance to warnings about global warming remain unquestioned throughout the performance; indeed, the monologue in which he figures forth the various disasters ahead is the most rhetorically compelling and memorable speech in the entire production.

At the level of plot and characterization, then, *Spider-Man* evinces ambivalence about scientific discovery and technological innovation. Still, Osborn's commitment to using scientific means to solve problems themselves discovered and described by scientists, and his resistance to the corporatization of his findings present themselves as positive traits: They invite us to believe in scientific inquiry and methodology. However, the zealotry with which Osborn pursues his research and his refusal to moderate his ambitions and his timeline to accommodate basic methodological protocols reminds us that those who pursue scientific research are imperfect humans. As a popular depiction of the visionary but obsessed researcher, Osborn offers the audience warnings about the trustworthiness of science and technology.

These warnings, though, are at odds with the show's manifestly and unambiguously celebratory disposition toward stage technology evinced by the visible production apparatus deployed throughout *Spider-Man*. These two sites of technological sophistication—diegetic and extra-diegetic—are unevenly matched. By the beginning of the second act, the production has entirely forgotten about Osborn's science. He appears, now as the Green Goblin, near the end of the intermission, as a genial, witty, wry lounge-singer, cracking wise about audience members still visibly taking their seats and even crooning "I'll Take Manhattan" as he plays a giant green piano. Thus begins the more technologically sophisticated of the show's two acts, no longer concerned with the ethical ambiguities of Osborn's research, opting instead for the one-dimensional, cartoon spectacle of the Green Goblin.

Predictably, chaos ensues as the Green Goblin and his minions wreak havoc all over the city. Spider-Man's fight to restore order culminates in an acrobatic extravaganza atop the Chrysler Building, which rises from the stage to offer the illusion of a bird's-eye, three-dimensional view of the Manhattan streetscape in what was clearly to be the show's coup de théâtre.

The transformations from human to superhero or monster in *Spider-Man* mirror the transformational aspirations of Müller's Hamlet-speaker and Ophelia-speaker and of Pinsky and Machover's Simon Powers.[75] In doing so, they highlight the way theater and performance in the postmodern era imagine Jameson's notions of the "new organs" and the advanced "sensorium" demanded by the increasingly nonintuitive dynamics of global capitalist culture and the decentering and automation of postmodern environments. These imaginary, aspirational transformations are linked to advanced technology in two ways: First, actual transformations in technology enabled by the digital revolution make them thinkable and, second, technological advancement in theatre makes them representable.

In *Spider-Man*, then, as in *Hamletmachine* and *Death and the Powers*, the framing/framed relationship heightens our awareness of the technologies of theatrical production and reproduction. *Hamletmachine's* frame text, the absent or deferred *Hamlet* of Shakespeare, is invoked, and indeed produced, by the performance-as-machine, whose function is to create an infinite regression of infinitely self-reproducing Hamlet machines. In *Death and the Powers*, the framing narrative stages robots who inexplicably speak in human language to express their own inability to understand the motivations of the human characters they are about to represent in a repeated ritual performance; and in the case of *Spider-Man*, the framing narrative is provided by the backstage and headline drama of the production's conception, rehearsal, and preview period, itself marked by the malfunction of stage machineries and which remains as a trace in the visible and audible machineries during live performance. Meanwhile, the story is precisely about the chaos that ensues when techno-scientific experiments go wrong, offering an ironic reflection on the production process itself. The self-referentiality is, arguably, a species of metatheatre, an ouroboros recursively devouring its own representational dynamics in order to reproduce them. The resulting mise en abyme—as distinct from a mise en scène—gestures toward the emerging fractal and spatial logic of 1970s postmodernity, themselves enabled by the digital revolution in computing and cybernetic theories of information, intelligence, and the human.

To conclude this chapter, I want now to turn my attention to the twentieth century's first disport with post-human drama. Karel Čapek's *Rossum's Universal Robots* (1920), commonly called *R.U.R.*, marks the first instance of the use of the term "robot" to refer to mechanically produced, artificially intelligent humanoid entities. Čapek's play, for all its concern about the impasses created by the invention of a race of robots intelligent enough to gain self-awareness and, finally, to experience emotional attachments to one another and a desire to procreate and sustain themselves, is remarkably simple in its staging. Most of its action takes place in the offices and rooms of the Rossum company, unit sets that employ relatively simple mechanisms to effect scene changes from act to act. The robots are played by human actors, and the play's expository scene emphasizes that robots are made of organic materials synthetically produced: nerve and muscle fiber, organs and blood, bones and cartilage that are in every way indistinguishable from those of humans. At the same time, the method by which Old Rossum first successfully created these tissues is intentionally vague in the dialogue, and the last scene of the play capitalizes on this vagueness as it is motivated by the search for the original plans. Machines are frequently referred to in the play—gunships, factory components, generators, communications networks, and electrified fences—but they remain offstage; with the exception of a pistol and some office machines, no piece of advanced technology ever appears on stage.

What strikes me as important about *R.U.R.*, prescient as it may seem, is that it offers the inverse of what *Spider-Man*, *Death and the Powers*, and *Hamletmachine* offer: namely, *R.U.R.* dramatizes the complications that arise when technology becomes human. By contrast, these three late works investigate the complications that arise when the human becomes technology: the databank, the machine, the robot, the cyborg, and the genetically enhanced organism. This inversion of the machine/human dynamic of becoming echoes a change in the way we conceive of theatre practice itself. If modernist theatre pieces like *The Gas Heart*, *The Eiffel Tower Wedding Party*, and *The Future Is in Eggs* deploy the human body and its apparatus of speech and movement to critique techno-rationalism and enact machine effects, such works as *Valparaiso*, *Death and the Powers*, and *Spider-Man* deploy the machine to critique traditional notions of the human and to enact humanity effects. Other plays mark moments along this trajectory of human/machine inversion in theatre, including *Death of a Salesman* or *Nixon in China*, where we see an uneasy equilibrium between machine and human in the deployment of the theatre's representational capabilities.

To be sure, this formulation of a linear narrative of theatrical evolution elides the complexities, ambiguities, and contradictions that a cross-section of theatre practices at any historical moment would immediately reveal. After *Spider-Man*, it would still be possible for a play like *War Horse*, whose effects are largely produced by onstage puppeteers manually manipulating wooden figures and figurines, to leave audience after audience in tears at the same National Theatre in London where, in 2017, a massively teched stage version of Paddy Chayefsky and Sidney Lumet's 1976 film *Network* would premiere. Each year, the Edinburgh Festival's technologically sophisticated mainstage productions vie with the simple barroom and basement stagings of the Edinburgh Fringe. Likewise, Bernard Shaw's and Henrik Ibsen's plays, with often simple box sets, were produced at the end of the nineteenth century in private theatre clubs simultaneously with sensational melodrama, complete with spectacular stage effects, on stage at the popular patent theatres. The synchronic diversity and stylistic divergence among theatre and drama, even when we consider only Western European and North American traditions, militates against metanarratives or grand theories about the arc of technological development in theatres and plays. Complicating the matter further, as the Introduction notes, theatre does not dispense with old ways of doing things even as it adopts and adapts cutting-edge innovations: manually controlled cables and pulleys are put to work alongside computerized light boards and digital sound production. In short, of all the arts, theatre is the one whose development over the years is perhaps the one least likely to be easily summarized in a few broad strokes; ironically, theatre is also the one that retains its earliest forms most recognizably.

And yet, theatre is susceptible to same forces that shape cultures at every level. In the developed West, a particularly powerful force of change has been the shift from analog to digital conceptions not just of information and industrial production, but of identity and value. In viewing late-twentieth- and early-twenty-first-century performance as manifesting the effects of digitality, we can begin to see how the concerns of plays that both dramatize and rely on technological innovation have registered and reacted to broad developments in the human–machine interface, whether literal, figurative, or hybrids of the two. The becoming-monster, becoming-robot, and becoming-machine enacted by *Spider-Man*, *Death and the Powers*, and *Hamletmachine* respectively, suggest a tendency in theatre toward the increasing integration of the human and the technological, an intensification of a integration already in process with the introduction of the first painted backdrop and first god descending via machine onto the Attic stage.

Coda: Medium, Machinery, and the Present Moment

To reflect on the technological dynamics of modern dramatic theatre at this moment in global history seems an exercise in nostalgia and blind optimism simultaneously. At the time of this writing—May 2020—theatres large and small around the world have been darkened by the spread of a novel coronavirus and the outbreak of the disease it causes, COVID-19. The threat of further infection, compounded by uncertainties about how exactly the virus spreads, who is vulnerable to it, and even how many have been infected and by fierce debate over what measures national and local governments should take to contain it, would seem to relegate discussions of any performing art to the margins of relevancy. The near certainty that this outbreak will not be the last of its kind, that the rapidly thawing permafrost has in store for us immunological challenges last experienced by our ice-age ancestors, raises the specter of the eventual end of collaborative art forms of all kinds, if not of humanity: In such a world, what use is the practice of live theatre, much less the academic study of it?

As I reflect on these questions, I am sitting in my den. It is late at night. The windows that surround me on three sides reveal only darkness outside. With Beckett's Krapp, I could well muse that the "world might be uninhabited." But noises off give the lie to this musing: The distant purr of traffic attests to the persistence of mechanized civilization. Closer at hand, the blinking lights of the internet modem remind me of the interconnections between my work, the very labor of research and writing, and the hugely diverse technological apparatus that makes it possible, particularly when libraries and archives remain closed. I have become aware of the battery-powered analog clock marking the seconds, of the almost inaudible hum of the incandescent lamp I am working by, and of the contrast in the quality of light between it and the indirect LED lighting recessed behind the room's crown molding. Nearby, my smartphone rests, a virtual portal into a world I am wary of venturing into physically, and a few feet further on, the only somewhat less smart television gazes blankly into the room. In the middle distance, the purr of the refrigerator and the basso continuo of the house's ventilation fade into and out of my awareness between tracks of the recording of Mozart's *Cosí Fan Tutte* I have put on to accompany my writing. Right now, Anna Sophie von Otter, Renée Fleming, and Michael Petrusi's digitized voices, recorded in the early 1990s, are singing the tender first act trio *Soave Sia Il Vento*, and on cue, the gentle breeze of the here and now rattles the louvers of the venetian blinds. It strikes me that my own home, during quarantine, has taken on the feel of the empty theatre the opening pages of this book evoked—"the still dance and dumb show ... of a millennia-long technological accrual," a phrase I wrote over two years before this book would be published. Even the drawstrings on the windows' venetian blinds resemble the rigging and guy wires that hang motionless about the quiet theatre's "wooden O."

In short, I am plugged in, alone as I am—connected to all kinds of machines: literal and metaphorical; simple, analog, digital; time machines, information machines, economic machines, political machines, transportation machines, entertainment machines, and delivery machines. My earbuds connect me to the digitally remastered sound of a piece of music recorded almost thirty years ago in a live performance, a piece composed for the Viennese stage over two hundred years earlier. And so I am also connected to the considerable technology of the classical operatic stage, which had already proved capable of producing elaborate effects of sea, wind, and weather. The cover of this very book speaks to that kind of trans-spatio-temporal rhizome: Robert Brill's set for Charles Gounod's *Faust* (1859) as performed at the New York Metropolitan Opera in its 2011–12 season figures Mephistophelean magic as a Manhattan-project-era deployment of nuclear physics within a mid-century military–industrial complex. The technologies of everyday life at the beginning of the third decade of the twenty-first century, taken so easily for granted, exceed the wildest of wild dreams of those inventors and "magicians"—John Dee and his astrology; Athasios Kircher and his acoustics; and Giovan Battista della Porta and his catoptrics—who elaborated seemingly unlimited ancient possibilities of sound and light in early modern and renaissance Europe.[1] In short, the deep time of theatre is part of what Siegfried Zielinski calls the "deep time of media," itself part of the deep time of Anthropocene technology.

Staging Technology's view of the way theatre's technologies imbricate military–industrial and media technologies may help address the question I raised at the beginning of this reflection: Namely, in the present world-historical moment, what is the point in investigating the technical dynamics of the rarefied and hermetic world of experimental modern drama created for live performance? For it allows us to begin to see not just the systematicity at work in the theatre, but also the theatrics at work in the everyday systems we inhabit. Our increasingly ubiquitous masks, the always carefully scripted and lighted presidential and prime ministerial soliloquies, and the manifestly staged executive administrations (especially in the United States and the United Kingdom) that have emerged during this global pandemic have made a theatre of public discourse and daily life. And that theatre articulates to the technologies we hope will save us: vaccines and treatments, personal protective equipment, ventilators and tests, and the mobilization of a massive global biotech, pharmaceutical, and transport infrastructure necessary for building the *machina* out of which some bioengineered *deus* might emerge to set things to right in answer to our imprecations.

Perhaps this, finally, is what we perceive when we begin to see dramatic theatre in this way: the ubiquity of the medium and the machine behind every effect. If "all the world is a stage" in the twenty-first century, it is not just because we are "players" who "pla[y] many parts." The world is a stage because the interplay between social and political representation and the media and technologies that enable it recapitulates that of the dramatic stage. If we are to "'cleanse the foul body of th'infected world," to continue this Shakespearean line of inquiry, we must train our gaze beyond the effects of representation—whether theatrical or ideological—and onto the apparatus that subtends it to reveal the sutures that hold ideologies and their discourses together. We must analyze these dynamics, in the etymological sense of breaking them up, and ask what values, assumptions, biases, and beliefs already inhere within the machineries and media that subtend the *opsis* of our sublunary existence.

That is certainly the lesson Tzara, Cocteau, and Ionesco teach us: to see the world of the stage and the stage of the world as part of a perhaps "infernal machine" whose workings emerge dimly in speech and thought and shape our habits and habitats and to retrain our gaze to see the unfamiliar in more familiar workings. Treadwell, Miller, Rice, and Gomez warn us of the dangers of turning away from an awareness of techno-rationality's ubiquity and toward nostalgia and longing for access to unmediated, unregulated human experience. In staging the mediation of media, Brecht and Weill, Adams and Goodman, DeLillo, and Fugard help us to recognize how already technologized and mediated are the aspirations, hopes, and desires we think of as quintessentially human: The very idea of the human is already a cyborg formation. And, as Beckett, Pinter, and Sircar demonstrate, that formation is always staged already, part of a recursive dynamic in which the life/theatre binary loops and intertwines. Perhaps, in a time of coronavirus, the fallen worlds of *Spider-Man*, *Hamletmachine*, and *Death and the Powers* serve as warnings about the fragility of the human as being and as idea, recapitulating as they do *R.U.R.*'s post-human conception of representation and meaning, where agency remains as a beleaguered trace in a techno-biosphere where not just the human and nonhuman but the organic and inorganic have lost their relative salience.

Dramatic theatre, in this view, is not just a microcosm of the "real" world that "hold[s], as 'twere, the mirror up to nature." The theatre of our everyday lives is also a surgical theatre, where we watch as treatments variously succeed and fail, as the infected recover or die, and as the *agon* of medical discovery and experimentation carry on. And like the technotexts *Staging Technology* explores, this everyday theatre teaches us how to see and think and invites us to look beyond the scrim and painted scene to the mechanics that put the whole show in motion. Theatre, under the analytical gaze, allows us to practice seeing the machine behind the effects, the machine the very effects are deployed to obscure. And where that obscurity has proven particularly impenetrable, a fun house of machines within machines within machines, doubling and splitting as we encounter them, there my project has tried to press pause on what Jean Baudrillard has called "the precession of simulacra"—"substituting of the signs of the real for the real"—and to get to the meaning of the materiality that becomes visible when the spin and torque of the axes of representation are stilled by the analytical gaze.[2]

To conclude, I will simply express my hope that the relevance of *Staging Technology*'s critical project outlasts the topical relevance of this coda. At the same time, with that hope comes my conviction that the project it advances is one of critical importance beyond the narrow scope of theatre and drama studies. For, if the world is a stage, and the stage is a machine, then it follows that the world—our world—is itself more machine than we are often aware: *Hier ist der apparat. Steig ein!*

Notes

Introduction: Staging Technology

1 Bertolt Brecht, *Lindbergh's Flight*, trans. John Willett, in Bertolt Brecht, *Collected Plays*, ed. John Willett, vol. 3 (of 8), part 2 (London: Methuen, 1997).

2 See Clement Greenberg, "Towards a newer Laocoön," *Partisan Review* 7 (July–August 1949), 296–310; Johannes Birringer, *Theatre, Theory, Postmodernism* (Bloomington: Indiana University Press, 1991); Marshall McLuhan, *Understanding Media* (New York: McGraw-Hill, 1964).

3 See, for instance, Johannes Birringer, *Theatre, Theory, Postmodernism* (Bloomington: Indiana University Press, 1991), esp. chapters 8 and 9; Matthew Causey, *Theatre and Performance in Digital Culture: From Simulation to Embeddedness* (London: Routledge, 2006); Gabriella Giannachi, *Virtual Theatres: An Introduction* (London: Routledge, 2004); and the work of The Wooster Group and Pina Bausch's *Tanztheater Wuppertal*, among others. This vein of performance theory, with its emphasis on medium and mediated performance, differs from that of theorists who, drawing from cultural anthropology or phenomenology or both, focus their attention primarily on avant-garde performance traditions that seek to establish and sustain intersubjective copresence among their performers and spectators. For influential examples of this work, see Erika Fischer-Lichte, *The Transformative Power of Performance*, trans. Saskya Iris Jain, intro. Marvin Carlson (London: Routledge, 2008); Mladen Ovadija, *Dramaturgy of Sound in the Avant-Garde and Postdramatic Theatre* (Montreal: McGill-Queen's University Press, 2013); and the foundational work of Richard Schechner and Marvin Carlson. Hans-Thies Lehman's *Postdramatic Theatre* (trans. Karen Jürs-Munby) (London: Routledge, 2006) tends toward the latter tradition, but usefully examines the way the materials of theatre production, such as space and acoustics, both contribute to and emerge as effects of experimental performance.

4 Gerard Genette, *Paratexts: Thresholds of Interpretation*, trans. Jane E. Lewin (Cambridge: Cambridge University Press, 1997), 1, 2.
5 Genette, 1.
6 Michel Foucault, *The Archaeology of Knowledge and the Discourse on Language*, trans. A. M. Sheridan Smith (New York: Pantheon Books, 1972), 4–5.
7 See Gilles Deleuze and Félix Guattari, *A Thousand Plateaus*, trans. Brian Massumi (Minneapolis: University of Minnesota Press, 1987). The term "assemblage" recurs throughout the book, assuming slightly different meanings and applications each time. However, its introduction in the book's opening pages and my discussion of the term in more detail in Chapter 1 will give the reader a sense of the term's applicability to the present study (3–4).
8 See Deleuze and Guattari, *Kafka: Toward a Minor Literature*, trans. Dana Polan (Minneapolis: University of Minnesota Press, 1986), esp. 16–27.
9 Janet H. Murray, *Hamlet on the Holodeck: The Future of Narrative in Cyberspace* (Cambridge: MIT Press, [1997] 2017), 346.
10 N. Katherine Hayles, *Writing Machines* (Cambridge: MIT Press, 2002), 19.
11 Hayles, *Writing Machines*, 23, 22.
12 Hayles, *Writing Machines*, 25.
13 Foucault, 222.
14 Foucault, 222–3.
15 I am cognizant, at the same time, of performance studies approaches, like that of Elinor Fuchs, which, while they validate the subjective and intersubjective experiences of performers and audiences alike, wish to preserve signification as a central component of those experiences.
16 Dennis G. Jerz, *Technology in American Drama, 1920–1950: Soul and Society in the Age of the Machine* (Westport, CN: Greenwood Press, 2003).
17 Christopher Baugh, *Theatre, Performance, and Technology: The Development of Scenography in the Twentieth Century* (London: Palgrave Macmillan, 2005), 8.
18 Baugh, 1.
19 Karel Čapek, *R.U.R.*, in Josef and Karel Čapek, *R.U.R. and The Insect Play*, trans. P. Selver, adapt. Nigel Playfair (Oxford: Oxford University Press, 1961 [1923]); Mervyn Millar, *The Horse's Mouth: How Handspring and The National made War Horse*, 2nd ed. (London: National Theatre, 2011).

20 Una Chaudhuri, *Staging Place: The Geography of Modern Drama* (Ann Arbor: University of Michigan Press, 1995).
21 Chaudhuri, xi.

1 Avant-Garde Assemblages: Tristan Tzara, Jean Cocteau, and Eugène Ionesco

1 *"J'ai quitté Paris et même la France, parce que la tour Eiffel finissait par m'ennuyer trop."* Guy de Maupassant, *La Vie Errante*, transcribed from Paris: Paul Ollendorff, 1890 (La Bibliothèque électronique de Québec, À tous les vents: 447:1.01), accessed October 14, 2018, https://www.google.com/url?sa=t&rct=j&q=&esrc=s&source=web&cd=1&ved=2ahUKEwj4867gw4beAhXQ1FkKHQ9yCegQFjAAegQIDBAC&url=https%3A%2F%2Fbeq.ebooksgratuits.com%2Fvents%2FMaupassant_La_vie_errante.pdf&usg=AOvVaw2mpsRXNNgcsxiH4kBlildL, 5.
2 Dwight D. Eisenhower, "The farewell address: reading copy of the speech," Dwight D. Eisenhower Presidential Library, Museum, and Boyhood Home [DDE's Papers as President, Speech Series, Box 38, Final TV Talk (1); NAID # 594599] (January 17, 1961) accessed October 14, 2018, https://www.eisenhower.archives.gov/research/online-documents/farewell-address/reading-copy.pdf, [1].
3 Jean Cocteau, *Les Mariés de la Tour Eiffel* in Cocteau, *Theatre*, vol. 1, 8th ed. (Paris: Gallimard, 1948), 52.
4 For a discussion of the design, construction, and early history of the Eiffel Tower, see Barry Bergdoll, "Introduction," Lucien Hervé, *The Eiffel Tower: A Photographic Survey* (New York: Princeton Architectural Press, 2003), 7–16.
5 Cocteau, *Mariés*, 32–33: *"La Tour Eiffel est une monde comme Notre-Dame. C'est Notre-Dame de la rive gauche."*
6 The impression of ceaseless movement, created both by the complex interrelationship among girders and joists, on the one hand, and by the movement of the central elevator shuttling visitors to and from the tower's platforms, on the other, presages Jean Tinguely's metamechanic sculptures of the 1970s and 1980s and Alexander Calder's high modernist mobile sculptures and installations. This kinetic aesthetic almost certainly

informed Fredric Jameson's description of John Portman's Westin Bonaventure Hotel lobby's escalators and elevators: "Given their very real pleasures in Portman, particularly the [elevators], which the artist has termed 'gigantic kinetic sculptures' and which certainly account for much of the spectacle and excitement of the hotel interior [...] I believe one has to see such 'people movers' [...] as somewhat more significant than mere functions and engineering components. [...I]t seems to me that the escalators and elevators here henceforth replace movement but also, and above all, designate themselves as new reflexive signs and emblems of movement proper. Here the narrative stroll has been underscored, symbolized, reified, and replaced by a transportation machine which becomes the allegorical signifier of that older promenade we are no longer allowed to conduct on our own: and this is a dialectical intensification of the autoreferentiality of all modern culture, which tends to turn upon itself and designate its own cultural production as its content." See Fredric Jameson, *Postmodernism: The Cultural Logic of Late Capitalism* (Durham: Duke University Press), 42. See also my discussion of Don DeLillo's play *Valparaiso* in Chapter 3 and of post-human theatre in Chapter 5.

7 Cocteau, *Mariés*, 52: "*Ils parlent très fort, très vite et prononcent distinctement chaque syllabe.*"
8 For concise but no less comprehensive discussion of the relationship of the actorly body to the iconic representation of character as it has been imagined throughout the past three hundred years on the Western dramatic stage, see Fischer-Lichte, esp. chapter 4, "The Performative Generation of Materiality."
9 William Shakespeare, *Hamlet*, ed G. R. Hibbard, *The Oxford Shakespeare* (Oxford: Oxford University Press, 2008), 2.2, ll. 593–4 (p. 236).
10 Julie Taymor, dir., *Oedipus Rex*, mus. Igor Stravinsky, libr. Jean Cocteau, cond. Seiji Ozawa, VHS (Polygram Video, 1994).
11 This ambiguity also obtains in the French, *nature morte*: the "dead" of *morte* connoting motionlessness and silence at the same time.
12 Cocteau, *Maries*, 53: "*PHONO UN: Voici le photographe de la Tour Eiffel. Il parle. Que dit-il? / PHONO DEUX: Vous n'auriez pas vu passer une autruche?*"

13 Cocteau, *Mariés*, 59: "PHONO UN: *L'enfant se sauve. Il hurle. Il trépigne. Il veut 'vivre ma vie.'* / PHONO DEUX: *Je veux vivre ma vie! Je veux vivre ma vie!*"
14 Cocteau, *Mariés*, 59–60: "PHONO UN: *Mais quel est cet autre tapage?* / PHONO DEUX: *Le directeur de la Tour Eiffel. Que dit-il?* / PHONO UN: *Un peu de silence, s'il vous plait. Ne faites pa peur aux dépêches.*"
15 Anson Rabinbach, *The Human Motor: Energy, Fatigue, and the Origins of Modernity* (Berkeley: University of California Press, 1990), 184–5.
16 Rabinbach, 244–53.
17 Rabinbach, 237.
18 Rabinbach, 253. See also Jean-Marie Lahy, 2nd ed. (Paris, 1921), 6, 143.
19 Rabinbach, 239.
20 Cocteau, *Les Mariés*, 55: "*Le discours du général est à l'orchestre. Il le gesticule seulement.*"
21 Cocteau, *Les Mariés*, 59.
22 Cocteau, *Les Mariés*, 60: "*Je veux qu'on me tire en photographie avec le général.*"
23 Cocteau, *Maries*, 66–6.
24 Cocteau, *Mariés*, 56:

PHONO UN: *Vous vous demandez où sont partis le chasseur d'autruche et le directeur de la Tour Eiffel. Le chasseur cherche l'autruche à tous les étages. Le directeur cherche le chasseur et dirige la Tour Eiffel. Ce n'est pas une sinécure. La Tour Eiffel est un monde comme Notre-Dame. C'est Notre-Dame de la rive gauche.*
PHONO DEUX: *C'est la reine de Paris.*
PHONO UN: *Elle était reine de Paris. Maintenant elle est demoiselle du télégraphe.*
PHONO DEUX: *Il faut bien vivre.*

25 Mick Hamer, "The biggest Meccano set in the world," *The New Scientist* (December 24–31, 1988, 65–8), 67–8: Eiffel's other engineering work included railway construction, railway station design, and producing the cast-iron frame of the Statue of Liberty; see also Hervé.
26 Cocteau, *Mariés*, 60.

PHONO DEUX: *Les dépêches prises tombent en scène et se débattent. Toute la noce courts après et leur saute dessus. [...] Les dépêches se*

Calment. Elles se rangent sur une ligne. La plus belle s'avance et fait le salut militaire.

PHONO UN: *voix de compère de revue: Mais qui donc êtes-vous?*

PHONO DEUX: *Je suis la dépêche sans fil et, comme ma soeur la cigogne, j'arrive de New-York.*

PHONO UN: *voix de compère de revue: New-York! Ville des amoureux et des contre-jour.*

27 Gilles Deleuze and Félix Guattari, *A Thousand Plateaus*, trans. Brian Massumi (Minneapolis: University of Minnesota Press, 1988 [1980]), 3–4.

28 Deleuze and Guattari, *Thousand*, 7.

29 Deleuze and Guattari, *Thousand*, 21.

30 Deleuze and Guattari, *Thousand*, 22.

31 For a complete discussion of the notion of "lines of flight" and "becoming," see Gilles Deleuze and Félix Guattari, *Kafka: Toward a Minor Literature*, trans. Dana Polan, Theory and History of Literature, vol. 30 (Minneapolis: University of Minnesota Press, 1986), esp. chapter 1 (3–15).

32 J. D. Hayhurst, *The Pneumatic Post of Paris*, ed. C. S. Holder, digitized by Mark Hayhurst (The France and Colonies Philatelic Society of Great Britain, 1974) accessed October 17, 2018, http://www.cix. co.uk/~mhayhurst/jdhayhurst/pneumatic/book1.html.

33 Edward Gordon Craig, "The actor and the marionette," in Craig, *On the Art of the Theatre*, ed. Franc Chamberlain (London: Routledge, 2009).

34 See Siegfried Zielinsky, *Deep Time of the Media*, trans. Gloria Custance (Cambridge, MA: MIT Press, 2006), 227–53.

35 Jean Cocteau, *The Infernal Machine*, trans. Albert Bermel, in *The Infernal Machine and Other Plays*, by Jean Cocteau (New York: New Directions, 1964), 6.

36 Tzara's title, *Le Coeur à Gaz* is ambiguous in French: It may suggest a heart *made of gas* (i.e., a gaseous heart) or a heart running on gas power, like a gas stove or a gas furnace. The second is more in line with the idiomatic use of the phrase "*à gaz*" in French; however, while some translators have chosen to make this meaning explicit in their rendering of Tzara's title (i.e., *The Gas Operated Heart* or *The Gas Powered Heart*), I prefer to allow the ambiguity to remain in my references to the play, following Michael Benedikt's translation: Tristan Tzara, *The Gas Heart*,

trans. Michael Benedikt, in *Modern French Theatre: The Avant-Garde, Dada, and Surrealism*, eds. Michael Benedikt and George E. Wellwarth (New York: Dutton, 1964), 146. For a discussion of the implications of these various translations, see Sarah Bay-Cheng, "Translation, typography, and the avant-garde's impossible text," *Theatre Journal* 59:3 [October 2007], 467–83, esp. 480 and 480n36.

37 Tzara, *The Gas Heart*, trans. Michael Benedikt, in *Modern French Theatre*, eds. Michael Benedikt and George Wellwarth (New York: E. F. Dutton, 1964), 9. Benedikt renders Tzara's *bouton* in lines 1–5 as *pimple*, perhaps because of its proximity to the word "nose" [*nez*], in French, *bouton* out of context is an ambiguous word, its possible meanings including not only *pimple*, but *button, crank-pin, knob,* and *switch,* among others.

38 See Robert A. Varisco, "Anarchy and resistance in Tristan Tzara's *The Gas Heart*," *Modern Drama* 40:1 (Spring, 1997), 139–48. Varisco's is a curious approach to reading *The Gas Heart*. While there is no question that many of his somewhat self-apparent observations about the way the play troubles assumptions about the relationship of drama to theatre, text to production, rehearsal to performance, actor to character, and production to audience are correct, the culminating "reading" he provides attempts to impose something like conventional sense on the piece. However, it succeeds in doing so only to the extent that it is able to take words and phrases out of the context within which they appear in Tzara's text and reorder them as extracted quotations in Varisco's own sensible formulations. In all, while his is an amusing experiment in reading something like sense into Tzara's play, it finally stretches credulity too far and does not, in fact, enable further critical inquiry.

39 Stanton B. Garner, Jr., "*The Gas Heart*: Disfigurement and the Dada body," *Modern Drama* 50:4 (Winter, 2007), 500–16, 501.

40 Garner, 501.

41 Garner, 510.

42 Garner, 509.

43 My translation; however, see Cocteau, *Eiffel Tower*, 107: Benedikt translates Tzara's "*un beau petit mort*" as "beautiful little victim" (Tzara, *Les Mariés*, 35). However, the French idiom *petit mort* is slang for *orgasm*, linking death in war with the moment of conception and with sexual pleasure.

44 Tristan Tzara, *Le Coeur à Gaz* (Paris: GLM, 1946 [1921]) 8: "*Le coeur chauffé au gaz ma[r]che lentement, grande circulation, c'est la seul et la plus grande excroquerie du siècle en 3 actes, elle ne portera bonheur qu'aux imbéciles industrialisés.*" Benedikt's translation renders "*le coeur chauffé au gaz*" as simply "the gas heart," while, as Stanton B. Garner, Jr., notes, John D. Erickson, in his study *Dada Performance, Poetry, and Art* (Boston: Twayne, 1984), renders the title *The Gaslight Heart*; see Garner, 513 (n. 6).
45 Bay-Cheng, 480.
46 Bay-Cheng, 481.
47 Bay-Cheng, 471.
48 Bay-Cheng, 472.
49 Bay-Cheng, 473.
50 Marshall McLuhan, *Understanding Media: The Extensions of Man* (New York: McGraw-Hill, 1964), 160.
51 McLuhan, 172.
52 McLuhan, 173.
53 McLuhan, 177.
54 Bay-Cheng, 482.
55 Bay-Cheng, 470.
56 McLuhan 171, quoting Beatrice Warde, "Twinkle in Andromeda," *Alphabet: International Annual of Letterforms* 1:1 (1964), 78–83. McLuhan does not provide citation for Warde's remark. And so, I am grateful to Amelia Hugill-Fontanel of The Rochester Institute of Technology's Cary Graphic Arts Collection, Ole Lund of the Department of Design of Norwegian University of Science and Technology, David Goodrich, and the American Printing History Association for tracking down Warde's original.
57 McLuhan, 171.
58 In this playful orientation to the promises of a technologically advanced industrial boom, these brief plays resemble Jacques Tati's film trilogy *Monsieur Hulot's Holiday* (1953), *Mon Oncle* (1958), and *Play Time* (1968).
59 Despite Donald M. Allen's decision to render the French name Jacques as Jack in his otherwise excellent translation of Ionesco's *Jacques, ou la Soumission*, I have chosen to retain the French cognate, wishing to

maintain an awareness of the French postwar context of these plays throughout this discussion. Derek Prouse's translation of *L'Avenir est dans les Ouefs, ou Il Faut de Tout pour faire un Monde* retains the French names. See Eugène Ionesco, *Jack, or The Submission* in *Four Plays* by Ionesco, trans. Donald M. Allen (New York: Grove Weidenfeld, 1958) and Ionesco, The Future Is in Eggs, or It Takes All Sorts to Make a World *in* Plays by Ionesco, vol. 4 (of 7), trans. Derek Prouse (London: Calder and Boyars, 1960). Unless otherwise noted, quotations in English will come from the aforementioned translation. In cases where I have provided my own translations, the accompanying French texts come from Ionesco, *Jacques, ou La Soumission* in *Théâtre* by Ionesco, vol. 1 (Paris: Gallimard, 1954) and *L'Avenir est dans les Ouefs, ou Il Faut de Tout pour Faire un Monde* in *Théâtre* by Ionesco, vol. 2 (Paris: Gallimard, 1958).

60 Ionesco, *Jacques*, 126.
61 Ionesco, *Jack*, 109.
62 Ionesco, *Jack*, 110.
63 Ionesco, *The Future*, 141.
64 Ionesco, *The Future*, 127.
65 Ionesco, *The Future*, 130.
66 Ionesco, *The Future*, 128–30 *passim*.
67 Ionesco, *The Future*, 138.
68 Ionesco, *The Future*, 139–40.
69 Ionesco, *The Future*, 140, 141.
70 Eisenhower, [1].

2 Machineries of Nostalgia and American Modernity: Sophie Treadwell, Elmer Rice, Arthur Miller, and Isaac Gomez

1 Herbert Hoover, "October 22, 1928: Principles and ideals of the United States government" (Campaign Speech Transcript), University of Virginia's Miller Center, accessed October 30, 2018 https://millercenter.org/the-presidency/presidential-speeches/october-22-1928-principles-and-ideals-united-states-government.

2   See Ralph Waldo Emerson, "Self-reliance," in *The Collected Works of Ralph Waldo Emerson*, vol. 2: *Essays: First Series*, eds. Joseph Slater, Alfred R. Ferguson, and Jean Ferguson Carr (Cambridge, MA: Harvard University Press, 1980); Alexis de Tocqueville, *Democracy in America*, vol. 1, trans. Henry Reeve, rev. Francis Bowen, ed. Phillips Bradly (New York: Vintage, [1945] 1954).
3   Elmer Rice, *The Adding Machine*, in *Seven Plays*, by Elmer Rice (New York: Viking Press, 1950), 75–76.
4   Rice, *Adding*, 76.
5   Rice, *Adding*, 76.
6   Rice, *Adding*, 76.
7   Anthony F. R. Palmieri, *Elmer Rice: A Playwright's Vision of America* (Rutherford: Farleigh-Dickinson Press, 1980).
8   Palmieri, 58–9.
9   Palmieri, 60.
10 Rice, qtd. in Palmieri, 57. Palmieri cites Rice's autobiography, *Minority Report*, as the source of all biographical quotations and material in his study.
11 Palmieri, 56.
12 Palmieri, 57.
13 Rice, *Adding*, 102.
14 Rice, *Adding*, 104.
15 Rice, *Adding*, 107–8.
16 Images of these Simonson's designs for Rice's play are widely available on the internet. See, for instance, Ian Ellis-Jones, "Don't be a mindless Zero," Dr. Ian Ellis-Jones…Living Mindfully Now (January 15, 2016), accessed November 1, 2018, http://ianellis-jones.blogspot.com/2016/01/dont-be-mindless-zero.html; Douglas Messerli et al., "Elmer Rice *The Adding Machine*," UStheater, Opera, and Performance (July 11, 2011), accessed October 31, 2018, http://ustheater.blogspot.com/2011/07/elmer-rice-adding-machine.html; and Gianni Truzzi, "The Adding Machine, 1923," GianT Thoughts (November 17, 2008), accessed November 2, 2018, http://giant-thoughts.blogspot.com/2008/11/adding-machine-1923.html.
17 See Lee Simonson, *The Art of Scenic Design* (New York: Harper and Brothers, 1950), esp. 21–47. See also Simonson, *The Part of a*

Lifetime: Drawings and Designs 1919–1940 (New York: Duell, Sloan and Pearce, 1943).
18 Simonson, *The Stage Is Set* (New York: Theatre Arts Books, 1963 [1932]), 124.
19 Simonson, *The Art*, ix; Simonson, *The Stage*, 125.
20 Sophie Treadwell, *Machinal*, intro. Judith E. Barlow (London: Nick Hern Books, 1993), 1.
21 Treadwell, 2.
22 See Edward P. Comentale, *Modernism, Cultural Production, and the British Avant-Garde* (Cambridge: Cambridge University Press, 2004), esp. 69–110. Comentale locates in T. S. Eliot's poetry traces of Eliot's own background as a banker, and argues that "Eliot's work at [Lloyds Bank]—in both content and structure—provided a way of transmuting the emotional wreckage of modern life into the formal economy of the marketplace. His repentant soul was drawn to the rational activity of tabulating account balances, which, in turn, became the model for an aesthetic activity" (73).
23 Cocteau *Eiffel*, 33; Tzara, 9.
24 Treadwell, 5, 6.
25 Treadwell, 6.
26 Treadwell, 11.
27 Treadwell, 25.
28 Treadwell, 25.
29 Charles Tung, "Modernism, time machines, and the defamiliarization of time," *Configurations* 23:1 (Winter 2015), 93–121, 99.
30 Treadwell, 53.
31 Treadwell, 53.
32 Treadwell, 40.
33 Treadwell, 50–1.
34 Treadwell, 69–70.
35 Cocteau, *The Infernal Machine*, 6.
36 See, for instance, Michael Evans, *Karl Marx* (London: George Allen and Unwin, Ltd., 2004 [1975]), esp. 69–72: "We can […] quarry out of Marx's writings general passages which state or imply that technology is the ultimately determining factor in all social change" (70).
37 Treadwell, 83.

38 Beckett, *Krapp*, 17.
39 Arthur Miller, *Death of a Salesman: Certain Private Conversations in Two Acts and a Requiem* (New York: The Viking Press, 1981 [1949]).
40 Miller, *Death*, 22.
41 Michael J. Meyer, "In his father's image: Biff Loman's struggle with inherited traits in *Death of a Salesman*," *Arthur Miller's* Death of a Salesman, ed. Eric J. Sterling (Amsterdam: Rodopi, 2008), 123.
42 Meyer, 135.
43 Miller, *Death*, 138.
44 Miller, *Death*, 31.
45 Matthew C. Roudané, "*Death of a Salesman* and the poetics of Arthur Miller," in *The Cambridge Companion to Arthur Miller*, ed. Christopher Bigsby (Cambridge: Cambridge University Press, 1997), 66.
46 Roudané, 66.
47 Roudané, 65.
48 Miller, *Death*, 17.
49 Miller, *Death*, 139.
50 Miller, *Death*, 139.
51 Miller, *Death*, 77.
52 It is Columbus.
53 Miller, *Death*, 83.
54 Miller, *Death*, 19.
55 Miller, *Death,* 73. For a fuller discussion of these particular encounters between Willy and domestic technologies, see Craig N. Owens, "Mystifying the machine: Staged and unstaged technologies in Arthur Miller's *Death of a Salesman*," in *Arthur Miller's* Death of a Salesman, ed. Eric Sterling (Amsterdam: Rodopi, 2008). See also Paula Morantz Cohen's essay "The dynamo, the salesman, and the playwright," in the same volume, for a reading of the way the human gets recuperated in both *Death of a Salesman* and in Miller's self-representations.
56 Miller, *Death*, 68.
57 Miller, *Death*, 11.
58 Simonson includes both Mielziner's design and a photograph of the lighted set in *The Art of Scenic Design*, 99.
59 Christopher Bigsby, *Arthur Miller: A Critical Study* (Cambridge: Cambridge University Press, 2005), 101.

60 Bigsby, *Arthur Miller*, 102. In quoting Miller, Bigsby cites Matthew Roudané, *Conversations with Arthur Miller* (Jackson, 1987), 129.
61 Una Chaudhuri, *Staging Place: The Geography of Modern Drama* (Ann Arbor: University of Michigan Press, 1991), 126. My emphasis.
62 Raymond Williams, *The Country and the City* (New York: Oxford University Press, 1973), 1.
63 Williams, *Country*, 1.
64 Isaac Gomez, *La Ruta*, dir. Sandra Marquez, scenic des. Regina Garcia (Chicago: Steppenwolf Theatre), January 5, 2019. I am grateful to the author for providing me with a reading script of the play.

3 Alienating Devices: Bertolt Brecht & Kurt Weill, John Adams & Alice Goodman, Don DeLillo, and Athol Fugard

1 Timothy A. Johnson, *John Adam's Nixon in China: Musical Analysis, Historical and Political Perspectives* (Farnham: Ashgate, 2011), 34. Unless otherwise noted, remarks on the performance of *Nixon in China* refer to the PBS broadcast of the 1987 Houston Grand Opera premiere, directed by Peter Sellars and featuring James Maddalena as Nixon; Sylvan Sanford as Chou En-Lai; John Duykers as Chairman Mao; Trudy Ellen Craney as Chiang Ch'ing (Madame Mao); Carolann Page as Pat Nixon; and Mari Opatz, Stephanie Friedman, and Marion Dry as Mao's Secretaries. See John Adams, *Nixon in China* (DVD), Houston Grand Opera, libretto by Alice Goodman, directed by Peter Sellars, choreography by Mark Morris, conducted by John DeMain, introduced by Walter Cronkite (PBS—*Great Performances*, April 15, 1988).
2 Johnson, 81.
3 Anthony Squiers, *An Introduction to the Social and Political Philosophy of Bertolt Brecht: Revolution and Aesthetics* (Amsterdam: Rodopi, 2014), 16.
4 Squiers, 17.
5 Brechtian aesthetics, for example, permeates Ronald Hayman's *British Theatre since 1955: A Reassessment* (Oxford: Oxford University Press, 1979), which takes as its starting point the middle of the decade

during which Brecht's *Berliner Ensemble* famously played in London, revolutionizing the concept of politically engaged theatre practice there, in 1956. More recently, Michael Patterson's *Strategies of Political Theatre: Post-War British Playwrights* (Cambridge: Cambridge University Press, 2003) serves as an example of the way Brechtian and neo-epic drama has become almost synonymous with "political theatre."

6 John Willett, "Introduction," *Brecht on Theatre*, by Bertolt Brecht, ed. and trans. John Willett (New York: Hill and Wang, 1964), xiii.

7 See Baugh, 1–4.

8 Guy-Ernest Debord, *Society of the Spectacle*, published by Black & Red, Nothingness.org, accessed November 27, 2018, http://library.nothingness.org/articles/SI/en/pub_contents/4.

9 For a pictorial survey of recent staged spectacles of all kinds, unreserved in its celebratory rhetoric, see *Spectacular! Stage Design: Concerts, Events and Ceremonies, Theaters* (Hong Kong: SendPoints Publishing, 2015).

10 See Viktor Shklovsky, "Art and device," in Shklovsky, *Theory of Prose*, trans. Benjamin Sher (Normal: Dalkey Archive Press, 1991).

11 Baugh, 76–7.

12 Baugh, 47, 17.

13 Bertolt Brecht, *Brecht on Theatre*, ed. and trans. John Willett (New York: Hill and Wang, 1964), 33.

14 *Apparatus* being a fourth-declension noun in Latin, the plural should be *apparatus*. In English, the plural would appear either as *apparatus* or *apparatuses*.

15 Brecht, *On Theatre*, 34.

16 Baugh, 75.

17 Eric Russell Bentley, "The theatres of Wagner and Ibsen," *The Kenyon Review* 6:4 (Autumn 1944), 542–69, 567, accessed October 1, 2018, https://www.jstor.org/stable/4332546.

18 For a detailed account of the evolution and development of the music and text of the piece, variously titled *Der Lindberghsflug, Der Flug der Lindberghs* and *Der Ozeanflug*, see Lynne Walker, "Brecht and Weill: The flight fantastic," *The Independent* (July 31, 2006), accessed February 14, 2008, http://www.independent.co.uk/arts-entertainment/music/features/brecht-and-weill-the-flight-fantastic-409959.html

19 By December 1928, Weill had replaced the sections composed by Hindemith with his own compositions. Subsequent productions have typically featured on Weill's music.
20 Willett's translation in Brecht, *On Theatre*, 31–2. The German can be found in Jan Knopf, *Brecht Handbuch: eine Ästhetik der Widersprüche* (Stuttgart: Metzler, 1996), 75: *Um Ablenkungen zu vermeiden, beteiligt sich der denkende an der Musik [hierin auch dem Grundsatz folgend: tun ist besser als fühlen] indem er die Musik mitliest und in ihr fehlende Stimmen mitsummt oder im Buch mit den Augen verfolgt oder im Verein mit anderen laut singt.*
21 See Brecht, *On Theatre*, fig. 9, n.p.
22 Josef Heinzelmann, "Kurt Weill's compositions for radio," trans. Lionel Salter, liner notes to Kurt Weill, *Der Lindberghflug and The Ballad of Magna Carta* (Königsdorf: Delta Music-Capriccio, 1990), 22.
23 Brecht, *On Theatre*, 18.
24 See Willett's editorial citation and note on the text in Brecht, *On Theatre*, 53.
25 Brecht, *On Theatre*, 51. Brecht describes the earliest role of the radio as "being a substitute: a substitute for theatre, opera, concerts, lectures, café music, local newspapers and so forth"—that is, as a time when the radio extended the reach of older forms and media but had not yet come into its own as a transformative innovation.
26 The reader will no doubt recognize the similarities between Brecht's conception of the radio of the future and the network of pneumatic tubes that composed Paris's pneumatic post, discussed in Chapter 1 in the context of the Cocteau's *Eiffel Tower Wedding Party*.
27 Brecht, *On Theatre*, 52.
28 Brecht, *On Theatre*, 52.
29 Brecht, quoted in Squiers, 22.
30 Brecht's thinking on the relationship between science and technology, on the one hand, and artistic and cultural production, on the other, echoes the early-twentieth-century work of the cubo-futurists, including Sergei Eisenstein, who "fell voraciously upon the findings of the scientific and technological avant-garde and attempted to translate these into artistic praxis or to find autonomous forms for them in art" (Siegfried Zielinksy,

Deep Time of the Media, trans. Charlotte Custance [Cambridge, MA: MIT Press, 2006], 234–5).
31 Mordecai Gorelik, "Bertolt Brecht's "Prospectus of the Diderot Society," *Quarterly Journal of Speech* 47:2 (April 1961), 113.
32 Brecht, quoted in Gorelik's translation in Gorelik, 114.
33 Brecht, quoted in Gorelik's translation in Gorelik, 115.
34 See Willet's notes on the essay in Brecht, *On Theatre*, 147.
35 Brecht's most coherent articulation of the purpose of the "gest" and of "gestic techniques" comes in his remarks "On gestic music" (Brecht, *On Theatre*, 104–6): "The social gest is the gest relevant to society, the gest that allows conclusions to be drawn about the social circumstances" (104–5). Willet's use of the term *gest* in rendering the German *Geste* is meant to distinguish the word from the everyday sense of *gesture* and to retain the sense of performance or gesticulation inherent in Brecht's usage.
36 Brecht, *On Theatre*, 136, 137.
37 Brecht, *On Theatre*, 136.
38 Brecht, *On Theatre*, 32.
39 See Walter Benjamin, "The work of art in the age of its technological reproducibility: Second version," trans. Edmund Jephcott and Harry Zohn, in Benjamin, *The Work of Art in the Age of its Technological Reproducibility and Other Writings on Media* (Cambridge, MA: Belknap Press/Harvard University Press, 2008). For a discussion of the relationship of capitalist ideology and subject formation, see also Louis Althusser, "Ideology and ideological state apparatuses: Notes toward an investigation," in *Lenin and Philosophy and Other Essays*, trans. Ben Brewster (New York: Monthly Review Press, 1971), 87–126.
40 The reader will recognize this embrace later, in Chapter 4, in the discussion of John Hurt's portrayal of Krapp in the filmed version of Beckett's *Krapp's Last Tape*.
41 Brian McMaster, "Brian McMaster introduces the 2006 Festival," accessed on February 14, 2008, www.eif.co.uk/audio/Brian3.mp3 [webpage no longer available].
42 Brecht, *On Theatre*, 34.
43 Squiers, 58.
44 See Zielinsky, *Deep Time*, 259: "Th[e] boundary between media users and media devices simultaneously divides and connects two different

spheres: that of the active users of the machines and that of the active machines and programs. In the 1990s, both technological developments and dominant media concepts were oriented toward making the boundary between the two imperceptible. The vision was to use a computer and be unaware that it is a machine based on algorithms for calculating and simulating. The user would be immersed in a so-called virtual reality of images and sounds without noticing the transition and, what is more, without knowing that one was dealing with a precisely prestructured, calculated construction of visual surfaces and temporal sequences.'

45 Goodman, 16–17.

46 See, for instance, Mao's remarks on Chiang Kai-shek in John Adams, *Nixon in China: An Opera in Three Acts*, vocal score, libretto by Alice Goodman (London: Boosey and Hawkes, 1999 [1987]), 45–7 (bars 46–61); his diplomatic directive to "save that for the Premier" (52–3 [bars 127–33]); and his remarks on diplomats, 'In the dark, all diplomats are grey' (54–5 [bars 149–61]), and elsewhere throughout Act One, Scene Two.

47 Goodman, 11.

48 Goodman, 20.

49 Adams 1.2, bb. 579–90.

50 Adams 1.2, bb. 998–1015.

51 Goodman, 20.

52 Adams 1.2, bb. 40–4; Goodman, 11.

53 John Duykers, perf., Act One, Scene Two (Tracks 7–12), *Nixon in China*, John Adams, comp., Alice Goodman, libr., and Peter Sellars, dir. Compact Disc (BMI-Red Dawn Music, 1987).

54 T. A. Johnson, 79.

55 Alice Goodman, *Nixon in China* in Goodman, *History Is Our Mother: Three Libretti* (New York City: New York Review of Books, 2017), 7–9.

56 Adams, 1.1, bb. 375–514.

57 Seymour Hersh, quoted in Timothy A. Johnson, 81. See Seymour M. Hersh, *The Price of Power: Kissinger in the Nixon White House* (New York: Summit Books, 1983).

58 Jerry Voorhis quoted in Timothy A. Johnson, 81. See Jerry Voorhis, *The Strange Case of Richard Milhous Nixon* (New York: Paul S. Eriksson, 1972).

59 See Adams, Vocal Score, 1.1, bb. 583–615.
60 Adams, Vocal Score, 1.1, bb. 245–58.
61 Goodman, 6–7.
62 Goodman, 30.
63 Goodman, 30.
64 Timothy A. Johnson, 82, citing Anne Halpin, his former student at SUNY Buffalo.
65 Adams, Vocal Score, 1.3, bb. 511–68.
66 Brecht, "Alienation effects in Chinese acting," *Brecht on Theatre*, 91. In his note on the text, Willett reports that, in May 1935, Brecht had attended a performance of Chinese actor Mei Lan-fang's company in Moscow. "Almost certainly," Willett informs us, "this […] is the first mention in [Brecht's] writings of the term 'Verfremdungseffekt'" (99).
67 Brecht, *On Theatre*, 91.
68 Brecht, *On Theatre*, 92.
69 Brecht, *On Theatre*, 92–3.
70 See, for instance, James Maddalena, perf., "News," New York Metropolitan Opera, January 31, 2011, YouTube, accessed November 28, 2018, https://www.youtube.com/watch?v=FJmXMo9nWRU
71 Chen Zhi-Zheng, director, *Nixon in China*, John Adams, composer, Alice Goodman, libretto, Théâtre du Chatelet, Chamber Orchestra of Paris, cond. Alexander Briger, and the Choir of the Châtelet (Paris, 2012), YouTube, accessed November 27, 2018, https://www.youtube.com/watch?v=Czi81hRErJk
72 Benjamin, 31–55.
73 Benjamin, 31.
74 Luigi Pirandello, quoted in Benjamin, 31. Benjamin's note cites Léon Pierre-Quint's '*Signification du cinéma*' in *L'Art cinématographique*, vol. 2, 14–15 as the source for this quotation from Pirandello's *Il Turno* (*The Turn*). See Benjamin, 47 n. 21.
75 Benjamin, *The Work of Art*, 31–2; Benjamin's emphasis.
76 Squiers, 67.
77 Squiers, 83; See Charles Tung, "Modernism."
78 Squiers, 67.
79 Timothy A. Johnson, 8.
80 Timothy A. Johnson, 8.

81 Timothy A. Johnson, 79, citing Stephen M. Prock, III, "Reading between the lines: Musical and dramatic discourse in John Adams's *Nixon in China*," PhD dissertation (Cornell University, 1993). See also William Germano, "Opera as news: *Nixon in China* and the contemporary operatic subject," *University of Toronto Quarterly* 81:4 (Fall 2012), 797–823.
82 Timothy A. Johnson, 185, citing Prock.
83 Timothy A. Johnson, 194, citing Prock.
84 Timothy A. Johnson, 247, citing Prock.
85 Don DeLillo, *Valparaiso* (New York: Scribner, 1999).
86 See Stuart Ewen, *All Consuming Images: The Politics of Style in Contemporary Culture* (New York: Basic Books, 1988), esp. chapter 9, "Form follows power," 185–232.
87 Rebecca Rey, *Staging Don DeLillo* (London: Routledge, 2016), chapter 4: "Technology and the celebrity circus in *Valparaiso*," 67–97.
88 Rey, 72.
89 Rey, 73.
90 Rey, 73.
91 Rey, 73.
92 Rey, 73.
93 Rey, 73.
94 DeLillo, 27.
95 DeLillo, 41.
96 Ewen, 209.
97 DeLillo, 44–45.
98 For a detailed analysis of the discontinuous, fragmented, and dispersed "text" offered by television programming in the late twentieth century, see Elizabeth Klaver, "Postmodernism and the intersection of television and contemporary drama," *Journal of Popular Culture* 27:4 (Spring 1994), 69–80.
99 DeLillo, 25.
100 See Germano's discussion of aria's tendency to effect "temporal dislocation," 808–11.
101 Fugard, with John Kani and Winston Ntshona, *The Island*, in *Statements*, 45–77.
102 Fugard, 42.

4 Machineries of Constraint: Samuel Beckett, Harold Pinter, and Badal Sircar

1. See *Quad, Rockaby*, and *Ohio Impromptu* in Samuel Beckett, *Collected Shorter Plays* (New York: Grove Press, 1984).
2. For a discussion of biomechanics in the context of Meyerhold's evolving concept of a machinic theatre in pre-Soviet and Soviet Russia, see Christopher Baugh, *Theatre, Performance and Technology: The Development of Scenography in the Twentieth Century* (Basingstoke: Palgrave Macmillan, 2005), 62–74.
3. Harold Pinter, *The Room*, in Pinter, *The Birthday Party and The Room: Two Plays* (New York: Grove Press, [1961] 1981).
4. Harold Pinter, *The Birthday Party*, in Pinter, *The Birthday Party and The Room: Two Plays*.
5. Harold Pinter, *Party Time*, in Pinter, *Party Time and The New World Order: Two Plays* (New York: Grove Press, 1993); Harold Pinter, *One for the Road* (New York: Grove Weidenfeld, 1985); Harold Pinter, *Mountain Language* (New York: Grove Press, 1988).
6. Samuel Beckett, *Krapp's Last Tape*, in *Krapp's Last Tape and Other Dramatic Pieces* (New York: Grove, 1958), 7–28.
7. Jürgen Habermas, "Technology and science as 'ideology,' " in Habermas, *Toward a Rational Society: Student Protest, Science, and Politics*, trans. Jeremy J. Shapiro (Boston: Beacon Press, 1970), 81.
8. Habermas, 81.
9. Habermas, 81.
10. Habermas, 82.
11. Habermas, 82–3.
12. See Shawn Kairschner, "Coercive somatographies: X-rays, hypnosis, and Stanislavsky's production plan for *The Seagull*," *Modern Drama* 51:3 (Fall 2008), 369–88; Amy Strahler Holzapfel, "Strindberg as vivisector: Physiology, pathology, and anti-mimesis in *The Father* and *Miss Julie*," *Modern Drama* 51:3 (Fall 2008), 329–52.
13. Beckett, *Krapp*, 14.
14. Beckett, *Krapp*, 16.
15. Jean Martin, "for reasons of immediacy and truth" opted, against Beckett's preferences, to control the playback from the stage for a 1970 production

in Paris, which Beckett directed (Knowlson, 511). In most productions, it is controlled backstage, and the machine onstage does not actually produce the sound. See James Knowlson, *Damned to Fame: The Life of Samuel Beckett* (New York: Simon and Schuster, 1996), 509–11.

16 Beckett, *Krapp*, 12–13, 18–19.
17 Beckett, *Krapp*, 25.
18 Beckett, *Krapp*, 10.
19 George Bernard Shaw, *Major Barbara, The Bodley Head Bernard Shaw: Collected Plays with Their Prefaces*, 7 vols. (New York: Dodd, Mead, 1970–4), vol. 3, 9–200.
20 John Osborne, *Look Back in Anger* (London: Faber and Faber, 1957).
21 Knowlson, *Damned*, 528.
22 Jonathan Bignell, *Beckett on Screen: The Television Plays* (Manchester: Manchester University Press, 2009), 89.
23 Atom Egoyan, dir. *Krapp's Last Tape*, by Samuel Beckett, *Beckett on Film*, DVD (Blue Angel Films, 2001), disc 2.
24 Beckett, *Krapp*, 9.
25 Beckett, *Krapp*, 9.
26 Beckett, *Krapp*, 9.
27 Beckett, *Krapp*, 11.
28 N. Katherine Hayles, "Voices out of bodies, bodies out of voices: Audiotape and the production of subjectivity," *Sound States: Innovate Poetics and Acoustical Technologies*, ed. Adelaide Morris (Chapel Hill: University of North Carolina Press, 1997) 74–96.
29 Hayles, "Voices," 75.
30 Beckett, *Krapp*, 18.
31 Beckett, *Krapp*, 20.
32 Hayles, "Voices," 78.
33 Jean Martin, quoted in Hayles, "Voices," 81. Hayles takes Martin's quotation from James Knowlson, "The beginnings of *Krapp's Last Tape*," *Krapp's Last Tape: A Theatre Notebook*, ed. James Knowlson (London: Brutus, 1980) 45–8 q.v.
34 Harold Pinter, *The Dumb Waiter*, in *Complete Works* by Harold Pinter, vol. 1 (New York: Grove Weidenfeld, 1976), 147.
35 Pinter *Dumb*, 154.
36 Pinter, *Dumb*, 133.

37 See Judith Roof, "The deficient ballcock: Pinter's comic turn," *The Harold Pinter Review: Essays on Contemporary Drama* 2 (2018), 16–21, for a discussion of the way much of the comedy of *The Dumb Waiter* hinges on the double entendre and scatological associations suggested by the malfunctioning machineries of the play.
38 Pinter, *Dumb*, 154.
39 Pinter, *Dumb*, 155.
40 Lance Norman, "Dumb waiters, dead children and Martinizing the Pinteresque," *Pinter Et Cetera*, ed. Craig N. Owens (Newcastle-upon-Tyne: Cambridge Scholars Press, 2009), 148.
41 McLuhan, 92.
42 Pinter, *Dumb*, 163.
43 Althusser, *passim*.
44 Samuel Beckett, *What Where*, in *Collected Shorter Plays*, by Samuel Beckett (New York: Grove, 1984), 316.
45 Beckett, *What*, 315.
46 We will see an almost identical structure—a performance initiated by and interpreted through a manifest piece of stage technology—in Tod Machover and Robert Pinsky's 2010 "Robots' Opera" *Death and the Powers* in Chapter 5.
47 Beckett, *What*, 310.
48 Beckett, *What*, 310.
49 Beckett, *What*, 310.
50 Beckett, *What*, 311.
51 Beckett, *What*, 316.
52 Damien O'Donnell, dir. *What Where*, by Samuel Beckett, *Beckett on Film*, DVD 2 of 4 (Blue Angel Films, 2001).
53 Samuel Beckett, *Play*, in Beckett, *The Collected Shorter Plays*, 153.
54 Samuel Beckett, *Play*, 160.
55 Beckett, *Play*, 158.
56 We have seen this inquisitorial dynamic linked to glowing instruments in the discussion of DeLillo's *Valparaiso* in Chapter 2.
57 Beckett, *Play*, 153.
58 Beckett, *Play*, 155.
59 Anthony Minghella, dir., *Play*, by Samuel Beckett, *Beckett on Film*, DVD 3 of 4 (Blue Angel Films, 2001). Herren, 188–97, usefully summarizes

critical responses to *Beckett on Film*, including a careful reading of Minghella's significant departures from Beckett's text and the debates they have given rise to. While these departures alter other aspects of *Play* and invite interpretations somewhat at odds with those a stage version would elicit, for my purposes, the introduction of the camera in place of the spot light is the departure most worth discussing here.

60 Herren, 193.
61 Martin Esslin, *The Theatre of the Absurd* (New York: Anchor, 1961) xix–xx.
62 Badal Sircar, *Evam Indrajit*, trans. Girish Karnad, *Three Modern Indian Plays* (Oxford: Oxford University Press, 1989) 1–60.
63 Sircar, 18, 28.
64 Sircar, 18.

5 Post-Human Recursivity: Heiner Müller, Julie Taymor, and Tod Machover & Robert Pinsky

1 For a fuller consideration of the way dramatic character, generally, has become an increasingly problematic concept in the past half century or so, see Fuchs, esp. Part II.
2 Robert Pinsky, *Death and the Powers: A Robot Pageant*, Poetry 196:4 (July/August, 2010), 285–332, 287.
3 Johannes Birringer, *Theatre, Theory, Postmodernism* (Bloomington: Indiana University Press, 1991), 182.
4 Birringer, 187.
5 Birringer, 190–1.
6 See Aleks Sierz, "In-yer-face theatre," In-Yer-Face Theatre, accessed November 9, 2018, http://www.inyerfacetheatre.com/intro.html; see also the works of such playwrights as Philip Ridley, Mark Ravenhill, and Sarah Kane, among others.
7 Heiner Müller, *The Hamletmachine*, trans. Carl Weber, *Performing Arts Journal* 4:3 (1980), 141–6, 144.
8 Müller, *Hamletmachine*, 143.
9 Müller, *Hamletmachine*, 146.
10 Müller, *Hamletmachine*, 144.

11 Müller, *Hamletmachine*, 143.
12 Müller, *Hamletmachine*, 141 (all caps in original).
13 Müller, *Hamletmachine*, 142.
14 Müller, *Hamletmachine*, 143.
15 Müller, *Hamletmachine*, 143.
16 Müller, *Hamletmachine*, 144.
17 Klaver, 69.
18 Klaver, 70.
19 Klaver, 71.
20 Nicholas Zurbrugg, "Post-modernism and the multi-media sensibility: Heiner Müller's *Hamletmachine* and the art of Robert Wilson," *Modern Drama* 31:3 (Fall 1988), 439–53.
21 Kirk Williams, "The ghost in the machine: Heiner Müller's devouring melancholy," *Modern Drama* 49:2 (Summer 2006), 188–205, 188.
22 Joseph Dudley, "Being and non-being: The Other and heterotopia in *Hamletmachine*," *Modern Drama* 35:4 (Winter 1992), 562–70, 569.
23 See Stephen Watt, *Joyce, O'Casey and the Irish Popular Theatre* (Syracuse: Syracuse University Press, 1991), 8–9.
24 See Alan R. Young, Hamlet *and the Visual Arts, 1709–1900* (Newark: University of Delaware Press, 2002), 279–345.
25 T. S. Eliot, *The Waste Land*, in Eliot, *The Complete Poems and Plays, 1909–1950* (New York: Harcourt, Brace, and World, 1971), line 128.
26 Althusser, 127 (emphasis mine).
27 James Slowiak, "To confront paradox: New World Performance Lab's *Hamletmachine*," in *Müller in America: American Productions of Works by Heiner Müller, Volume One*, ed. Dan Friedman (New York: Castillo Cultural Center, 2003), 89.
28 Linda Eisenman quoted in Slowiak, 89.
29 Jeff Burke, "A play that is not a play: Heiner Müller's *Hamletmachine* as digital installation," in *Müller in America: American Productions of Works by Heiner Müller*, vol. 1, ed. Dan Friedman (New York: Castillo Cultural Center, 2003), 85–6. See also Scott Magelssen and John Troyer's "BLA BLA," a textual "performance" of *Hamletmachine*, in the same volume, 95–105.
30 Magelssen and Troyer, 98–100.

31 Zurbrugg, 443, quotes Peter Kemp, "Rude mechanicals," *The Independent* (November 6, 1987), 15: 'Indeed, as Peter Kemp remarks, Müller's imagery has a "quaint 1930s ring," and often appears "Rear-guard, not avant-garde."'
32 Craig N. Owens, "The eyes have It: 'Ocular proof' and the practice of criticism," in Judith Roof, ed., *Talking Drama* (Newcastle-upon-Tyne: Cambridge Scholars, 2009), 117.
33 Benoit B. Mandelbrot, qtd. in Daniel Schiffman, "Fractals," The Nature of Code, accessed November 16, 2018, https://natureofcode.com/book/chapter-8-fractals/. This definition is widely quoted without page citation, and often without attribution, or with references vaguely pointing toward Mandelbrot, *The Fractal Geometry of Nature* (New York: W. H. Freeman, 1983).
34 Mandelbrot, 14.
35 Mandelbrot, 15, 409–13.
36 See Kirk Williams, "The ghost in the Machine: Heiner Müller's Devouring Melancholy," *Modern Drama* 49:2 (Summer 2006), 188–205, 201–3.
37 Birringer, 65–6.
38 Dudley, 569.
39 Andreas Höfele, "A theater of exhaustion? '*Posthistoire*' in recent German Shakespeare productions" (*Shakespeare Quarterly* 43:1 [Spring, 1992]) 80–6, 84.
40 Höfele, 84.
41 Höfele, 85.
42 N. Katherine Hayles, *How We Became Posthuman* (Chicago: University of Chicago Press, 1999), 2–3.
43 Fredric Jameson, *Postmodernism, or, the Cultural Logic of Late Capitalism* (Durham: Duke University Press, 1991), 44.
44 Jameson, 39.
45 Jameson, 44.
46 Tod Machover, composer, and Robert Pinsky, libretto, *Death and the Powers*, DVD (Dallas: Winspear Opera House, 2014). This recording was made on the occasion of a live simulcast of the opera, closely following its 2010 Monte Carlo premiere and featuring three of the four original cast members of the original production.
47 Pinsky, 286.

48 Müller, *Hamletmachine*, 144.
49 Müller, *Hamletmachine*, 144.
50 Jean-François Lyotard, *The Inhuman: Reflections on Time*, trans. Geoffrey Bennington and Rachel Bowlby (Stanford, CA: Stanford University Press, 1991), 8–23.
51 N. Katherine Hayles, *How We Became Posthuman: Virtual Bodies in Cybernetics, Literature, and Informatics* (Chicago: University of Chicago Press, 1999), 7.
52 Hayles, *Posthuman*, 1.
53 Hayles, *Posthuman*, 53.
54 Hayles, *Posthuman*, 54.
55 Müller, *Hamletmachine*, 144.
56 Philip Kenicott, "Man and machine," *Opera News* (October, 2013), accessed November 15, 2018, web.media.mit.edu/~tod/media/pdfs/October2013_OperaNews.pdf.
57 Tod Machover qtd. in Robbie Hudson, "Opera gets a Machover," *The Sunday Times* (November 8, 2010), accessed November 15, 2018, https://operaofthefuture.com/2010/11/08/the-sunday-times-opera-gets-a-machover/.
58 Tod Machover, "On future performance," *New York Times*: Opinionator (January 13, 2010), accessed November 15, 2018, https://opinionator.blogs.nytimes.com/2010/01/13/on-future-performance/.
59 Ada Brunstein and Tod Machover, "Singing the body electric: Emotion-reading technology gives Tod Machover's opera an animatronic stage with heart," *New Scientist* (December 18, 2010), accessed November 15, 2018, operaofthefuture.files.wordpress.com/2010/12/newscientistqamachover.pdf.
60 Pio Barone Lumaga, "Dallas Opera's simulcast—Tod Machover's *Death and the Powers*," accessed November 15, 2018 http://web.media.mit.edu/~tod/media/pdfs/LOFT-DATP-simulcast_upcoming.pdf.
61 Patrick Healy and Kevin Flynn, "A Broadway superlative for all the wrong reasons," *New York Times* (March 13, 2011), accessed November 15, 2018, https://www.nytimes.com/2011/03/14/theater/spider-man-a-superlative-for-all-the-wrong-reasons.html.
62 Healy and Flynn.
63 Healy and Flynn.

64 Michael Riedel, "Broadway bombshell," *New York Post* (May 30, 2010), accessed November 16, 2018, https://nypost.com/2010/05/30/broadway-bombshell/.
65 Robert Hughes, "Swinging for the rafters: Spider-Man set designer opts for a pop-up Peter Parker," *The Observer* (September 28, 2010), accessed November 16, 2018, https://observer.com/2010/09/swinging-for-the-rafters-ispidermani-set-designer-opts-for-a-popup-peter-parker/.
66 Hughes. Here, we leave aside the fact that leaving the theatre and turning left, one might have had a much more immersive experience of New York City by finding oneself literally immersed in it.
67 Hughes.
68 Glen Berger, *The Song of Spider-Man: The Inside Story of the Most Controversial Musical in Broadway History* (New York: Simon and Schuster, 2013). See especially chapter 5 ("Stages," 61–86), in which Berger refers to the production as a "Rube Goldberg contraption" (75) and remarks on Marvel's contractual requirement that "the technology in all respects be cutting edge" (79). Elsewhere, Berger describes the fraught interplay of manual and automated technologies (185) and references neurology to explain the metaphoric qualities of Peter Parker's transformation into Spider-Man (53).
69 Berger, 268 (italics in original).
70 Jean Genette, *Paratexts: Thresholds of Interpretation*, trans. Jane E. Lewin (Cambridge: Cambridge University Press, 1997); originally published as *Seuils* (Paris: Editions du Seuil, 1987).
71 I use the scare quotes advisedly here to register my own skepticism about whether "disbelief" is something one can "suspend," willingly or not, and indeed whether disbelief is itself susceptible to suspension of any kind.
72 The set and technical design for this scene, along with the tilting proscenium and pop-up design of the whole production, earned George Tsypin's set a place in *Spectacular! Stage Design: Concerts, Events & Ceremonies, Theatres* (Hong Kong: SendPoints, 2015), 182–91.
73 See Christopher Baugh, *Theatre, Performance and Technology: The Development of Scenography in the Twentieth Century* (London: Palgrave, 2005), esp. chapter 3, "Scene as machine, 1: Scenography as a machine of performance," 46–61.

74 See Judith Roof, *The Poetics of DNA* (Minneapolis: University of Minnesota Press, 2007).
75 As an aside, it is worth noting that French mathematician Henri Poincaré (1854–1912) characterized his peers' early work with what would become fractal math as producing "monsters."

Coda: Medium, Machinery, and the Present Moment

1 See Zielinski, esp. pp. 57–157, for lucid, rigorously researched analyses of the positions Kircher, Dee, and della Porta occupy in media's deep time.
2 Jean Baudrillard. "The Precession of Simulacra." *Simulacra and Simulation*, trans. Sheila Faria Glaser (Ann Arbor: University of Michigan Press, [1981] 1994) 1–42, 2.

Bibliography

Adams, John, comp., and Alice Goodman, libr. *Nixon in China*. Compact Disc. BMI-Red Dawn Music, 1987.

Adams, John, comp., and Alice Goodman, libr. *Nixon in China*. DVD. Houston Grand Opera. Libr. Alice Goodman. Dir. Peter Sellars. Cond. John DeMain. Intr. Walter Cronkite. PBS—*Great Performances*: April 15, 1988.

Adams, John, comp., and Alice Goodman, libr. *Nixon in China: An Opera in Three Acts*. London: Boosey and Hawkes, 1999.

Althusser, Louis. "Ideology and Ideological State Apparatuses: Notes Toward an Investigation." Louis Althusser. *Lenin and Philosophy and Other Essays*. Trans. Ben Brewster. New York: Monthly Review Press, 1971.

Baudrillard, Jean. "The Precession of Simulacra." In Baudrillard (ed.). *Simulacra and Simulation*, trans. Sheila Faria Glaser. Ann Arbor: University of Michigan Press, [1981] 1994 1–42.

Baugh, Christopher. *Theatre, Performance, and Technology: The Development of Scenography in the Twentieth Century*. London: Palgrave Macmillan, 2005.

Bay-Cheng, Sarah. "Translation, Typography, and the Avant-Garde's Impossible Text." *Theatre Journal* 59:3 (October 2007), 467–83.

Beckett, Samuel. *Collected Shorter Plays*. New York: Grove Press, 1984.

Beckett, Samuel. *Krapp's Last Tape*. Samuel Beckett. *Krapp's Last Tape and Other Dramatic Pieces*. New York: Grove, 1958.

Beckett, Samuel. *Quad*. In Beckett. *Collected Shorter Plays*.

Beckett, Samuel. *Ohio Impromptu*. In Beckett. *Collected Shorter Plays*.

Beckett, Samuel. *Play*. In Beckett. *The Collected Shorter Plays*.

Beckett, Samuel. *Rockaby*. In Beckett. *Collected Shorter Plays*.

Beckett, Samuel. *What Where*. In Beckett. *Collected Shorter Plays*.

Benjamin, Walter. "The Work of Art in the Age of Its Technological Reproducibility: Second Version." Trans. Edmund Jephcott and Harry Zohn. Walter Benjamin. *The Work of Art in the Age of Its Technological Reproducibility and Other Writings on Media*. Cambridge, MA: Belknap Press of Harvard University Press, 2008.

Bentley, Eric Russell. "The Theatres of Wagner and Ibsen." *The Kenyon Review* 6:4 (Autumn 1944), 542–69.

Bergdoll, Barry. "Introduction." Lucien Hervé. *The Eiffel Tower: A Photographic Survey*. New York: Princeton Architectural Press, 2003.

Berger, Glen. *The Song of Spider-Man: The Inside Story of the Most Controversial Musical in Broadway History*. New York: Simon and Schuster, 2013.

Bignell, Jonathan. *Beckett on Screen: The Television Plays*. Manchester: Manchester University Press, 2009.

Bigsby, Christopher. *Arthur Miller: A Critical Study*. Cambridge: Cambridge University Press, 2005.

Birringer, Johannes. *Theatre, Theory, Postmodernism*. Bloomington: Indiana University Press, 1991.

Brecht, Bertolt. "Alienation Effects in Chinese Acting." In Bertolt Brecht. *Brecht on Theatre*.

Brecht, Bertolt. *Brecht on Theatre*. Ed. and trans. John Willett. New York: Hill and Wang, 1964.

Brecht, Bertolt. *Lindbergh's Flight*. Trans. John Willett. Brecht. *Collected Plays*. Ed. John Willett. Vol. 3 of 8. Part 2. London: Methuen, 1997.

Brunstein, Ada and Tod Machover. "Singing the Body Electric: Emotion-reading technology gives Tod Machover's opera an animatronic stage with heart." *New Scientist*. December 18, 2010. Accessed November 15, 2018. operaofthefuture.files.wordpress.com/2010/12/newscientistqamachover.pdf.

Burke, Jeff. "A Play that is Not a Play: Heiner Müller's *Hamletmachine* as Digital Installation." In Friedman.

Čapek, Karel. *R.U.R.* in Josef and Karel Čapek. *R.U.R. and The Insect Play*. Trans. P. Selver. adapt. Nigel Playfair. Oxford: Oxford University Press, [1923] 1961.

Chaudhuri, Una. *Staging Place: The Geography of Modern Drama*. Ann Arbor: University of Michigan Press, 1995.

Cocteau, Jean. *The Infernal Machine*. Trans. Albert Bermel and Jean Cocteau. *The Infernal Machine and Other Plays*. New York: New Directions, 1964.

Cocteau, Jean. *Les Mariés de la Tour Eiffel*. In Cocteau, *Theatre* vol. 1. 8th ed. Paris: Gallimard, 1948.

Cocteau, Jean. *The Wedding on the Eiffel Tower*. Trans. Michael Benedikt. *Modern French Theatre*. Eds. Michael Benedikt and George Wellwarth. New York: E. P. Dutton, 1962.

Cohen, Paula Morantz. "The Dynamo, the Salesman, and the Playwright." *Arthur Miller's* Death of a Salesman. Ed. Eric Sterling. Amsterdam: Rodopi, 2008.

Comentale, Edward P. *Modernism, Cultural Production, and the British Avant-Garde*. Cambridge: Cambridge University Press, 2004.

Craig, Edward Gordon. "The Actor and the Marionette." *On the Art of the Theatre*. Ed. Franc Chamberlain. London: Routledge, 2009.

de Maupassant, Guy. *La Vie Errante*. La Bibliothèque électronique de Québec. Transcribed from Paris: Paul Ollendorff, 1890. *À tous les vents*: 447:1.01. Accessed October 14, 2018. https://www.google.com/url?sa=t&rct=j&q=&esrc=s&source=web&cd=1&ved=2ahUKEwj4867gw4beAhXQ1FkKHQ9yCegQFjAAegQIDBAC&url=https%3A%2F%2Fbeq.ebooksgratuits.com%2Fvents%2FMaupassant_La_vie_errante.pdf&usg=AOvVaw2mpsRXNNgcsxiH4kBlildL, 5.

de Tocqueville, Alexis. *Democracy in America*. Vol. 1. Trans. Henry Reeve. Rev. Francis Bowen. Ed. Phillips Bradly. New York: Vintage, [1945] 1954.

Debord, Guy-Ernest. *Society of the Spectacle*. Nothingness.org. Published by Black & Red. Accessed November 27, 2018. http://library.nothingness.org/articles/SI/en/pub_contents/4.

Deleuze, Gilles and Félix Guattari. "Kafka: Toward a Minor Literature." Trans. Dana Polan. *Theory and History of Literature*. Vol. 30. Minneapolis: University of Minnesota Press, 1986.

Deleuze, Gilles and Félix Guattari. *A Thousand Plateaus: Capitalism and Schizophrenia*. Trans. Brian Massumi. Minneapolis: University of Minnesota Press, 1987.

DeLillo, Don. *Valparaiso*. New York: Scribner, 1999.

Dudley, Joseph. "Being and Non-Being: The Other and Heterotopia in *Hamletmachine*." *Modern Drama* 35:4 (Winter 1992), 562–70.

Egoyan, Atom, dir. *Krapp's Last Tape*. Samuel Beckett. Beckett on Film. DVD. Blue Angel Films, 2001. Disc 2.

Eisenhower, Dwight D. "The Farewell Address: Reading Copy of the Speech." Dwight D. Eisenhower Presidential Library, Museum, and Boyhood Home. DDE's Papers as President. Speech Series. Box 38. Final TV Talk 1); NAID # 594599. January 17, 1961. Accessed October 14, 2018. https://www.eisenhower.archives.gov/research/online-documents/farewell-address/reading-copy.pdf.

Eliot, T. S. *The Waste Land*. In *The Complete Poems and Plays, 1909–1950*. Ed. T. S. Eliot. New York: Harcourt, Brace, and World, 1971.

Ellis-Jones, Ian. "Don't Be a Mindless Zero." Dr. Ian Ellis-Jones…Living Mindfully Now. January 15, 2016. Accessed November 1, 2018. http://ianellis-jones.blogspot.com/2016/01/dont-be-mindless-zero.html.

Emerson, Ralph Waldo. "Self-Reliance." *The Collected Works of Ralph Waldo Emerson*. Vol. 2: Essays: First Series. Eds. Joseph Slater, Alfred R. Ferguson, and Jean Ferguson Carr. Cambridge, MA: Harvard University Press, 1980).

Evans, Michael. *Karl Marx*. London: George Allen and Unwin, [1975] 2004.

Ewen, Stuart. *All Consuming Images: The Politics of Style in Contemporary Culture*. New York: Basic Books, 1988.

Foucault, Michel. *The Archaeology of Knowledge and the Discourse on Language*. Trans. A. M. Sheridan Smith. New York: Pantheon Books, 1972.

Friedman, Dan, ed. *Müller in America: American Productions of Works by Heiner Müller, Volume One*. New York: Castillo Cultural Center, 2003.

Fugard, Athol. *Statements: Sizwe Bansi Is Dead, The Island, and Statements after an Arrest under the Immorality Act*. New York: Theatre Communications Group, 1986.

Gans, Andrew. "President Bill Clinton Comments on Opening of *Spider-Man Turn Off the Dark*." Playbill June 15, 2011. Accessed November 16, 2018. http://www.playbill.com/article/president-bill-clinton-comments-on-opening-of-spider-man-turn-off-the-dark-com-180102.

Garner, Stanton B., Jr. "*The Gas Heart*: Disfigurement and the Dada Body." *Modern Drama* 50:4 (Winter 2007), 500–16.

Genette, Gerard. *Paratexts: Thresholds of Interpretation*. Trans. Jane E. Lewin. Cambridge: Cambridge University Press, 1997.

Germano, William. "Opera as News: *Nixon in China* and the Contemporary Operatic Subject." *University of Toronto Quarterly*. 81:4 (Fall 2012), 797–823.

Gomez, Isaac. *La Ruta*. Dir. Sandra Marquez. Scenic des. Regina Garcia. Chicago, IL: Steppenwolf Theatre, January 5, 2019.

Goodman, Alice. *Nixon in China*. In Goodman. *History is our Mother: Three Libretti*. New York City: New York Review of Books, 2017. 1–69.

Gorelik, Mordecai. "Bertolt Brecht's 'Prospectus of the Diderot Society.'" *Quarterly Journal of Speech* 47:2 (April 1961).

Jerzy Grotowski, "Towards a Poor Theatre." Trans. T. K. Wiewiorowsky. *Towards a Poor Theatre*. Ed. Eugenio Barba. New York: Routledge, 2002, 15–25.

Habermas, Jurgen. 'Technology and Science as "Ideology."' *Toward a Rational Society: Student Protest, Science, and Politics*. Trans. Jeremy J. Shapiro. Boston: Beacon Press, 1970.

Hamer, Mick. "The Biggest Meccano Set in the World." *The New Scientist*. December 24–31, 1988, 65–68.

Harmon, Maurice, ed. *No Author Better Served: The Correspondence of Samuel Beckett and Alan Schneider*. Cambridge, MA: Harvard University Press, 1998.

Hayhurst, J. D. *The Pneumatic Post of Paris*. Ed. C. S. Holder. Digitized by Mark Hayhurst. The France and Colonies Philatelic Society of Great Britain, 1974. Accessed October 17, 2018. http://www.cix.co.uk/~mhayhurst/jdhayhurst/pneumatic/book1.html.

Hayles, N. Katherine. *How We Became Posthuman: Virtual Bodies in Cybernetics, Literature, and Informatics*. Chicago: University of Chicago Press, 1999.

Hayles, N. Katherine. "Voices out of Bodies, Bodies Out of Voices: Audiotape and the Production of Subjectivity." *Sound States: Innovate Poetics and Acoustical Technologies*. Ed. Adelaide Morris. Chapel Hill: University of North Carolina Press, 1997.

Hayles, N. Katherine. *Writing Machines*. Cambridge: MIT Press, 2002.

Hayman, Ronald. *British Theatre since 1955: A Reassessment*. Oxford: Oxford University Press, 1979.

Healy, Patrick and Kevin Flynn. "A Broadway Superlative for All the Wrong Reasons." *The New York Times*. March 13, 2011. Accessed November 15, 2018. https://www.nytimes.com/2011/03/14/theater/spider-man-a-superlative-for-all-the-wrong-reasons.html.

Heinzelmann, Josef. "Kurt Weill's Compositions for Radio" (Liner notes). Trans. Lionel Salter and Kurt Weill. *Der Lindberghflug and The Ballad of Magna Carta*. Königsdorf: Delta Music-Capriccio, 1990.

Herren, Graley. *Samuel Beckett's Plays on Film and Television*. New York: Palgrave, 2009.

Hersh, Seymour M. *The Price of Power: Kissinger in the Nixon White House*. New York: Summit Books, 1983.

Höfele, Andreas. "A Theater of Exhaustion? '*Posthistoire*' in Recent German Shakespeare Productions." *Shakespeare Quarterly* 43:1 (Spring 1992), 80–6.

Holzapfel, Amy Strahler. "Strindberg as Vivisector: Physiology, Pathology, and Anti-Mimesis in *The Father* and *Miss Julie*." *Modern Drama* 51:3 (Fall 2008), 329–52.

Hoover, Herbert. "October 22, 1928: Principles and Ideals of the United States Government." Campaign Speech Transcript. University of Virginia's Miller Center. Accessed October 30, 2018. https://millercenter.org/the-presidency/presidential-speeches/october-22-1928-principles-and-ideals-united-states-government.

Hudson, Robbie. "Opera gets a Machover." *The Sunday Times* November 8, 2010. Accessed November 15, 2018. https://operaofthefuture.com/2010/11/08/the-sunday-times-opera-gets-a-machover/.

Hughes, Robert. "Swinging for the Rafters: Spider-Man Set Designer Opts for a Pop-Up Peter Parker." *The Observer*. September 28, 2010. Accessed November 16, 2018. https://observer.com/2010/09/swinging-for-the-rafters-ispidermani-set-designer-opts-for-a-popup-peter-parker/.

Ionesco, Eugène. "L'Avenir est dans les Ouefs, ou Il Faut de Tout pour Faire un Monde." Théâtre. Vol. 2. Paris: Gallimard, 1958.

Ionesco, Eugène. "The Future is in Eggs, or It Takes All Sorts to Make a World." Trans. Derek Prouse. Eugène Ionesco. *Plays*. Vol. 4 of 7. London: Calder and Boyars, 1960.

Ionesco, Eugène. "Jack, or The Submission." *Four Plays*. Trans. Donald M. Allen. New York: Grove Weidenfeld, 1958.

Ionesco, Eugène. "Jacques, ou La Soumission." *Théâtre*. Vol. 1. Paris: Gallimard, 1954.

Jameson, Fredric. *Postmodernism: The Cultural Logic of Late Capitalism*. Durham: Duke University Press, 1989.

Johnson, Timothy A. *John Adam's* Nixon in China: *Musical Analysis, Historical and Political Perspectives*. Farnham: Ashgate, 2011.

Kairschner, Shawn. "Coercive Somatographies: X-rays, Hypnosis, and Stanislavsky's Production Plan for *The Seagull*." *Modern Drama* 51:3 (Fall 2008), 369–88.

Kemp, Peter. "Rude Mechanicals." *The Independent*. November 6, 1987.

Kenicott, Philip. "Man and Machine." *Opera News*. October, 2013. Accessed November 15, 2018.web.media.mit.edu/~tod/media/pdfs/October2013_OperaNews.pdf.

Klaver, Elizabeth. "Postmodernism and the Intersection of Television and Contemporary Drama." *Journal of Popular Culture* 27:4 (Spring 1994), 69–80.

Knowlson, James. *Damned to Fame: The Life of Samuel Beckett.* New York: Simon & Schuster, 1996.

Knopf, Jan. *Brecht Handbuch: eine Ästhetik der Widersprüche.* Stuttgart: Metzler, 1996.

Lumaga, Pio Barone. "Dallas Opera's Simulcast—Tod Machover's *Death and the Powers*." Accessed November 15, 2018. http://web.media.mit.edu/~tod/media/pdfs/LOFT-DATP-simulcast_upcoming.pdf.

Lyotard, Jean-François. *The Inhuman: Reflections on Time.* Trans. Geoffrey Bennington and Rachel Bowlby. Stanford: Stanford University Press, 1991.

Machover, Tod, comp., and Robert Pinsky, libr. *Death and the Powers.* DVD. Dallas: Winspear Opera House, 2014.

Machover, Tod. "On Future Performance." *New York Times*: Opinionator. January 13, 2010. Accessed November 15, 2018. https://opinionator.blogs.nytimes.com/2010/01/13/on-future-performance/.

Maddalena, James. perf. "News." Comp. John Adams and libr. Alice Goodman. *Nixon in China.* New York Metropolitan Opera. January 31, 2011. YouTube. Accessed November 28, 2018. https://www.youtube.com/watch?v=FJmXMo9nWRU.

Magelssen, Scott and John Troyer's "BLA BLA, a textual 'performance' of *Hamletmachine*." In Friedman.

Mandelbrot, Benoit B. *The Fractal Geometry of Nature* New York: W. H. Freeman, 1983.

Marx, Karl. *Capital: Volume I.* Trans. Samuel Moore and Edward Aveling. In Karl Marx and Frederick Engels. *The Marx–Engels Reader.* 2nd ed. Ed. Robert C. Tucker. New York: Norton, 1978.

McLuhan, Marshall. *Understanding Media: The Extensions of Man.* New York: McGraw-Hill, 1964. 160.

McMaster, Brian. "Brian McMaster Introduces the 2006 Festival." Accessed February 14, 2008. www.eif.co.uk/audio/Brian3.mp3 [webpage no longer available].

Messerli, Douglas, et al. "Elmer Rice *The Adding Machine*." UStheater, Opera, and Performance. July 11, 2011. Accessed October 31, 2018. http://ustheater.blogspot.com/2011/07/elmer-rice-adding-machine.html.

Meyer, Michael J. "In His Father's Image: Biff Loman's Struggle with Inherited Traits in *Death of a Salesman*." In *Arthur Miller's* Death of a Salesman. Ed. Eric J. Sterling. Amsterdam: Rodopi, 2008. 123.

Millar, Mervyn. *The Horse's Mouth: How Handspring and The National Made War Horse*. 2nd ed. London: National Theatre, 2011.

Miller, Arthur. *Death of a Salesman: Certain Private Conversations in Two Acts and a Requiem*. New York: Viking Press, [1949] 1981.

Minghella, Anthony, dir. *Play*. by Samuel Beckett. *Beckett on Film*. DVD 3 of 4 Blue Angel Films, 2001.

Müller, Heiner. *The Hamletmachine*. Trans. Carl Weber. *Performing Arts Journal* 4:3 (1980), 141–6.

Norman, Lance. "Dumb Waiters, Dead Children and Martinizing the Pinteresque." In *Pinter Et Cetera*. Ed. Craig N. Owens. Newcastle-upon-Tyne: Cambridge Scholars Press, 2009.

O'Donnell, Damien, dir. *What Where*. Samuel Beckett. *Beckett on Film*. DVD. Blue Angel Films, 2001. Disc 2.

Osborne, John. *Look Back in Anger*. London: Faber & Faber, 1957.

Owens, Craig N. "The Eyes Have It: 'Ocular Proof' and the Practice of Criticism." In *Talking Drama*. Ed. Judith Roof. Newcastle upon Tyne: Cambridge Scholars, 2009.

Owens, Craig N. "Mystifying the Machine: Staged and Unstaged Technologies in Arthur Miller's *Death of a Salesman*." In *Arthur Miller's* Death of a Salesman. Ed. Eric Sterling. Amsterdam: Rodopi, 2008.

Palmieri, Anthony F. R. *Elmer Rice: A Playwright's Vision of America*. Rutherford: Farleigh-Dickinson Press, 1980.

Patterson, Michael. *Strategies of Political Theatre: Post-War British Playwrights*. Cambridge: Cambridge University Press, 2003.

Pinsky, Robert. *Death and the Powers: A Robot Pageant. Poetry* 196:4 (July/August 2010), 285–332.

Pinter, Harold. *The Birthday Party. The Birthday Party and The Room: Two Plays*. New York: Grove Press, 1981 [1961].

Pinter, Harold. *The Dumb Waiter. Complete Works*. Vol. 1. New York: Grove Weidenfeld, 1976.

Pinter, Harold. *Mountain Language*. New York: Grove Press, 1988.

Pinter, Harold. *One for the Road*. New York: Grove Weidenfeld, 1985.

Pinter, Harold. "Party Time." *Party Time and The New World Order: Two Plays*. New York: Grove Press, 1993.

Pinter, Harold. "The Room." *The Birthday Party and The Room: Two Plays.* New York: Grove Press, [1961] 1981.

Pirandello, Luigi. *Six Characters in Search of an Author.* In *Three Plays.* Trans. Edward Storer. New York: Dutton, 1922.

Rabinbach, Anson. *The Human Motor: Energy, Fatigue, and the Origins of Modernity.* Berkeley: University of California Press, 1990.

Rey, Rebecca. *Staging Don DeLillo.* London: Routledge, 2016.

Rice, Elmer. "The Adding Machine." *Seven Plays.* New York: Viking Press, 1950.

Riedel, Michael. "Broadway Bombshell." *New York Post.* May 30, 2010. Accessed November 16, 2018. https://nypost.com/2010/05/30/broadway-bombshell/.

Roof, Judith. "The Deficient Ballcock: Pinter's Comic Turn." *The Harold Pinter Review: Essays on Contemporary Drama* 2 (2018).

Roof, Judith. *The Poetics of DNA.* Minneapolis: University of Minnesota Press, 2007.

Roudané, Matthew C. "*Death of a Salesman* and the Poetics of Arthur Miller." *The Cambridge Companion to Arthur Miller.* Ed. Christopher Bigsby Cambridge: Cambridge University Press, 1997.

Schiffman, Daniel. "Fractals." The Nature of Code. Accessed November 16, 2018. https://natureofcode.com/book/chapter-8-fractals/.

Shakespeare, William. *Hamlet. The Oxford Shakespeare.* Ed. G. R. Hibbard. Oxford: Oxford University Press, 2008.

Shaw, George Bernard. *Major Barbara. The Bodley Head Bernard Shaw: Collected Plays with their Prefaces.* Vol. 3 of 7. New York: Dodd, Mead, 1970–74.

Shklovsky, Viktor. "Art and Device." In *Theory of Prose.* Trans. Benjamin Sher. Normal: Dalkey Archive Press, 1991.

Sierz, Aleks. "In-Yer-Face-Theatre." Accessed November 9, 2018. http://www.inyerfacetheatre.com/intro.html.

Simonson, Lee. *The Art of Scenic Design.* New York: Harper and Brothers, 1950.

Simonson, Lee. *The Part of a Lifetime: Drawings and Designs 1919–1940.* New York: Duell, Sloan and Pearce, 1943.

Simonson, Lee. *The Stage Is Set.* New York: Theatre Arts Books, [1932] 1963.

Sircar, Badal. *Evam Indrajit [and Indrajit].* Trans. Girish Karnad. *Three Modern Indian Plays.* Oxford: Oxford University Press, 1989, 1–60.

Slowiak, James. "To Confront Paradox: New World Performance Lab's *Hamletmachine*." In Friedman.
Spectacular! Stage Design: Concerts, Events and Ceremonies, Theaters. Hong Kong: SendPoints Publishing, 2015.
Squiers, Anthony. *An Introduction to the Social and Political Philosophy of Bertolt Brecht: Revolution and Aesthetics*. Amsterdam: Rodopi, 2014.
Taymor, Julie, dir. *Oedipus Rex*. Comp. Igor Stravinsky. Libr. Jean Cocteau. Cond. Seiji Ozawa. VHS Polygram Video, 1994.
Treadwell, Sophie. *Machinal*. Intr. Judith E. Barlow. London: Nick Hern Books, 1993.
Truzzi, Gianni. "*The Adding Machine*, 1923." GianT Thoughts. November 17, 2008. Accessed November 2, 2018. http://giant-thoughts.blogspot.com/2008/11/adding-machine-1923.html.
Tung, Charles. "Modernism, Time Machines, and the Defamiliarization of Time." *Configurations* 23:1 (Winter 2015), 93–121.
Tzara, Tristan. *Le Coeur à Gaz* Paris: GLM, 1946 [1921].
Tzara, Tristan. *The Gas Heart. Modern French Theatre: The Avant-Garde, Dada, and Surrealism*. Trans. Michael Benedikt. Eds. Michael Benedikt and George E. Wellwarth. New York: Dutton, 1964.
Voorhis, Jerry. *The Strange Case of Richard Milhous Nixon*. New York: Paul S. Eriksson, 1972.
Varisco, Robert A. "Anarchy and Resistance in Tristan Tzara's *The Gas Heart*." *Modern Drama* 40:1 (Spring 1997), 139–48.
Walker, Lynne. 'Brecht and Weill: The Flight Fantastic.' *The Independent*. July 31, 2006. Accessed February 14, 2008. http://www.independent.co.uk/arts-entertainment/music/features/brecht-and-weill-the-flight-fantastic-409959.html.
Watt, Stephen. *Joyce, O'Casey and the Irish Popular Theatre*. Syracuse: Syracuse University Press, 1991.
Willett, John. "Introduction." *Brecht on Theatre*. Ed. and trans. John Willett. New York: Hill and Wang, 1964.
Williams, Kirk. "The Ghost in the Machine: Heiner Müller's Devouring Melancholy." *Modern Drama* 49:2 (Summer 2006), 188–205.
Williams, Raymond. *The Country and the City*. New York: Oxford University Press, 1973.
Young, Alan R. Hamlet *and the Visual Arts, 1709–1900*. Newark: University of Delaware Press, 2002.

Zhi-Zheng, Chen, dir. *Nixon in China*. Comp. John Adams and libr. Alice Goodman. Théâtre du Chatelet. Chamber Orchestra of Paris. Paris, 2012. YouTube. Accessed November 27, 2018. https://www.youtube.com/watch?v=Czi81hRErJk (the video is unavailable at present).

Zielinski, Siegfried. *Deep Time of the Media*. Trans. Gloria Custance. Cambridge, MA: MIT Press, 2006.

Zurbrugg, Nicholas. "Post-Modernism and the Multi-Media Sensibility: Heiner Müller's *Hamletmachine* and the Art of Robert Wilson." *Modern Drama* 31:3 (Fall 1988), 439–53.

Index

absurdist theatre 29–30, 161–2, 168, 172–3, 175, 180
actors
  absurdist theatre for 168
  alienation and 164–6
  in *Beckett on Film* (Egoyan) 158
  for Brecht 115–16, 131
  characterization and 131–2, 159–60, 232 n.8
  dislocution for 161–2
  dramatic text and 225–6
  machines as 190–1
  rehearsal for 162–3
  script analysis and 44
  singing for 125–6
  stage directions for 157–8
  symbolism and 40
  in *Valparaiso* (DeLillo) 156
Adams, John 11–12, 28–9
  Goodman and 67, 122, 241 n.1
  music by 127–8, 135
  see also Nixon in China
The Adding Machine (Rice) 23–4, 27
Death of a Salesman (Miller) and 98–9
Machinal (Treadwell) and 89, 94–5
modernity in 71–7
philosophy in 86
sound in 182
Taylorism in 81
Adler, Stella 155
Aeschylus 192
aesthetics 231 n.6
  of art 41
  of *Hamletmachine* (Müller) 183
  mise en scène for 176
  of modernity 67
  politics and 107–9, 241 n.5
Africa 21–2

Aguirre-Sacaso, Roberto 186
Albee, Edward 180
alienation
  actors and 164–6
  in *Lindbergh's Flight* (Brecht and Weill) 107–16
  in *Nixon in China* (Goodman and Adams) 132–6
  in spectacle 105–6
  in theatre 101–3
Allen, Donald M. 236 n.59
All My Sons (Miller) 93–5
Althusser, Louis 118, 170–1
ambiguity 50–1
  in absurdist theatre 172–3
  in dialogue 142
  in *Eiffel Tower Wedding Party* (Cocteau) 55–6
  in language 232 n.11, 234 n.36
  in narrative performance 206
  production of 52–3
  for Tzara 56–63
  of voice 42–4
Anderson, June 132
and Indrajit (Sircar) 149, 180–3
animals 38
Anthropocene technology 225
apparatus 242 n.14
  family as 143
  ideological 12, 154–5
  "Ideology and Ideological State Apparatuses" 170–1
  of machines 64, 141
  in production 47–8
  scientific 49–50, 114–15
  social 168
  technological 223–4
  theatrical 5, 10, 17, 144, 150, 161–2, 176–7, 200–1

Appia, Adolphe 20, 214
Aristotle 4, 106
Armitage, Karole 207
art
 aesthetics of 41
 of ballet 37
 choreography in 2
 during the Enlightenment 35
 during industrialism 26–7
 innovation in 4
 machines in 25
 modernity and 114–15
 Renaissance paintings 61
 sculptures 231 n.6
 systems in 15
 "The Work of Art in the Age of its Technological Reproducibility" 133
 in United States 12
Asia 21–2
assemblage 6–7, 27, 51–2, 230 n.7
Auburn, David 21
audiences
 for Brecht 109
 consciousness of 208
 dramatic text and 174–5, 212–13, 226–7
 emotions for 65–6
 interaction with 209
 Krapp's Last Tape (Beckett) for 167–8
 as listeners 111
 performance for 15
 plot stability for 189–90
 spectacle for 105–6
 suspension of disbelief for 212–13, 255 n.71
 television for 190–1
 theatrical apparatus for 176–7
 in United States 129
Auric, Georges 35, 37
Australia 193–4
authorial identity 10

authority 9–10
autonomy 88

Baden-Baden Chamber Music Festival 28, 111–13, 121
ballet 37
Baudrillard, Jean 227
Baugh, Christopher 17–19, 109
Bauhaus University 193–4
Bay-Cheng, Sarah 60–2
Bayreuth Festspielhaus 215
Beckett, Samuel 11, 13, 23, 193
 Pinter and 147, 149–51, 179–80, 182–3, 226
 production for 248 n.15
 reputation of 157–8, 194
 see also Breath; *Catastrophe*; *Come and Go*; *Krapp's Last Tape*; *Not I*; *Ohio Impromptu*; *Play*; *Quad*; *Rockaby*; *That Time*; *Waiting for Godot*; *What Where*
Benedikt, Michael 59
Benjamin, Walter 9, 29, 118–19, 133, 141
Berger, Glen 186, 211–12, 255 n.68
Bignell, Jonathan 158
Bigsby, Christopher 13, 94
biomechanics 248 n.2
Birringer, Johannes 187–8, 197–8
The Birthday Party (Pinter) 150
Bond, Edward 104, 200–1
Bono (musician) 30, 183, 186, 209; *see also Spider-Man*
Börlin, Jean 37
Boucicault Dion 20
bourgeois values 180–2
Breath (Beckett) 179
Brecht, Bertolt 1, 13, 29, 193
 actors for 115–16, 131
 audiences for 109
 Benjamin and 118–19
 Fugard and 102
 Galileo (Brecht) 21
 gest for 244 n.35

Index

Greek theatre for 109–10
  innovation for 113–14, 243 n.30
  radio for 243 n.25
  spectacle for 120–1
  theory of 105, 107–8
  Weill and 67, 157
  Willett on 246 n.66
  see also Galileo; *The Good Person of Szechuan*; *Lindbergh's Flight*; *Short Organum for Theatre*
Brenton, Howard 105
Brill, Robert 224–5
Broadway theatre 171–2, 209–10
Brook, Peter 201
Buontalenti, Bernardo 20
Burkman, Katherine 32

Calder, Alexander 231 n.6
cameras 176, 178–9
Camus, Albert 180
Cantor set 195
Čapek, Karel 31, 219–20, 226
capitalism
  culture of 218
  entertainment and 106–7
  expressionism and 73–4
  ideology of 28–9, 141, 193, 244 n.39
  individual
    disempowerment and 71
  machines and 27–8, 94, 188–9
  NAFTA and 96–7
  politics of 170–1
Catastrophe (Beckett) 179
The Chairs (Ionesco) 53
Chaplin, Charlie 154–5
characterization 16
  actors and 131–2, 159–60, 232 n.8
  dialogue and 125–6
  in *Krapp's Last Tape* (Beckett) 169
  plot and 217
  stage directions for 88
Chaudhuri, Una 31–3, 95, 196–7
Chayefsky, Paddy 220

Chen Zhi-Zheng 132
Ch'iang Ching *see Nixon in China*
Chong, Ping 188
choreography 2, 59, 207
choruses 140, 144
Churchill, Caryl 105, 174
Cleveland Public Theater 193
Cocteau, Jean 12, 27, 35, 226
  machines for 160
  Rice and 74
  see also Eiffel Tower Wedding Party; *The Infernal Machine*
Come and Go (Beckett) 179
communication
  dialogue and 169–70
  with family 153–4
communication (technologies)
  innovation in 141
  production and 149
Conrad, Joseph 193
consciousness 204–5, 208
constraint
  in *The Dumb Waiter* (Pinter) 164–72, 182
  in *and Indrajit* (Sircar) 180–3
  in *Krapp's Last Tape* (Beckett) 151–60
  machines and 149–51
  in *Play* (Beckett) 176–80
  in *What Where* (Beckett) 172–7
COVID-19 223
Craig, Gordon 20, 55, 214
Craney, Trudy Ellen 241 n.1
Cronkite, Walter 135–6, 241 n.1
cubo-futurists 243 n.30
culture
  bourgeois values in 180–2
  of capitalism 218
  ideology and 22
  masculinity in 137–8
  modernism in 51
  modernity in 39
  of prisons 145–6
  rhizomes and 52

in scholarship 21–2
cybernetics 204, 219
cyborgs 139, 220, 226
cynicism 85–6

D'Alembert, Jean le Rond 35
dance
 choreography in 59
 dialogue and 39–40
 interpretation of 62
 scholarship on 60
death 142–3
Death and the Powers (Pinsky and Machover) 11, 30–1
 Hamletmachine (Müller) and 215, 218–21, 226
 machines in 214
 performance in 250 n.46
 post-human recursivity in 201–9
 production of 253 n.46
 Spider-Man and 183, 186, 214–16
Death of a Salesman (Miller) 27
The Adding Machine (Rice) and 98–9
 interpretations of 40
 minimalism in 98
 modernity in 69, 95
 Nixon in China (Goodman and Adams) and 220
 nostalgia in 84, 86–94
 Valparaiso (DeLillo) and 152–3
Debord, Guy 106
deconstruction 6, 12–13
Dee, John 225
Deleuze, Gilles 6–7, 9, 27, 51–2, 51–3, 95, 193, 230 n.7
DeLillo, Don 23, 28, 40, 67, 138–9; see also *Valparaiso*
della Porta, Giovan Battista 225
DeMain, John 241 n.1
Derrida, Jacques 6–7, 9
Descartes, René 35
Diaghilev, Sergei 35
dialogue 16
 ambiguity in 142
 characterization and 125–6
 communication and 169–70
 dance and 39–40
 expressionism and 79–80
 for family 92–3
 language in 166
 machines and 164
 by Miller 93–4
 modernity in 81–2
 in music 130–1
 politics in 126–7
 stage directions for 177–8
 tone from 79, 82–3
 in *Valparaiso* (DeLillo) 91–2
Diderot, Denis 35
Diderot Society 115–16
digitality 12, 26, 165, 203–4, 221
 coding and 194–5
 digital sound 1–2, 183
 remastering with 224
diplomacy 245 n.46
dislocution 144, 160–2
disruption 23–4
dramatic text
 actors and 225–6
 audiences and 174–5, 212–13, 226–7
 by Goodman 135
 interior monologues in 160
 interpretive thresholds in 6
 machines in 179–80
 modernity in 89–90
 by Müller 194–5, 197, 199
 nostalgia in 67
 paratext in 5
 performance and 1, 6–7, 15–16, 20, 162–3
 production and 4–9, 173–4
 for readers 61
 repetition in 128–9
 scholarship on 3–4, 19, 104–5, 196–7
 script analysis of 12–13, 155–6

Index

stage directions in 24
theory and 8
transportation in 102–3
Dry, Marion 241 n.1
Duchamp, Marcel 35
Dudley, Joseph, M. 192, 197–8
The Dumb Waiter (Pinter) 23, 29–30, 149–51
  comedy in 250 n.37
  constraint in 164–72, 182
Hamletmachine (Müller) and 167
Krapp's Last Tape (Beckett) and 179–80
  philosophy in 83
  themes in 82
Durey, Louis 35
Duykers, John 126, 241 n.1

Eastern Europe 174
economic violence 96–7
The Edge (musician) 30, 183, 186, 200–1, 209; *see also* Spider-Man
Edinburgh International Festival 117, 120, 220
Edison, Thomas 49
education 22–5
Egoyan, Atom 158
Eiffel, Gustave 49
Eiffel Tower Wedding Party (Cocteau) 12, 27, 58, 66
  ambiguity in 55–6
  The Future Is in Eggs and 101
  The Gas Heart and 79, 220
  innovation in 53–4
  Ionesco and 69
  language in 46–9
  machines in 54–5, 154
  setting in 35–43
  sound in 42–5
  symbolism in 49–53
  themes in 62–3
Eisenhower, Dwight D. 37, 66–7
Eisenstein, Linda 193
Eisenstein, Sergei 243 n.30

electric chair 84–5
Eliot, T. S. 192–3, 239 n.22
emasculation 95
Emerson, Ralph Waldo 27–8, 70
emotions 64–6
England 55, 171, 174
the Enlightenment 35, 140
entertainment 106–7
Esslin, Martin 180
ethics 212
Euripides 193
Europe
  assemblage in 51–2
  Eastern Europe 174
  the Enlightenment for 140
  France for 35–42
  history of 57–8
  innovation for 61–2
  language in 60
  United States and 10, 21–2, 26, 35, 146–7, 171–2
  war for 45
Evans, David Howell *see* The Edge
Ewen, Stuart 29, 137–8
existentialism 180
expressionism
  capitalism and 73–4
  dialogue and 79–80
  in Germany 84
  machines and 80–1
  in theatre 69–70

family
  in *All My Sons* (Miller) 93–4
  as apparatus 143
  communication with 153–4
  dialogue for 92–3
  modernity for 86–7
female agency 84
film 179, 220
Fitzgerald, F. Scott 54
Fleming, Renée 224
Flynn, Kevin 210
Foucault, Michel 6–7, 9, 14–15

The Archaeology of Knowledge
   (Foucault) 6
The Discourse on Language
   (Foucault) 14–15
Foxwoods theatre 214–15
fractals 195–9, 201, 219, 256 n.75
France
   for Europe 35–42
   French 234 n.36, 235 n.37,
      235 n.43
   "The Glorious Thirty Years"
      in 62–3
   idioms from 59
   labor in 44–5
   Taylorism in 45–6
   see also Eiffel Tower Wedding Party
Frayn, Michael 21
Freeman, Barry 32
free will 185–6
French modernist theatre 27
Friedman, Stephanie 241 n.1
Fuchs, Elinor 230 n.15
Fugard, Athol 29, 102, 145–6
The Future Is in Eggs (Ionesco) 23, 27,
   36, 220
   Eiffel Tower Wedding Party
      (Cocteau) and 101
   Jack, or The Submission and 63–6
   modernity in 62–3
   stage directions in 73
   see also *The Island*
Futurism 55

Galileo (Brecht) 21
Garner, Stanton B. Jr. 57–8, 60
Garrick Theatre (New York) 76–7
The Gas Heart (Tzara) 12, 27, 66, 190,
   235 n.38
   Eiffel Tower Wedding Party
      (Cocteau) and 79, 220
   performance in 56–63
   satire in 101
   title of 234 n.36
Geikekam, Greg 32

gender 189
Genet, Jean 180
Genette, Gerard 5, 212–13
Germany 45, 63, 84, 113–14, 193–4
gest 244 n.35
Girard, François 117, 119–21
Glass, Philip 188
globalism 28
Gomez, Isaac 28, 226; see also
   La Ruta
Goodman, Alice 11–12, 28–9,
   128, 213
   Adams and 67, 122, 241 n.1
   dramatic text by 135
   see also *Nixon in China*
The Good Person of Szechuan
   (Brecht) 133
Gorelik, Mordecai 114
Gounod, Charles 224–5
Grass, Günther 180
Greek theatre 59–60, 103, 106,
   109–10, 140
Greenberg, Clement 2–3
Gropius, Walter 20
Grotowsky, Jerzy 193
Guattari, Félix 6–7, 9, 27, 51–2, 51–3,
   95, 193, 230 n.7
Gutenberg press 61

Habermas, Jürgen 9, 151–3
Hamletmachine (Müller) 12, 30–1
   aesthetics of 183
   Death and the Powers (Pinsky and
      Machover) and 215, 218–21, 226
   The Dumb Waiter (Pinter) and 167
   labor in 171
   post-human recursivity in
      188–97, 200–1
   systems in 197–9
Hare, David 105, 174
Harold Pinter Society 13
Hausdorff–Besicovitch
   dimensions 196
Hayles, N. Katherine 9, 163, 200

How We Became Posthuman (Hayles) 204–6
"Voices out of Bodies, Bodies out of Voices" (Hayles) 160
Writing Machines (Hayles) 3, 7–8, 10
Healy, Patrick 210
hegemony 107
Hemingway, Ernest 193
Herren, Graley 179
Hewson, Paul David *see* Bono
Hindemith, Paul 111
historiography 6
history
  of Europe 57–8
  of France 62–3
  of innovation 66–7
  of labor 44–5
  of modernity 51
  of performance 15, 26–7, 31–2
  of production 12–13
  real 96
  of theatre 1–5, 19–20, 25–7, 220–1
Höfele, Andreas 198–9
Holzapfel, Amy Strahler 153
Honneger, Arthur 35, 37
Hoover, Herbert 27–8, 70
Hudson, Robbie 207–8
Hughes, Robert 211
humans
  consciousness of 204–5
  COVID-19 for 223
  free will for 185–6
  humanist optimism 211–12
  innovation for 17
  language for 48–9
  machines and 23–4, 29–30, 44, 62, 69–70, 92–3, 95–6, 117–18, 159–60, 166–9
  for Miller 240 n.55
  mortality for 205–6
  robots and 10–12, 201–2
  subjectivity of 16
  systems for 31, 225
  see also post-human recursivity
Hurt, John 158–60, 244 n.40

Ibsen, Henrik 220
identity 10
ideology
  of capitalism 28–9, 141, 193, 244 n.39
  of Cocteau 55
  culture and 22
  ideological apparatus 12, 154–5
  ideological hegemony 107
  in *Krapp's Last Tape* (Beckett) 170–2
  machines and 18
  modernity and 151–2
  performance and 187–8
  power and 10–11
  psychology and 154
  of rugged individualism 27–8, 70, 185
  "Technology and Science as Ideology" 151–2
  techno-rationalist 151, 181–2, 226
  from theatre 67
  in United States 70–1, 86, 95
idioms 59, 235 n.43
India 180–2
individual disempowerment 71
industrialism 26–7, 36–7, 66–7
The Infernal Machine (Cocteau) 55–6, 212
innovation, technological
  Anthropocene technology 225
  in art 4
  for Brecht 113–14, 243 n.30
  in communication 141
  in *Eiffel Tower Wedding Party* (Cocteau) 53–4
  for Europe 61–2
  history of 66–7
  for humans 17
  from industrialism 66–7
  for lighting 132, 176

in *Lindbergh's Flight* (Brecht and Weill) 101–2
in *Machinal* (Treadwell) 69
machines in 10–11
Mandelbrot set and 195–6
motifs of 38–9
for Müller 187
in music 112
nostalgia and 75–6
ontology and 18
for performance 30–1
for playback 121–2
politics and 130–1
in production 31, 46–7, 186
scholarship on 20–1, 25
sound and 1–2, 49–50
spectacle and 106–7, 117–19, 217–18
stage directions and 21
from Technological Revolution 40
in technotexts 20–1
in theatre 19–22, 114–15
theory and 12–13
for violence 84–5
from war 50, 94
interaction 209
interpretation 62
interpretive thresholds 6
Ionesco, Eugène 23, 180, 226, 236 n.59
absurdism for 36
Eiffel Tower Wedding Party (Cocteau) and 69
Jack, or the Submission (Ionesco) 27, 36, 63–6
themes of 37, 62, 66
Tzara and 74
see also *The Chairs*; *The Future Is in Eggs*; *It Takes All Sorts to Make a World*; *Jack, or the Submission*
Irving, Henry 192
The Island (Fugard) 29, 102, 145–7, 180
Italy 55

It Takes All Sorts to Make a World (Ionesco) 36, 62

Jack, or the Submission (Ionesco) 27, 36, 63–6
Jameson, Fredric 9, 201, 218, 231 n.6
Japanese theatre 42
Jefferson, Thomas 27–8
Jerz, Dennis 16–17
Johnson, Timothy A. 126, 129–30, 134–5
Jones, Inigo 20
Joyce, James 35
Juárez, Mexico 98

Kandinsky, Wassily 35
Kane, Sarah 104
Kani, John 145
Kasubowski-Houston, Magdalena 32
Kazan, Elia 88
Kennicott, Philip 207
Kim, Alfred 132
Kircher, Athasios 225
Klaver, Elizabeth 191
Knowlson, James 13
Koch curve 195
Krapp's Last Tape (Beckett) 11, 23, 29–30, 149–50, 182
for audiences 167–8
characterization in 169
constraint in 151–60
The Dumb Waiter (Pinter) and 179–80
Hurt in 244 n.40
ideology in 170–2
interpretations of 40
modernity in 69, 160–3
sound in 85
themes in 223
Kyung Chun Kim 132

labor
in *Hamletmachine* (Müller) 171
history of 44–5

machines and 91–2
politics of 45–6
productivity and 54–5
Lahy, Jean-Marie 45–6
Langridge, Philip 42
language
  ambiguity in 232 n.11, 234 n.36
  in dialogue 166
  in *Eiffel Tower Wedding Party* (Cocteau) 46–9
  for emotions 64–5
  in Europe 60
  for humans 48–9
  in *Machinal* (Treadwell) 182
  of machines 72–3, 250 n.37
  Oxford English Dictionary 54
  psychology and 140
  Sanskrit 181
  Spanish 97
  of terminology 106
  of titles 58–9
  translation of 234 n.36, 235 n.37, 236 n.44, 236 n.59
Les Six (collective) 37
Lewis, Gary 176
lighting
  cameras and 178–9
  innovation for 132, 176
  props and 146
  sound and 30
  spot lights 177–8
  for tone 77
Lindbergh, Charles 101–2, 116
Lindbergh's Flight (Brecht and Weill) 2, 28, 33, 67
  alienation in 107–16
  innovation in 101–2
  Nixon in China (Goodman and Adams) and 104–5, 122–4, 136, 140, 143–5
  politics in 116–20
  production of 121–2, 157
  themes in 126
listening 160–1

literary scholarship 7–8
Lucille Lortel Theatre 4–5
Lumaga, Pio Barone 209
Lumet, Sidney 220
Lyotard, Jean-François 203

Machinal (Treadwell) 23, 27, 182
  The Adding Machine (Rice) and 89, 94–5
  innovation in 69
  modernity in 77–86
  nostalgia in 98–9
  La Ruta and 96
  Taylorism in 190
machines
  as actors 190–1
  apparatus of 64, 141
  in art 25
  biomechanics and 248 n.2
  capitalism and 27–8, 94, 188–9
  for Cocteau 160
  constraint and 149–51
  cyborgs 139
  in *Death and the Powers* (Pinsky and Machover) 214
  dialogue and 164
  in dramatic text 179–80
  in *Eiffel Tower Wedding Party* (Cocteau) 54–5, 154
  electric chair as 84–5
  ethics and 212
  expressionism and 80–1
  Gutenberg press 61
  humans and 23–4, 29–30, 44, 62, 69–70, 92–3, 95–6, 117–18, 159–60, 166–9
  ideology and 18
  in industrialism 36–7
  in innovation 10–11
  labor and 91–2
  language of 72–3, 250 n.37
  math and 195–6
  in media studies 244 n.44
  as metaphors 191–2

modernity and 52–3
phenomenology of 208–9
for Rabinbach 65
radio as 113–14
robots and 10–12, 221
Rube Goldberg contraptions 255 n.68
sound and 90–1, 248 n.15
in spectacle 211
"Staging the Machine" 23
Technological Revolution for 40
in theatre 157, 223–7
Turing test for 167
in *Valparaiso* (DeLillo) 136–45, 220
violence and 57–8
Writing Machines (Hayles) 3, 7–8, 10
Machover, Tod 11, 30–1, 183, 186
music of 202
phenomenology for 208–9
Pinsky and 187, 200–1, 205–8, 216, 250 n.46
see also Death and the Powers
McKinley, Philip William 186, 210; *see also Spider-Man*
McLuhan, Marshall 2–3, 27, 60–2, 169, 236 n.56
McMaster, Brian 120
Maddalena, James 131–4, 207, 241 n.1
Malpurgo, Michael 31
Mandela, Nelson 145
Mandelbrot, Benoit B. 195–6, 201
Mandelbrot set 195–6
Manifest Destiny 70, 86–7
Mao Tse-Dong 193; *see also Nixon in China*
Marcuse, Herbert 151–2
Maré, Rolf de 37
Martin, Jean 161–2
Marvel 255 n.68
Marx, Karl 193, 239 n.36
Marxism 28, 85, 110, 118

masculinity 137–8
Massachusetts Institute of Technology Media Lab 202, 206–9
math 195–6
Maupassant, Guy de 36
media studies 11, 244 n.44
medium (artistic or creative) 3–4, 6, 22, 121–2, 144, 223–7
consciousness as 205
filmic 179
performance and 229 n.3
tape recording as 161
Meisner, Sanford 168
mêkanê 103
meta-theatre 168–9, 173–7, 181–2
The Method theory 88
Mexico 28, 96–8
Meyer, Michael J. 87
Meyerhold, Vsevolod 20, 150
Middle East 21–2
Mielziner, Jo 93
Milhaud, Darius 35, 37
Miller, Arthur 13, 27–8, 139, 185, 193
Arthur Miller (Bigsby) 94
DeLillo and 40
dialogue by 93–4
humans for 240 n.55
nostalgia for 226
see also All My Sons; Death of a Salesman
Minghella, Anthony 178–9, 250 n.59
minimalism 98, 102, 145–6
Miranda, Lin-Manuel 4–5
mise en scène 176
mobility 88
modernist/modernism 10, 13, 19, 35–7, 39, 188
in culture 51
experiments 160
high 107–8
logic of 149
machineries of 95
plays 26–7, 101, 185, 220

sculptures 231 n.6
  stage aesthetics of 67, 69, 113
  theatrical 46
  themes 71, 194
modernity 39
  in *The Adding Machine* (Rice) 71–7
  aesthetics of 67
  art and 114–15
  in *Death of a Salesman*
    (Miller) 69, 95
  in dialogue 81–2
  in dramatic text 89–90
  for family 86–7
  in *The Future Is in Eggs*
    (Ionesco) 62–3
  history of 51
  ideology and 151–2
  in *Jack, or the Submission*
    (Ionesco) 27, 36
  in *Krapp's Last Tape* (Beckett)
    69, 160–3
  in *Machinal* (Treadwell) 77–86
  machines and 52–3
  music and 46
  nature and 87–8
  nostalgia and 69–71
  in *La Ruta* (Gomez) 96–9
  Taylorism and 51, 64
  techno-modernity 71, 140
  in United States 185
Monk, Meredith 188
monologues, interior 160
Moravec, Hans 204–5
Morris, Mark 241 n.1
mortality 205–6
Moscow Art Theatre 88
motifs 38–9
Mountain Language (Pinter) 150, 174
Mozart, Wolfgang Amadeus 224
Müller, Heiner 12, 30–1, 186
  dramatic text by 194–5, 197–8, 199
  innovation for 187
  scholarship on 192
  see also Hamletmachine

Murray, Janet H. 8
music
  by Adams 127–8, 135
  dialogue in 130–1
  innovation in 112
  of Machover 202
  modernity and 46
  by orchestras 214–15
  singing and 124
  of Weill 108, 111
Mussolini, Benito 193
mustard gas 57–8

NAFTA *see* North American Free
  Trade Agreement
narration 91, 136, 160
nature 87–9, 95–6
Nazism 63, 113–14
Neher, Caspar 28, 102, 109–11,
  145
New Brutalism 104–5, 189
New Historicism 14, 19
New Wave Festival 187
The New World Order (Pinter) 174
New York City 255 n.66
New York Observer 211
New York Post 210
New York Times 208, 210
New York University 191
nihilism 197
Nixon, Richard 11–12; *see also*
  specific topics
Nixon in China (Goodman and
  Adams) 11–12, 28–9, 67, 213
  alienation in 132–6
  Death of a Salesman (Miller)
    and 220
  Lindbergh's Flight (Brecht and
    Weill) and 104–5, 122–4, 136,
    140, 143–5
  production of 241 n.1
  script analysis of 125–32
Valparaiso and 102, 161
verisimilitude in 103–4

Norman, Jessye 42
Norman, Lance 168–9
North American Free Trade
    Agreement (NAFTA) 28, 96–7
nostalgia
    in *Death of a Salesman* (Miller)
        84, 86–94
    in dramatic text 67
    innovation and 75–6
    in *Machinal* (Treadwell) 98–9
    for Miller 226
    modernity and 69–71
    production of 144
    protagonists and 69–70
    in *La Ruta* (Gomez) 71
    theatre and 27–8
Not I (Beckett) 150, 157–8
Notre Dame Cathedral 39
Ntshona, Winston 145

The Ocean Flight (Brecht) *see*
    Lindbergh's Flight
O'Donnell, Damien 175–6, 179
offstage narration 91
Ohio Impromptu (Beckett) 150
One for the Road (Pinter) 150, 174
ontology 18
Opatz, Mari 241 n.1
opera
    Dallas Opera 207–9
    Houston Grand Opera 103,
        122–3, 135–6
    Opera News 207
Opéra National de Lyon 28, 102,
    117, 119–20
orchestras 214–15
Orth, Robert 207
Osborne, John 105
Oxford English Dictionary 54

pacing 135
Page, Carolann 241 n.1
Palmieri, Anthony F. R. 73–5
paratext 5

Paris, France *see* Eiffel Tower
    Wedding Party
Party Time (Pinter) 150, 174
Paulus, Diane 207
performance
    for audiences 15
    avant-garde 3
    in *Death and the Powers* (Pinsky
        and Machover) 250 n.46
    deconstruction of 12–13
    disembodied 208
    dramatic text and 1, 6–7, 15–16,
        20, 162–3
    emasculation in 95
    embodied 4
    in *The Gas Heart* (Tzara) 56–63
    history of 15, 26–7, 31–2
    ideology and 187–8
    innovation for 30–1
    medium (artistic or creative) and
        229 n.3
    narrative 10, 15, 20, 26–7,
        50–1, 206
    for New Historicism 14
    New World Performance Lab 193
    preperformance preparations 155
    for protagonists 168–9
    on radio 101–2, 111–13, 116–17
    rehearsal and 235 n.38
    scholarship on 230 n.15
    spectation and 4–5
    stylized 42
    on television 135–6
    theatre and 9–10, 17–19
    theory 229 n.3
peripherals 213–14
Petrusi, Michael 224
phenomenology 13–14, 19, 208–9
philosophy
    in *The Adding Machine* (Rice) 86
    in *The Dumb Waiter* (Pinter) 83
    existentialism 180
    of Marxism 118
    nature in 89

Index

nihilism 197
post-structuralist theory and 6
of Rice 76
theory and 9
Picabia, Francis 35
Picasso, Pablo 35
Pinsky, Robert 11, 183, 186
   Machover and 187, 200–1, 205–8, 216, 250 n.46
   stage directions by 201–2
Pinter, Harold 23, 29–30, 104
   Beckett and 147, 149–51, 179–80, 182–3, 226
   Harold Pinter Society 13
   themes of 174
   see also *The Birthday Party*; *The Dumb Waiter*; *Mountain Language*; *The New World Order*; *One for the Road*; *Party Time*; *The Room*
Pirandello, Luigi 180–1
Piscator, Erwin 20
Play (Beckett) 30, 149–51, 172, 176–80, 182, 250 n.59
playback 121–2
playwrights 9–10, 13
plot 189–90, 217
pneumatic tubes 243 n.26
Poincaré, Henri 256 n.75
politics
   aesthetics and 107–9, 241 n.5
   of capitalism 170–1
   in dialogue 126–7
   of diplomacy 245 n.46
   innovation and 130–1
   in *The Island* (Fugard) 145–7
   of labor 45–6
   in *Lindbergh's Flight* (Brecht and Weill) 116–20
   of Marxism 110
   radio for 114
   script analysis for 129–30
   in theatre 104–5
   in United States 122
   for Weill 117
   of Western democracies 174
Pomponi, Franco 132
Portman, John 231 n.6
post-human recursivity
   in *Death and the Powers* (Pinsky and Machover) 201–9
   in *Hamletmachine* (Müller) 188–97, 200–1
   in *Rossum's Universal Robots* (Čapek) 219–20
   in *Spider-Man* (Taymor) 209–14, 216–19
   in theatre 185–8, 220–1
post-human theatre 30–1
post-structuralist theory 6–7
Poulenc, Francis 35, 37
power 10–11
prisons 145–6
Prock, Stephan M. 135
production
   in absurdist theatre 175
   of ambiguity 52–3
   apparatus in 47–8
   for Beckett 248 n.15
   for Broadway theatre 209–10
   cameras in 176
   communication and 149
   of *Death and the Powers* (Pinsky and Machover) 253 n.46
   dramatic text and 4–9, 173–4
   history of 12–13
   innovation in 31, 46–7, 186
   of *Lindbergh's Flight* (Brecht and Weill) 121–2, 157
   of *Nixon in China* (Goodman and Adams) 241 n.1
   of nostalgia 144
   playwrights and 13
   process of 218–19
   set design and 255 n.72
   of theatre 10–12, 28–9, 118
   translation in 124–5
   in *Valparaiso* (DeLillo) 67

value 41
productivity 54–5
props 146
protagonists 69–70, 168–9
Prouse, Derek 236 n.59
psychology 140, 154

Quad (Beckett) 150

Rabinbach, Anson 9, 27, 45–6, 65
radio 243 n.25
  as machines 113–14
  performance on 101–2,
    111–13, 116–17
  for politics 114
  television and 66–7
  in theatre 112
rationalization 151–2
Ravenhill, Mark 104
readers 61
realism 104
rehearsal 162–3, 235 n.38
Renaissance paintings 61
repetition 128–9
Rey, Rebecca 91, 138–40, 153, 211–12
rhizomes 52, 57
Rice, Elmer 23, 27–8, 73–6, 139,
    185, 226; see also *The Adding
    Machine*
Richard Wagner Festspielhaus 111
Riedel, Michael 210
robots
  animal 38
  cybernetics 204
  cyborgs 139, 220, 226
  humans and 10–12, 201–2
  machines and 10–12, 221
  Rossum's Universal Robots (Čapek)
    31, 219–20, 226
  in *Spider-Man* (Taymor) 187
  "Robot's Opera" *see Death and
    the Powers*
Rockaby (Beckett) 150
Roof, Judith 32, 216

The Room (Pinter) 150–1
Roset, Olivier 132
Roudané, Matthew C. 88
Rousseau, Jean-Jacques 35
Rube Goldberg contraptions 255 n.68
rugged individualism 27–8, 70, 185
La Ruta (Gomez) 28, 71, 96–9

Sanford, Sylvan 241 n.1
San Francisco 83–4
Sanskrit 181
Sartre, Jean-Paul 180, 193
satire 101
Schiele, Egon 84
scholarship
  culture in 21–2
  on dance 60
  on dramatic text 3–4, 19,
    104–5, 196–7
  on innovation 20–1, 25
  literary 7–8
  media studies 11
  on Müller 192
  on performance 230 n.15
  on *Play* (Beckett) 250 n.59
  on theatre 2–3, 5–9, 12–16,
    22–5, 31–3
scientific apparatus 49–50, 114–15
script analysis 12–13, 44,
    125–32, 155–6
sculptures 231 n.6
Sellars, Peter 103, 122–3, 241 n.1
set design 76–7
  by Appia 214
  by Mielziner 93
  minimalism in 145–6
  by Neher 102, 109, 145
  production and 255 n.72
setting 35–43, 76–7, 83–4, 96–8, 161
Shakespeare, William 198, 225–6
  Hamlet (Shakespeare) 167, 189,
    192–3, 199
  Midsummer Night's Dream
    (Shakespeare) 201

The Tempest (Shakespeare) 202
Shaw, Bernard 156-7, 220
Short Organum for Theatre
　(Brecht) 116
Sierpinsky triangle 195
Sierz, Aleks 189
Simonson, Lee 76-7
singing 124-6
Sircar, Badal 149, 180-3, 226; *see also*
　and Indrajit
social apparatus 168
sound
　in *The Adding Machine* (Rice) 182
　analogue 183
　digital 1-2, 183
　in *Eiffel Tower Wedding Party*
　　(Cocteau) 42-5
　innovation and 1-2, 49-50
　in *Krapp's Last Tape* (Beckett) 85
　lighting and 30
　listening and 160-1
　machines and 90-1, 248 n.15
　offstage 65-6
　pacing and 135
　for Rice 74-5
　setting and 161
　stage directions for 78-9
　voice and 40
South Africa 145-7
South America 21-2
Spanish language 97
spectacle
　alienation in 105-6
　for audiences 105-6
　for Brecht 120-1
　innovation and 106-7,
　　117-19, 217-18
　machines in 211
　for Neher 110-11
spectation 4-5, 11, 175, 179, 191
Spider-Man (Taymor) 30, 220-1, 226
　Death and the Powers (Pinsky and
　　Machover) and 183, 186, 214-16
　for Marvel 255 n.68

popularity of 188
post-human recursivity in
　209-14, 216-19
robots in 187
spot lights 177-8
Squiers, Anthony 104, 121, 133-4
Stadttheater Breslau 112-13, 121
Stafford, Nick 31
stage directions 16
　for actors 157-8
　for characterization 88
　for dialogue 177-8
　in dramatic text 24
　in *The Future Is in Eggs*
　　(Ionesco) 73
　innovation and 21
　by Paulus 207
　by Pinsky 201-2
　for sound 78-9
Stalin, Joseph 198
Stanislavsky, Konstantin 88
Stein, Gertrude 35
Steppenwolf Theatre series 97
Stoppard, Tom 174, 192
Strasberg, Lee 155
Stravinsky, Igor 35
　Oedipus Rex (Stravinsky) 42
　Rite of Spring (Stravinsky) 37
subjectivity 16, 189
Sunday Times of London 207-8
suspension of disbelief 212-13,
　255 n.71
Svoboda, Josef 20-1
Swenson, May 203
symbolism 39-40, 49-53
systems 15, 24, 31, 197-9, 225

tableau vivant 53
Tailleferre, Germaine 35, 37
Talbot, Jeff 4-5
Tati, Jacques
　Mon Oncle (Tati) 236 n.58
　Monsieur Hulot's Holiday (Tati)
　　236 n.58

Play Time (Tati) 236 n.58
Taylorism
  in *The Adding Machine* (Rice) 81
  in France 45–6
  logic in 54–5, 72, 78
  in *Machinal* (Treadwell) 190
  modernity and 51, 64
Taymor, Julie 30, 183, 186
  Oedipus Rex (Stravinsky) for 42
  reputation of 209–11
  theatrical apparatus for 200–1
  see also Spider-Man
technology
  technological apparatus 223–4
  Technological Revolution 40
  see also specific topics
techno-modernity 71, 140
techno-rationalist ideology 151, 181–2, 226
technotexts 8, 10, 20–1
television 66–7, 135–6, 179, 190–1; *see also* Nixon, Richard
Terfel, Bryn 42
That Time (Beckett) 150, 179
theatre
  absurdist 29–30, 161–2, 168, 172–3, 175, 180
  alienation in 101–3
  Broadway theatre 171–2, 209–10
  of cruelty 189
  death in 142–3
  expressionism in 69–70
  Foxwoods theatre 214–15
  French modernist 27
  Greek 59–60, 103, 106, 109–10, 140
  The Group Theatre 155
  history of 1–5, 19–20, 25–7, 220–1
  Houston Grand Opera 103
  ideology from 67
  innovation in 19–22, 114–15
  Japanese 42
  Lucille Lortel Theatre 4–5
  machines in 157, 223–7
  meta-theatre 168–9, 173–7, 181–2

  Moscow Art Theatre 88
  New Brutalism 189
  in New York City 255 n.66
  nostalgia and 27–8
  offstage sound in 65–6
  Opéra National de Lyon 28, 102
  orchestras in 214–15
  performance and 9–10, 17–19
  peripherals in 213–14
  politics in 104–5
  post-human 30–1
  post-human recursivity in 185–8, 220–1
  production of 10–12, 28–9, 118
  radio in 112
  realism in 104
  repetition in 128–9
  Richard Wagner Festspielhaus 111
  scholarship on 2–3, 5–9, 12–16, 22–5, 31–3
  Short Organum for Theatre (Brecht) 116
  Steppenwolf Theatre series 97
  Theatre Champs-Élysées 37
  theatrical apparatus 5, 10, 17, 144, 150, 161–2, 176–7, 200–1
  war in 57–8
  West End 171–2
  see also specific topics
theory
  assemblage 6–7, 27
  of Brecht 105, 107–8
  of cybernetics 204, 219
  deconstruction 6
  dramatic text and 8
  of fractals 195–9, 201, 219, 256 n.75
  innovation and 12–13
  Marxism 85
  The Method 88
  New Historicism 14, 19
  performance 229 n.3
  phenomenology 13–14, 19
  philosophy and 9
  post-structuralist 6–7

Tinguely, Jean 231 n.6
Tintoretto (painter) 198–9
titles 58–9
tone 77, 79, 82–3, 85–6
Toqueville, Alexis de 27–8, 70
translation 124–5, 234 n.36, 235 n.37, 236 n.44, 236 n.59
transportation 102–3
Treadwell, Sophie 23, 27–8, 139, 185, 226; see also Machinal
Tsypin, George 186, 210–11, 255 n.72
Tung, Charles 81
Turing test 167
typography 27, 60–2, 91
Tzara, Tristan 12, 27, 35–6, 226
  ambiguity for 56–63
  Ionesco and 74
  themes of 37
  see also The Gas Heart

U2 (band) 30, 183, 186, 209
Übermarionettes 55
Undershaft, Andrew 156–7
United States
  art in 12
  audiences in 129
  England and 174
  Europe and 10, 21–2, 26, 35, 146–7, 171–2
  The Group Theatre in 155
  ideology in 70–1, 86, 95
  Mexico and 96–7
  modernity in 185
  politics in 122
  rugged individualism in 27–8, 70, 185
University of California, Los Angeles 193–4
University of South Wales 193–4

Valparaiso (DeLillo) 23, 28, 212
  actors in 156
  Death of a Salesman (Miller) and 152–3
  dialogue in 91–2

  interpretations of 40
  machines in 136–45, 220
  Nixon in China (Goodman and Adams) and 102, 161
  production in 67
Varisco, Robert A. 57, 235 n.38
Verfremdungseff 105; see also alienation
verisimilitude 103–4
vibe 119–20, 141, 179, 214
video recording 122
violence 57–8, 84–5, 96–7
virtual education 22–4
voice 40–4, 207
von Otter, Anna Sophie 224

Wagner, Richard 215
Waiting for Godot (Beckett) 151
war 45, 50, 57–8, 94, 113–14
Weber, Max 151–2
Weill, Kurt 2, 28, 33, 243 n.19
  Brecht and 67, 157
  music of 108, 111
  politics for 117
  see also Lindbergh's Flight
West End theatre 171–2
Western democracies 174
Westin Bonaventure Hotel 201, 231 n.6
What Where (Beckett) 30, 149–51, 172–7, 179, 182, 202
Whitelaw, Billie 157
Willett, John 105, 244 n.35, 246 n.66
Williams, Kirk 191–2
Williams, Raymond 28, 95–6
Wilson, Robert 188, 191, 197–8; see also Hamletmachine
Wonder, Erich 198
Workman, Charles 119–20

Yeats, W. B. 203

Zielinski, Siegfried 9, 225
Zurbrugg, Nicholas 191

www.ingramcontent.com/pod-product-compliance
Lightning Source LLC
Chambersburg PA
CBHW072126290426
44111CB00012B/1797